the bent World

THE COLLEGE THEOLOGY SOCIETY

ANNUAL PUBLICATIONS

1979
the bent World

Edited by
John R. May

JOHN R. MAY

the bent World

ESSAYS ON RELIGION AND CULTURE

The Annual Publication of the
College Theology Society

1979

SCHOLARS PRESS

Distributed by
Scholars Press
101 Salem St.
Chico, California 95926

the bent World

ESSAYS ON RELIGION AND CULTURE

The Annual Publication of the College Theology Society

Printed in the United States of America
1 2 3 4 5 6
Edwards Brothers Inc.
Ann Arbor, Michigan 48104

PREFACE

The title of this collection of essays--a phrase from Gerard
Manley Hopkins' "God's Grandeur"--preserves the capitalization of
its poetic origin for at least two reasons: it is thus closer, I
believe, to the poet's meaning and to the intention of this collection. Hopkins' poem celebrates God's all-renewing Spirit who unex-
pectedly, but surely refreshes the world despite the blight of man's
persistent sinfulness. Hopkins splits the phrase at line's end so
that "World" begins a new line, the sonnet's last, and is capital-
ized--no doubt to signal the fact that the world, as God's creation,
is irrepressibly "charged" with his grandeur and thus remains forever
fresh even if "bent" by man's searing trade and blearing toil.

Hopkins' poem is, as we know, about the interaction of *God* and
world rather than *religion* and world or culture, and many of us
realize also--at least in our more lucid moments--that God and religion are not synonymous. Even if its primary concern is *with* God,
religion is *not* God, precisely because it is never more than--but
always at least--our historically, and therefore culturally, conditioned response to our experience of transcendence. Religion may,
however, be considered the God-oriented aspect of culture. The "bent
World" of this collection therefore--not unlike Hopkins'--is that
contemporary intersection of religion and culture that is both an
indictment of the detritus of civilization and a stimulus to the
quickening of the human spirit.

This collection celebrates far less assuredly, but nonetheless
definitely the perennial vitality of the human spirit in its varied
cultural manifestations despite our pervasive presumption in dealing
with one another and with nature. Nowhere in this collection is the
horror of that presumption more clearly exposed than in Richard L.
Rubenstein's introductory essay, "Reason's Deadly Dreams." The
College Theology Society was privileged to have such an eminent the-
ologian--perhaps the premier religious commentator on the Holocaust--
give the first plenary address at its 1979 annual meeting at Trinity
College in Washington, D.C.; it was a keynote address that takes its
rightful place at the head of this collection as a continuing challenge to our theological tradition. We must face the darkness, its
position reminds us, if we are ever to reach the day. Even in the
face of the recent, terrifying institutionalization of mass murder,
the contributors to this collection search their Judeo-Christian
tradition for current relevance--and not without hope. "The most

v

likely framework for the fruitful renewal of the millenarian impulse," Rubenstein himself suggests, "will probably be within the body of Christendom itself."

What follows Rubenstein's essay is an attempt to recover some of the richness of that tradition. Most of the essays were presented as papers at the 1979 annual meeting of CTS, though some in quite different form; the others were solicited with a view toward a more balanced presentation. Structured as the volume is in terms of contemporary challenge and response, it obviously does not conceive tradition in any static sense, as if it were a deposit preserved in perennially decipherable language. The essays that form the heart of this volume accept the cultural dynamism of religious tradition; they seek to carry values from the shore of the past over into the idiom of the present and to illuminate ways in which apparently autonomous cultural developments can be seen as contiguous with the spirit of a religious tradition.

The interrelationship of religion and culture is indeed a vast area of consideration, and the diversity of insights and approaches here--obviously suggestive rather than prescriptive--may serve at best to indicate the potential of the Judeo-Christian tradition for responding to the institutional perversity of our century. The divisions of the collection proceed from the more abstract to the particular. Part One views the interrelationship of religion and culture primarily from a philosophical perspective; Part Two offers contemporary insights into some major religious texts of our tradition, from Sacred Scripture through the writings (and lives) of saints and mystics. Part Three considers the dynamism of religion and culture as a manifestation of the imagination in art and ritual, while Part Four deals with the more concrete interactions of religion with psychology, sociology, and literature.

My work as editor, I hasten to add in conclusion, would have been far less rewarding without the gracious assistance of my secretary, Mary Scardina, and the firm support of my colleague and friend Lawrence Cunningham, presently serving as chairman of the Publications Committee of CTS.

John R. May
Louisiana State University
December 31, 1980

TABLE OF CONTENTS

And for this, nature is never spent;
  There lives the dearest freshness deep down things;
And though the last lights off the black West went
  Oh, morning, at the brown brink eastward, springs--
Because the Holy Ghost over the bent
  World broods with warm breast and with ah! bright wings.

                    Gerard Manley Hopkins, "God's Grandeur"

INTRODUCTION

The Challenge

REASON'S DEADLY DREAMS*

Richard L. Rubenstein

In addressing this body, I would like to begin by identifying
the abiding preoccupation that has shaped my career as a theologian.
Some scholars concentrate their attention on a single discipline,
others on a single issue. My choice has been the latter, but I
would hasten to add that, when a thinker attempts to solve one problem, he or she will be led to others that were not on the horizon
at the beginning of his/her quest. The question that has dominated
all of my work can best be formulated as follows: what are the
full implications for the understanding of contemporary western
civilization of the destruction of the European Jews during World
War II?

When I first posed the question, my interest was primarily
theological. Regretably, there has been some misunderstanding concerning my theological response. I did not, as some maintain, argue
that Auschwitz rendered belief in God impossible. It is my conviction that what set my response apart from that of other Jewish
thinkers was my insistence that no compromising ambiguities be introduced into the interpretation of the doctrines of the sovereignty
of God and the election of Israel in considering the problem of God
and the Holocaust. I saw no way to avoid the conclusion that, if
the doctrines of the sovereignty of God and the election of Israel
are affirmed with the seriousness they deserve, Auschwitz must be
seen as a purposeful expression of God's will. If God is absolutely
sovereign, then no act, not even his readiness to condemn innocent
millions to agonizing and premature death can be thought of as beyond either his capacity or his inclination.

There is a profound scandal in faith in the Old Testament as
well as the New. If God is Lord of all Creation, men have no more
reason to expect that they can fully comprehend his ways than that
they would be able to make themselves at home in one of the universe's imploding Black Holes. The mental and physiological capacities of ordinary men are designed to cope with only the smallest
part of creation. If God is the Sovereign and Universal Creator, it
is hardly likely that his ways could be symmetrical with the everyday experience of ordinary men. This was clearly understood by

*Delivered as a plenary address to the College Theology Society at
 its 1979 Annual Meeting.

3

Isaiah when he declared: "For my thoughts are not your thoughts,
and your ways are not my ways sayeth the Lord.   For as the heavens
are higher than the earth, so are my ways higher than your ways
and my thoughts than your thoughts" (Isa. 55:8,9).

I have never objected to those who can honestly affirm that
the destruction of Europe's Jews was an expression of divine
purposes, even though I profoundly disagreed with them.   My quarrel
has been with those theologians and literateurs who have attempted
to affirm the radical sovereignty of the God of covenant and election while denying that that God could be the ultimate author of
the Holocaust.   If (a) God is unconditionally sovereign and (b)
if He has chosen Israel, it is ridiculous to pretend that he was
uninvolved in so overwhelmingly central an event in Israel's history
as the Holocaust.   There is a point in theological reflection at
which a certain literal-mindedness is inescapable if theological
propositions are to retain more than emotive significance.   The
Holocaust would appear to be one of them.   If, however, one cannot
accept the Holocaust as a deliberate intention of God, one must at
the very least reject a literal interpretation of the doctrine
of covenant and election, and perhaps the doctrine of absolute
divine sovereignty as well.   In my theological writings, I have not
argued that belief in God is impossible; I have argued that if one
believes in the biblical God, one had better be prepared to pay
one's theological dues all the way.   I was unable to pay those
dues, and concluded that I had no choice but to reject not God,
but the belief that God has chosen Israel.[1]

Let us, however, not dwell on my personal theological reflections which are ultimately unimportant.   Instead, let us consider
briefly the theological situation of those who affirm Israel's
election in the face of the Holocaust.   These include some very
Orthodox Jews as well as triumphalist Christians.   Both groups
have sought to interpret the Holocaust in terms of their distinctive
understanding of God's covenant with Israel.   For the very Orthodox
Jews, the Holocaust is seen as God's response to Israel's failure
to keep God's Law as that Law has been authoritatively interpreted.
For triumphalist Christians, Christ is the true meaning and the
fulfillment of God's covenant with Israel.   The triumphalists assert that by rejecting Christ, Israel has rejected God's covenant,
and Auschwitz must therefore be seen as a contemporary example of
God's continuing chastisement of Israel for its infidelity.   Although this view is seldom expressed in the public arena, it would
be a mistake to underestimate its pervasiveness.

As we know, the triumphalist interpretation is consistent
with the classical Christian interpretation of Israel's misfortunes,
just as the Orthodox interpretation is consistent with the classical
Jewish view. For example, in Matthew, Jesus is depicted as teaching
the Parable of the Marriage Feast in which the kingdom of heaven
is likened to a king who gave a marriage feast for his son, but
became angry when many of those whom he had invited refused un-
graciously the second as well as the first summons to the feast.
Matthew depicts the king's response: "The king was angry and he
sent his troops and destroyed those murderers and burned their city"
(Matt. 22:7).

Many contemporary New testament scholars see in this sentence
a reference to the fall of Jerusalem and take it as evidence for a
date after the year 70 for the writing of Matthew.[2] For our purposes, the dating is less important than the fact that the greatest
Jewish catastrophe of all time before the Holocaust is depicted in
a classical document of the Christian faith as God's punishment of
the Jews for having refused his invitation to the messianic banquet.
Put differently, the classical Christian response to overwhelming
Jewish catastrophe has been, since the very beginning, to see the
Jewish misfortune as confirming evidence of Christian truth. I
could multiply examples, but before a group like this such repeti-
tion is hardly necessary. Your knowledge of the Christian tradition
far exceeds mine.

Now, if I were a professional working for a national Jewish
inter-faith relations organization, I might at this juncture be
tempted to lecture to you on the anti-Semitism to be found in
Christian teachings and, with as much discretion as I could muster,
I might even suggest ways in which such teachings ought to be modi-
fied for the sake of better inter-group relations. Although I am
strongly interested in Christian involvement in and response to
Jewish misfortune, I bring you no such suggestions. On the contrary, in my role as theologian, I would be more inclined to say to
other Jewish thinkers that perhaps the time has come to consider
seriously the possible significance of the classical Christian interpretation of Jewish misfortune for contemporary Judaism apart
from the question of whether or not it is anti-Jewish.

I would point out that the Christian interpretation rests
on the same theology of covenant and election as does the Jewish.
Both believing Jews and Christians look to the record of history
for confirmation of their faith. I would also say to them, "If
you believe in such a God, is it not possible that the Christian

interpretation of Jewish history is more plausible than the Jewish?" For example, if one asserts that Christ is the divinely
authorized *telos*, that is, both the end and the goal of the Law,
and if within a single generation after the majority of the Jewish
community had rejected him, the principal religious institution in
which the Laws of Judaism were observed was destroyed, the sacer-
dotal leaders of the community were effectively stripped of all
authority, and the capital city fell to the avenging sword of con-
querors, would it not be plausible to see these events as evidence
that the God-who-acts-in-history was confirming Christ's role as
the end of the Law? Moreover, if one asserted that baptism in
Christ is the true circumcision and within two generations after the
fall of Jerusalem, the Jews, provoked by the Emperor Hadrian's
prohibition of circumcision, took up arms and were again bitterly
defeated by Rome, would it not be plausible to conclude, as did
Justin Martyr, that the hand of the God-who-acts-in-history was
in the defeat, certifying once again that there is no hope in the
old circumcision but only in the new baptism, especially when the
leader of the Jews, Bar Cochba, was a man whose messianic preten-
sions had been clearly disconfirmed by the events?[3]

Nor would it necessarily be "anti-Semitism" were Christians to
argue in this fashion. Such Christians would in effect be saying
to Jews, "Given the universe of theological discourse we hold in
common, which, in fact, we learned from you, is not our interpretation of your fate more plausible than your own?" It should be
obvious that a like question can be posed by Christians to Jews
about Auschwitz. At the moment, it is only being posed by the
fundamentalists, but, if one accepts a theology of covenant and e-
lection, it is certainly both a fair and a plausible query.

There is, of course, good reason why Christians ought to be
reluctant to utilize Auschwitz as evidence for triumphalist claims.
To take Auschwitz as confirmation of Christian truth involves seeing one of the greatest murders of all history as, at times, he
saw himself, namely as doing God's work by destroying the Jews, a
claim made by not a few of the National Socialist inner circle.[4]
To use Auschwitz as confirming evidence of triumphalist claims is
to admit the death camps into the domain of God's beneficent purposes, a step which ought to give even the most ardently consistent
believer at least a brief pause.

Nevertheless, the allegedly anti-Jewish passages in Christian
writings ought to be taken very seriously by Jewish thinkers, not
as evidence of Christian malice, which at times they undoubtedly

were, but for the absolutely fundamental challenge they present to
the Jewish understanding of God's relation to Israel, especially
after the Holocaust. It is at least conceivable, given the faith
in covenant, election, and the God-who-acts-in-history common to
both traditions, that the Holocaust is most important evidence of
both the validity of the Christian message and of a defect of Jewish self-understanding that has persisted for almost two thousand
years. Let us not fail to recognize the extent to which the spiritual foundations of Israel have been decisively challenged by the
Holocaust. I might add that my own rejection of the doctrine of
covenant and election is rooted in my inability to regard Auschwitz
as fulfilling any meaningful role in what is called in German the
Heilsgeschichte of mankind.

Reflections such as these may help us to answer a question
which is sometimes raised about the Holocaust: "Why," it is sometimes asked, "should we be all that concerned about Auschwitz?
Admittedly, it was one of the most hideous events of our times,
but do we not err when we focus so much attention on it to the
exclusion of the other mass sufferings of the twentieth century?
Did not Stalin murder and enslave more people than Hitler? Shall
we ignore the massacre of at least 1,500,000 Armenians? Are we
not racists when we dwell on Jewish misery and ignore the fact that
King Leopold I of the Belgians may have brought about the death of
as many as twenty million blacks in the Belgian Congo? What about
the recent genocidal horrors in Cambodia?"

We know, of course, that many people in both Europe and North
America are tired of hearing about the Holocaust. Yet, there is a
sense in which the Holocaust has a different meaning for believing
Jews and Christians than the other tragedies of our century. No
other contemporary event is so inextricably linked to the classical
interpretation of God's action in history for humanity's salvation
in both traditions. The Holocaust highlights a fundamental difference between philosophy and theology. A philosopher might be trou-
bled by the problem of reconciling the presence of radical evil with
the existence of an omnipotent, yet beneficent God, but his concern
would be ahistorical and no single historical instance of human misfortune would seem more significant than any other. This is not the
case in either Judaism or Christianity. God's relation to Israel
is a fundamental issue in both the Old and the New Testament. As
tragic as have been the other horrors of the twentieth century,
they do not have the same theological import for the community that
considers itself to be Israel after the Spirit as does the fate of

Israel after the Flesh. Unlike all the other horrors of the twentieth century, the Holocaust is inextricably linked with the classical mythic structures of the major faiths of the western world.

At this point, it may be helpful to say a word about what I
mean when I use the term "the death of God." When I used that
term in my theological writings over a decade ago, I chose my
words with a good deal of deliberation. It was not my intention
to say that God does not exist. In the light of the Holocaust,
the problem seemed to be not whether God exists but how he is to
be understood. *When I used the term "the death of God," I was
seeking an appropriate symbol to indicate that I no longer found
credible a very specific conception of God, namely, the biblical
doctrine that God is the Sovereign Lord of covenant and election.*
At no time did I deny that God is the ultimate Source of all creation. To have done so would have been tantamount to atheism. And
death-of-God theology was never really atheistic.

In the light of the Holocaust, a particular image of God had
died for me--the image of a God whose purposes in the drama of
human history are symmetrical with the ultimate aspirations of the
community of Israel. Put differently, I no longer found any plausibility in the proposition that the historical vicissitudes of the
Jewish people are central to the divine economy of human history.

The term "death of God" has, however, another related meaning
which is highlighted by the fact of the Holocaust. It can also
refer to a condition of radical secularity. When I wrote that we
live in the time of the death of God, I meant that we live in a
radically secular era. Some sociologists have challenged this view
with convincing statistics about the continuing strength of religious faith among large numbers of Americans, but this criticism is
beside the point.[5] In a secular age the majority of the population
might hold strong *private* beliefs. Nevertheless, as long as these
beliefs have a minimal effect on the *public* decision-making processes of government and private corporations, our era can legitimately be regarded as secular. For example, about a year ago, the
Zenith Television Company was forced to shut down its color TV manufacturing plant in the Chicago area, thereby rendering 3,900 people
unemployed. It then opened a new plant in Taiwan. Zenith found
that it could no longer meet Asian competition by manufacturing col-
or TV sets in Chicago. In making the decision, Zenith executives
had no choice but to ignore the appalling human consequences of the
move for the American workers and their families.

Although I do not know any Zenith executives, it is reasonable
to assume that they are decent men and women who are sincerely committed to their religious institutions. Nevertheless, no appeal
based upon religion, ethics, or simple compassion could override
the fact that our economic system does not measure success in terms
of the happiness of the labor force, but on the ability of a business enterprise to sustain a profit over term. This simple fact
was graphically illustrated when the utility company that owns the
Three Mile Island Nuclear Plant began operations at the plant two
days before the end of the 1978 fiscal year in order to receive tax
benefits amounting to about $40,000,000, although there were indi-
cations that there was considerable risk of some kind of breakdown
as a result of the premature operation of the plant.[6] In this
case, considerations of profit and loss overrode considerations of
safety not only for the present population of the area but also
conceivably for any future population for thousands of years.
Given the capital intensive nature of utility operations as well as
the firm's apparent exemption from financial responsibility to the
public for radiation damage, the executives determined that their
primary obligation was to what they regarded as the financial well-
being of their company. As we know, their calculations were in-
credibly short-sighted.

I assume that the executives in question are decent, religious
men and women in their private lives. Nevertheless, no appeal
to the sacredness of human life or to religious principles would
have prevented them or their opposite numbers in government from
basing their public decisions on a calculus of trade-offs between
the anticipated benefits of nuclear power and the possible hazards
of an "acceptable" level of radiation-induced cancer deaths. In
such a calculus, the lives of individual citizens are not considered
to be sacred. Some level of pollution-induced deaths per unit of
population is deemed to be acceptable.

Nor ought we to forget Alfred Sloan's honest and candid observation that General Motors is not in the business of making cars
but profit. This was not Mr. Sloan's confession of personal or
corporate greed, but a frank recognition of the ultimate imperative
of any properly functioning business enterprise in our society,
such as the corporation that owns the Three Mile Island Plant. The
production of electrical power is a means to an end; there is only
one end, profit. Moreover, we have currently no realistic alternative but to continue to regard profit as the appropriate end of
economic enterprise in our system.

The above are dramatic examples of some of the consequences
of the secularization process in our society. That process has
been defined as the removal of ever wider domains of human activity
from religious influence. Secularization is evident in a crucial
feature of the modern economy long observed by social theorists,
namely, the separation of the home and its values from the place
of work and its values. This separation has permitted and even
encouraged private religious experience to flourish while, in decisive arenas of public endeavor such as bureaucratic and corporate
decision-making, religious values play an ever-decreasing role.
When, over a decade ago, I wrote that we live in the time of the
death of God, it was to this phenomenon that I was referring, not
the private religious feelings of the individual. Incidentally,
I have come to the conclusion that many of those directly involved
in the destruction of Europe's Jews were decent and even religious
men in their private lives; in public, however, they recognized
only one binding imperative, their obligation to fulfill faithfully
and effectively their assigned tasks, no matter what the human
cost.[7]

Let us now return to a consideration of the destruction of
the European Jews. As I have indicated, my original interest was
religious and theological. One aspect of the religious concern was
understandably the question of the negative image of Jews and
Judaism in Christian literature and its relation to the events of
this century. However, the more I reflected on the question of
Christian attitudes and actions towards Jews, the more I was compelled to conclude that all attempts to explain the Holocaust primarily as a reflection of Christian anti-Semitism were inadequate.
At no time in the entire history of Christendom until the dread
Wansee Conference of January 1942 did the Church or any legitimate
government ever advocate a policy of systematic extermination of
the Jews. Far from being a throwback to the Middle Ages, the
Holocaust was a distinctly modern enterprise.

For those who seek to understand the event, the crucial question is: Given the power equation between Christians and Jews
ever since the days of Constantine, why did outright genocide not
occur before the twentieth century and in what way must the Holocaust be regarded as a distinctly modern undertaking? To pose such
a question is to take the investigation of the Holocaust beyond
the confines of theology and the history of religion. At the very
least, it involves entertaining the hypothesis that the twentieth
century is radically different than any previous era in human

history and that it has witnessed a quantum leap in the destructive
capacities of both human weaponry and human consciousness.

This neightened capacity for systematized murder by functionaries devoid of all feeling of either guilt or responsibility has
been observed by students of the overall phenomenon of twentieth-
century mass destructiveness. For example, although the Armenians
had been the object of murderous official hostility under the
corrupt, inefficient, old-fashioned regime of Sultan Abdul Hamid,
it was only after he was deposed by the modern, rational, western-
trained Young Turks, that the Armenians were compelled to endure
cold-blooded, systematic, deliberate genocide. Over 1,000,000
Armenians were slaughtered in 1915 by a government which was determined to utilize mass murder to restructure Turkish society and
politics.[8]

If we define functional rationality as the methodical attainment of a practical end by means of a precise calculation of adequate means, then the massacre of the Armenians, the destruction
of Europe's Jews, and the recent Cambodian genocide can all be seen
as important expressions of the triumph of functional rationality
as the predominant mode of problem-solving in human affairs. Similarly, Aleksandr Solzhenitsyn has pointed out that no crimes
committed by the Czarist regime ever approached the magnitude and
the horror of the violence done by the Stalinist regime.[9] Perhaps
instead of Goya's aphorism--"the sleep of reason brings forth monsters"--an appropriate aphorism for our times might be "the dreams
of reason bring forth monsters."

It may be asked, "If functional rationality involves the methodical attainment of a precisely calculated end, what possible end
could the Turkish and the German governments have had in mind when
they resorted to systematic mass murder in World Wars I and II
respectively?" In both cases, the end was the riddance of an unwanted population. In the case of the Armenians, they inhabited a
border region between Turkey and Russia. Because of their Christian
religion and culture, the Young Turks, whose Moslem faith had been
intensified by modern nationalism, decided to take advantage of
the cover of war and bring about a "final solution" of their Armenian
problem.

In the case of the Jews, the reasons they were unwanted were
somewhat more complicated. They were, of course, unwanted because
of their alien religion and culture, but that was an old story. A
further ingredient was required before social animosity and religious
rivalry could yield to systematic mass murder. It is my conviction

that the new element derived from the fact that the modernization
process which has created the culture of the twentieth century
carries with it the danger of a periodic state-sponsored resort to
mass murder or other forms of mass population elimination such as
war. If this hypothesis has merit, the murder of the Jews can be
understood as a particularly dramatic expression of the potentialities for mass destructiveness intrinsic to the modernization
process.[10]

In order to make clear why modernization runs the periodic
danger of so murderous an outcome, let me first define what I mean
by the process. Modernization can be understood as the growth and
diffusion of a distinctive set of institutions and values rooted
in the rational transformation of the economy through human inventiveness or technology.[11] Modernization requires an economy in
which the value of all goods and services without exception can be
calculated in monetary terms, the most rational method of calculation devised by men. The observations of the German sociologist
Max Weber on the nature of a money economy are instructive:

> The market community as such is the most impersonal
> relationship of practical life into which human beings
> can enter with one another. . . . The reason for
> the impersonality of the market is . . . its orienta-
> tion to the commodity and only that. Where the
> market is allowed to follow its own autonomous ten-
> dencies, its participants do not look towards the
> persons of each other but only towards the commodity;
> there are no obligations of brotherliness or reverence,
> and none of those spontaneous human relations that
> are sustained by personal unions. . . . Such ab-
> solute depersonalization is contrary to all the
> elementary forms of human relationship.[12]

The supremacy of the commodity over all human relationships
in a market economy noted by Weber takes on an almost sinister
aspect in an age of capital-intensive investment in nuclear energy.
It should be apparent that where modernization leads to the rationalization of human action, as it does under our economic system, it
also presupposes thorough-going secularization, at least in the
public sphere. Once purposes of collective action have been defined
by either government or business, behavioral constraints deriving
from religious traditions can only serve to impede the employment
of the most rational means for attaining whatever end is envisaged,
even if that end is the elimination of unwanted sectors of the
population.

The rationalization of means, which is an intrinsic element in
the modernization process, has had some profoundly disturbing social
consequences which continue to beset us almost two hundred years

after western Europe took its first decisive steps in modernization
with the Industrial Revolution. Briefly stated, there has seldom
been a period since the beginning of the Industrial Revolution
that most European countries were without a huge redundant population. As capital-intensive enterprise displaced labor-intensive
enterprise in both agriculture and manufacturing, there was the
ever-repeating story of men and women who found that their labor was
no longer needed in the countryside and were driven to the cities
in search of work.

As a result of the differentiation of labor roles, there was
a continual expansion in the demand for non-agricultural workers.
Unfortunately, in most periods, demand was never as great as the
supply. Had it not been for the availability of vast lands outside
of Europe for exploitation by Europeans, Europe would have had to
confront long before the twentieth century the massive social crises
which were a by-product of the processes of modernization and rationalization we call the Industrial Revolution.[13]

In 1891, the Chancellor of the German Reich, Leo von Caprivi,
Bismark's successor, said that Germany must either export people
or goods.[14] At the time, Germany was in the midst of the most extraordinary industrial development of any nation in the history of
Europe, but Caprivi understood that his was a society in the midst
of profound crisis. Unless those Germans, who could no longer
find work in agriculture, found it in industry or in other urban
pursuits, the country would have to face the social crisis attendant
upon the presence in its midst of millions of people cut off from
all hope of participating in the rewards of industrialization. Unfortunately, the inventiveness which had created German industry
had also made it so efficient that its productivity outstripped the
nation's ability to consume. As a result, industrial productivity
would only be sustained by foreign demand. Were that demand to fal-
ter, millions of men and women would have had no useful role in
German society. Somehow, they would have had to be eliminated to
avoid a social crisis.

Moreover, the situation in Germany was not very different
from the situation elsewhere in Europe. As a result of the modernization process in both agriculture and industry, millions of
Europeans could no longer find a viable existence in the communities
in which they were born.[15] Many of us are descendents of those
fortunate enough to find a new beginning in America. Other Europeans met a more tragic fate. Germany did get rid of a portion of
its unwanted people; so too did France, Britain, Austria, Italy,

Russia, and England. Over twenty-five million Europeans were deemed
expendable in the utterly horrendous battles of World War I.[16]
Still, the problem was not solved even by that monumental blood-
letting. World War I was followed by the Great Depression, and
structurally-induced unemployment became a world-wide phenomenon.
Europe could no longer export its redundant population to America,
because over twenty-five percent of the American work force was
unemployed. Let us not forget that it was neither free enterprise
nor bloated government bureaucracies that dismantled the American
unemployment problem, but America's entry into World War II. In
Europe, the crisis was of such a magnitude that 8,500,000 Poles
out of a population of 35,000,000 were either unemployed or woe-
fully underemployed immediately before World War II.[17]

If a person finds himself in an overcrowded lifeboat with
more hands and fewer supplies than are needed to survive, he
may behave in a very different way than when space and supplies
are plentiful. In a lifeboat situation, those who possess weapons
may be tempted to eliminate those without weapons, especially if
the latter were culturally and religiously alien. This may be
an oversimplification of what took place in Europe during World
War II, but it does suggest some of the social and economic reasons
why outright genocide occurred in the twentieth century rather
than earlier. It was only in the twentieth century that the
modernization process confronted European society with the problem
of millions of surplus people who could neither be exported to
America nor gainfully employed at home. It was also only in the
twentieth century that a corps of functionaries with a fully
rationalized, depersonalized consciousness became available for
the new tasks.

It is not at all surprising that murder became a preferred
solution. If rationality is the methodical attainment of a practical end by a precise calculation of adequate means, then the
most cost-effective "solution" of the problem of eliminating surplus people is murder. In the case of the Jews, their hazard did
not come from the fact that they were useless to the productive
process but because it was understood that, were they removed,
others less alien could easily and willingly take their place.
In truth, the dreams of reason bring forth monsters.

The Germans were not the only ones to realize that a rationalized, secularized market economy might require mass murder as a
solution. Let me quote from a distinguished American writer. I
shall withhold his name and the date of his essay until I have

completed the quotation.

> Unless we deal with the permanently unemployed,
> we shall have trouble. The masses of the unem-
> ployed are not consuming. They are beginning to
> engage in anti-social pursuits . . . . And in
> twenty years, . . . this class may increase to
> fifty million men. If the number increases or is
> even allowed to remain constant, it will . . .
> constitute a dire menace to public order. . . .
> Society would suffer the least rupture . . . , if
> it quietly, and in the ordinary routine of in-
> dustrial technology, *killed off about eight
> million workers and their families.*
>
> It should be done, all things considered, gradually,
> but completed in a year lest there should be an
> abnormal increase of that class of persons, with
> the attendant perils. . . .
>
> I need not suggest that the method be painless.
> We are too humane for the axe, guillotine, rope
> or firing squad. I should personally prefer
> some kind of lethal gas, but not being a chemist,
> I leave that proposal to the specialists. . . .
>
> I have said that this method of disposing of the
> residue x would relieve us of the whole problem
> of unemployment. That is not strictly true. It
> assumes as accomplished a long moratorium on the
> invention of labour-eliminating devices; it re-
> quires for its success a stabilization of our
> technology. Yet should our technical equipment
> still further improve, the method is still workable.
> There would merely be a certain number of newly
> unemployed to kill off every year.

The author was a member of that group of Southern writers known as
the Agrarians. They did not admire industrial society and were
deeply concerned with its social costs. The author wrote "tongue
in cheek," to be sure, and in imitation of Jonathan Swift's classic
satirical piece, but he was keenly aware of some of the more destructive tendencies imminent in our rationalized technological
society. The name of the article is "The Problem of the Unemployed: A Modest Proposal." It appeared in *The American Review*,
Volume One, Number Two, May, 1933. The author was the celebrated
American poet Allen Tate.[18]

Moreover, the problem of surplus people is currently still
one of the most intractable structural problems of technological
civilization. We attempt to ameliorate the situation by the dole
and by bloated bureaucracies. We may even soon return to the draft
to find work for the cadres of young people who would otherwise
waste their time on the streets or worse. The problem is complicated by the fact that the very rationality that has driven us
to define worth in the most impersonal way possible, namely in
monetary terms, has condemned millions to be regarded as worthless

both in the eyes of society and in their own as well.

"What is a man worth?" Thomas Hobbes asked at the beginning
of the era of possessive individualism. His answer for our time
as well as his was: the price his labor will get in the market-
place.[19] But if his labor can fetch no price, is he then worthless? Do we treat him as we would any commodity which has lost
all value? Do we consign him to the junk heap? That solution
was tried in Europe and could be tried again, were war and its
aftermath once again to provide such an operation with a cover, as
it did for the Turks in World War I and the Germans in World War II
and recently for the Long ..ol government in Cambodia. In peacetime
such a "solution" is hardly likely. In fact, a brief look at
some aspects of actual and potentially redundant populations, rather
than at the governments that could threaten their existence, may
be more interesting for our purposes.

Hobbes' idea that a man is worth the price of his labor was
based upon a conception Hobbes shared with Adam Smith; namely, that
labor is a commodity like any other.[20] The Oxford English Dictionary succinctly defines a commodity as "anything that one 'trades'
or 'deals' in." There is, however, a sense in which, if human
labor is a commodity, it is not like any other. If I run my car
to the ground and throw it away, I need have no further concern
that it will trouble me. However, if I cast a man aside, I cannot be certain how he will act. That is why Caprivi was convinced
that Germany's excess population had to be safely dispatched to
the New World if work could not be found for them at home. Incidentally, a key element in Hitler's program from start to finish
was *Lebensraum*. Unlike Caprivi, Hitler was not content to see
Germany's surplus population exported to the New World. He thought
he had a more "rational" solution, in the technical sense in which
we have been using the term. Hitler was intent upon creating his
own new world for surplus Germans in those areas to the east of
Germany that were inhabited by the Slavic peoples. Taking as his
model the American elimination of the native Indian population, he
was convinced that the eventual enslavement and slaughter of the
Slavs would give the Germans the new world they required.[21]

What can a person do whom society casts aside? He can of
course try to ameliorate his situation by political action. However, as early as 1905 when he wrote *What Is To Be Done*? Lenin understood that, having failed in the economic sphere, an unaided
underclass was hardly likely to succeed in politics.[22] Another
response)f the underclass might be to retreat into one of the

many forms of escapism which are currently available. We need not
dwell on the subcultures of drugs or small scale crime which are
expressions of this escapism. From our perspective, religious
responses to superfluity may be more interesting and instructive.

Let me put forth the hypothesis that the growth of cults in
the United States is at least in part a religious response to the
perception of superfluity. As has been often observed, a particularly large proportion of those involved in the cults tend to be
young adults, often of college age. But, is not this the age for
whose labor our society has least use? Is not the difference between middle-class youth and lower-class youth that, whereas both
are superfluous to the labor market, society provides a respectable
precinct where middle-class youth can be segregated from the
working populations while they acquire the complex skills required
for entry into the labor market? We call those precincts colleges
and universities. Thus, even middle-class youth, who can in fact
expect eventually to find respectable slots in the labor market,
nevertheless feel the cultural and psychological pressure of the
threat of superfluity in a way that other age groups may not.

Moreover, many of the contemporary cults can be classified
as millenarian; that is, as religious movements which promise the
imminent liberation of humanity from the moral and existential
limitations of the present order and its transformation into a
condition of perfect goodness and happiness.[23] It is important
to add that usually the charismatic leader of the millenarian community is taken to be the divinely-appointed agent of the promised
transformation. His role is usually depicted as messianic.
Millenarian movements are said to be pre-political; that is, they
are attempts at social transformation of those who seek change but
are without effective access to the political and social instruments
of change. They are also pre-political in the sense that the skills
learned in the movement may at a later time be applied to the political arena.[24]

However, millenarian movements can also be post-political. It
may, for example, be no accident that, whereas in the sixties young
people tended to seek political change through the great movements
of protest, in the seventies criticism and even rejection of the
established order has tended to take religious forms. Even the
convert to a high-intensity fundamentalist religious group is involved in a symbolic rejection of the established order, if only in
his rejection of lukewarm mainstream religion. In the case of the
millenarians, the rejection is explicit. Young people who

participate in such movements have come to the conclusion that, if
society is to be changed at all, it must be through religious
means. Furthermore, the sectarian character of these movements is
an expression of the fact that their adherents have come to the
conclusion that the majority of mankind is not likely to be saved
under any circumstances, that the system cannot be transformed,
and that salvation is possible only for the counter-community of
the elect. Here again, the very nature and organization of these
movements bears witness to their criticism of the current social
order.

Rejection of contemporary society involves rejection of its
standards of worth. People who are afraid of becoming superfluous
in a society that measures all things human by the utterly rational
standard of money are going to seek a standard of worth other than
money. If you tell a person, "Since your labor is worthless, you
are worthless," as we do with the unemployed, that person may respond: "You don't know how to measure human worth. Men cannot
measure other men. Only God can do that, and we shall yet see who
are God's elect." Thus, secular rationality which defines worth
in monetary terms pushes beyond itself to an attempt to recon-
stitute a religious definition of worth. According to the old-new
definition, he has worth who is part of God's plan for mankind's
salvation. It is easy to recognize that the history of Christianity
is not without its parallels to the logic of the contemporary
millenarians.

I think it reasonable to predict that, as the dilemmas of
twentieth-century capitalism intensify, we shall see more millenarian movements. If by the death of God we mean the triumph of
the secular spirit and its rationalizing modes of behavior and
consciousness, we can hardly rejoice at all that triumph has
meant. We ought, however, to recognize that many of those threatened by the practical consequences of that secular spirit, namely,
those millions who have been rendered redundant by our technological
and organizational genius, may adopt new modes of religious consciousness which offer them the hope of personal and social
transformation. Unfortunately, there is little assurance that they
will ultimately succeed in their quest. Millenarian movements tend
to promise more than they can deliver.[25]

This fact was exemplified by the People's Temple Cult and its
hideous denouement.[26] The group was clearly millenarian in its
aspirations. It was largely composed of surplus people many of
whom were recipients of welfare. Nor is it accidental that their

final journey was from California to Guyana. If America was the
safety valve offering hope of a new beginning to Europe's surplus
people, California is geographically and perhaps psychologically
the last stop in the American dream. That may be why cults are
more likely to flourish in California. Exclusivistic expressions of
religious fervour are more likely to appear in strength in the
Deep South, where a sense of history has limited the credibility of
utopian optimism concerning the public domain. In the Deep South,
transformations are more likely to take place in the soul of man
than in the public world. In the case of the members of Jim
Jones' Temple, when even California failed to yield the New Jerusalem, Jones was determined to create his elect community in the
wilderness. And, as has so often happened in the past, Jones'
heaven on earth was hell from the very start. Instead of a New
Heaven and a New Earth, the members of the People's Temple found
a dead end.

Typical of millenarian movements in the past, bizarre sexual
practices played an important ritual and symbolic role in the Jones'
cult.[27] Jones used sexual degradation to explode the only nuclear
unit that might have served as a focus of opposition to his absolute domination--the family. By compelling chosen followers to
commit adultery and to indulge in bizarre sexual practices with
him, often in the presence of the marital partner, Jones accomplished what Creon of Thebes was unable to achieve with Antigone,
who obeyed the unwritten, eternal law of family loyalty rather than
submit to the state and its necessities. This ought to give those
of us pause who are quick to relegate the family to the past. In
a world of total domination, the dominators would always prefer
to deal with isolated individuals than with families or other me-
diating structures such as the churches. The bizarre sexual de-
gradations also served dramatically to symbolize the cult members'
total break with the world that had rejected them. Jones' followers had been judged worthless by the standard of measure of our
society. They were under strong temptation to reject its norms.
By rejecting society's behavioral norms, they were dramatizing, as
have millenarian groups so often in the past, their belief that
the end of the Old Adam and the birth of the New was taking place
in their community.

There may even be a relationship between the mass suicide of
the Jones' cult and the Three Mile Island crisis. The triumph of
functional rationality can result in what can best be called the
madness of reason. Again, I repeat, "The dreams of reason bring

forth monsters." The worst danger involved in the triumph of
practical rationality is the possibility that it may result in irreversible damage to the ecosphere, the most fearsome being drastic
nuclear pollution. Three Mile Island dramatized the widespread
apprehension that a nuclear accident can render a large population
center uninhabitable for thousands of years, which is irrevocable
damage, given the temporal horizons of our culture. The Guyana
suicides demonstrate what a group of human beings might do if they
or their leaders came to regard the negative aspects of their condition as irreversible, that is, that they are indeed at a dead
end. The final irony of the triumph of practical rationality
might be that, in an era of irreversible transformations and mass
impotence, the decisive model would be neither Moses, nor Jesus,
nor Buddha, nor Mohammed, but Samson, and that the destructive resources available to tomorrow's Samsons would be infinitely greater
than those available to the Jones' cult.

I do not want to end this discussion on an altogether pessimistic note. As I indicated at the beginning of this essay, I
have been led to these reflections by an attempt to understand the
Holocaust and, through the Holocaust, the general phenomenon of
mass destructiveness in our times. I would stress that my concluding scenario is a possible scenario, not one that must necessarily unfold. Furthermore, not all of today's millenarian cults
are suicidal. Many will yield socially constructive long-range
results. Let us not forget that Christianity itself began as a
millenarian movement. The most likely framework for the fruitful
renewal of the millenarian impulse will probably be within the
body of Christendom itself. Let us also remember that monsters
can be defeated, as the legend of St. George and the dragon reminds
us, and that every thinker who has ever seriously reflected on the
"death of God" has awaited the moment of divine rebirth. Perhaps
I have dwelt as unsparingly on the destructive aspects of our culture as I have out of the conviction that only by fully comprehending our hazards can we hope to overcome them.

NOTES

[1]That the doctrine of the election of Israel is central to my
theological concerns is evident in my earliest and most influential
discussion of the problem of God and the Holocaust. See Richard
L. Rubenstein, "The Dean and the Chosen People," in *After Auschwitz*
(Indianapolis: Bobbs-Merrill, 1966), pp. 47-60. For a statement
of my position concerning the affirmation of belief in God after

the Holocaust, see "God after the Death of God" in Richard L.
Rubenstein, *Morality and Eros* (New York: McGraw-Hill, 1970),
pp. 183-196.

[2]See Norman Perrin, *Rediscovering the Teachings of Jesus* (New
York: Harper and Row, 1976), pp. 110 ff., and S. G. F. Brandon,
The Fall of Jerusalem and the Christian Church (London: Society
for Promoting Christian Knowledge, 1968), pp. 230 f.

[3]See Justin Martyr, *Dialogue with Tryphon*, trans. A. L.
Williams (London: 1930), II, p. 107.

[4]On April 26, 1933, in an interview with Bishop Berning of
Osnabruck, Hitler declared, "As for the Jews, I am just carrying
on with the same policy which the Catholic Church has adopted for
fifteen hundred years." See J. S. Conway, *The Nazi Persecution
of the Churches 1933-45* (New York: Basic Books, 1968), p. 26.
See also Raul Hilberg, *The Destruction of the European Jews* (Chicago: Quadrangle Books, 1967), pp. 12 f.

[5]See Andrew Greeley, *Unsecular Man* (New York: Dell, 1972),
and Greeley, *The Denominational Society* (Glenview, IL: Scott,
Foresman & Co., 1972).

[6]See Rod Nordland, "Nuclear Patchwork," in *Tallahassee
Democrat*, April 22, 1979. This is a syndicated article which first
appeared in the *Philadelphia Inquirer*.

[7]This conviction has been reinforced as a result of a long
conversation with Professor H. Martin Rumscheidt of the Atlantic
School of Theology, Halifax, Nova Scotia, in which he recounted
his childhood memories of Dr. Walter Dürrfeld, a neighbor of the
Rumscheidt family in Leuna, Germany. Leuna was the seat of the
corporate headquarters of the I. G. Farben petro-chemical cartel.
During World War II Dürrfeld served as chief executive officer of
I. G. Farben's slave-labor factory at the Auschwitz death camp.
Within his own circle Dürrfeld had an exemplary reputation, yet
he was altogether willing to administer a factory which was so
organized that its workers would drop dead or be weakened so that
they were exterminated as unfit on a calculated, predetermined
schedule. On the subject of I. G. Auschwitz and Dürrfeld, see
Richard L. Rubenstein, *The Cunning of History* (New York: Harper and
Row, 1975), pp. 48-57; and Joseph Borkin, *The Crime and Punishment
of I. G. Farben* (New York: Free Press, 1978), pp. 11-127.

[8]See Michael Arlen, *Passage to Ararat* (New York: Farrar,
Straus & Giroux, 1975), pp. 135-185; see also Henry Morgenthau,
Ambassador Morgenthau's Story (New York: Doubleday, Page, 1918);
Viscount (Spring) Bryce, *The Treatment of Armenians in the Ottoman
Empire 1915-16: Documents Presented to the Secretary of State
for Foreign Affairs by Viscount Bryce* (London: 1916).

[9]See Aleksandr Solzhenitsyn, *The Gulag Archipelago* (New York:
Harper & Row, 1973), I, pp. 431 ff.

[10]The hypothesis that the Holocaust is both a response to and
an expression of the modernization process is fundamental to my
interpretation of that event. See *The Cunning of History*, pp. 1-21.

[11]See Peter Berger, Brigitte Berger and Hansfried Kellner,
The Homeless Mind: Modernization and Consciousness (New York:
Irvington, 1973), pp. 8 ff.

[12] Max Weber, *Economy and Society: An Outline of Interpretive Sociology*, ed. Guenther Roth and Claus Wittich (New York: Bedminster, 1968), II, pp. 636-37.

[13] See Rubenstein, *The Cunning of History*, p. 10. For an overview of mass migration in modern times, see *World Migration in Modern Times*, ed. Franklin D. Scott (Englewood Cliffs, NJ: Prentice-Hall, 1968).

[14] See A. J. Ryder, *Twentieth Century Germany: From Bismarck to Brandt* (New York: Columbia University Press, 1973), p. 40.

[15] See Oscar Handlin, *The Uprooted* (Boston: Little, Brown, 1951), pp. 7-33.

[16] See Gil Eliot, *Twentieth Century Book of the Dead* (New York: Scribner, 1972).

[17] See Celia S. Heller, *On the Edge of Destruction: Jews of Poland Between the Two World Wars* (New York: Schocken, 1977), pp. 94 f.

[18] This passage was pointed out to me by Mr. William Moss, a graduate student at Florida State University.

[19] Thomas Hobbes, *Leviathan*, ed. C. B. Macpherson (Harmondsworth, Middlesex: Penguin, 1968), Part I, Chapter X, pp. 151 f.

[20] Adam Smith, *The Wealth of Nations*, ed. Andrew Skinner (Harmondsworth, Middlesex: Penguin, 1970), pp. 225 f.

[21] The Nazis apparently had no explicit plan for the extermination of the Slavs, but they did have a plan for their mass enslavement. All authorities are agreed that in the process a very large proportion of the Slavs would have been exterminated, as indeed the number of victims during World War II clearly indicates. On Nazi policy towards the Slavs, see Bohdan Wytwycky, *The Other Holocaust: Many Circles of Hell* (Washington: 1980); Alexander Dallin, *German Rule in Russia: 1941-1945* (New York: St. Martin's, 1957); Ihor Kamenetsky, *Secret Nazi Plans for Eastern Europe: A Study of Lebensraum Policies* (New York: Bookman Associates, 1961); Kamenetsky, *Hitler's Occupation of the Ukraine*, 1941-1944 (Milwaukee: Marquette University Press, 1956). Hitler's ideas about the creation of a *Lebensraum* to the east were influenced by the novels of Karl May. May never visited America, but wrote graphically about the exploits of the white settlers in defeating the Indians. In private conversation Hitler would frequently refer to the Russians as "redskins." See Robert G. L. Waite, *The Psychopathic God-Adolf Hitler* (New York: Basic Books, 1977), pp. 11 f., 40; Robert Payne, *The Life and Death of Adolf Hitler* (New York: Popular Library, 1973), pp. 27 f.

[22] V. I. Lenin, "What is to be Done?" in *Lenin on Politics and Revolution*, ed. James E. Connor (Indianapolis: Pegasus, 1968), pp. 31-78.

[23] See Yonina Talmon, "The Pursuit of the Millenium: The Relation Between Religion and Social Change," in *Sociology and Religion*, ed. Norman Birnbaum and Gertrud Lenzer (Englewood Cliffs, NJ: Prentice-Hall, 1969), pp. 238-254.

[24] *Ibid.*, pp. 249 ff.

[25]*Ibid.* That is why they are so frequently confronted with crises of disconfirmation.

[26]See Marshal Kilduff and Ron Javers, *The Suicide Cult: The Inside Story of the Peoples Temple Sect and the Massacre in Guyana* (New York: 1978), pp. 50-90.

[27]*Ibid.*, pp. 53-57.

PART ONE

Technological Society

and

Theological Method

A CHRISTIAN RESPONSE TO TECHNOLOGICAL SOCIETY:

A MYSTICISM OF TECHNOLOGY

Martin C. Kastelic

In the broadest sense of the terms, this essay deals with
the relationship between religion and culture. More specifically,
it focuses on the relationship between Christianity and technological society. Its purpose is to suggest the positive contribution
that Christian faith can make to a society which is technologically
determined.

The desire to address such an issue does not come from some
nostalgic attachment to Christendom, a pining away for another
medieval synthesis in which the church would find itself in charge
of culture. Nor is the desire a result of some kind of superman
complex, an eagerness to come to the world's rescue just in the
nick of time, thereby restoring faith in a somewhat Clark Kentish
establishment. The desire stems, rather, from a keen awareness
that Christianity gone awry is responsible for technology gone awry.

No attempt will be made here to prove this last statement.
Studies enough have shown the part played by the Christian religion
in the development of technological society and how, as Christianity
failed in its mission, this development manifested a tendency toward the dystopian. Those who have analyzed the history of technology have at last seen fit to note the positive thrust given to technological progress by the Christian worldview.[1] Those who have re-
searched contemporary religiosity continue to illustrate how scientific technology contributed to the demise of Christian culture.[2]
And those who have noted the dehumanizing tendencies of present
technological society willingly admit the guilt of Christians in
this regard.[3] To give but one example, Richard Rubenstein's *The
Cunning of History* could be cited. In this little book, Rubenstein
argues persuasively that the Holocaust is the logical outcome of
a technological society with a surplus population, finite resources,
and expanding state powers; and that this technological society is
a development out of fundamentally biblical traditions.[4]

In view of the work done by Rubenstein and others, it seems
more appropriate and, one would hope, more interesting to move a-
head. Rather than spend more time trying to figure out how we arrived at the present juncture, let us turn to consider what may be
done in the future. But it will be necessary, first, to establish

a starting point. What is the nature of technological society?

To my mind, the most insightful interpreter of technological society continues to be Jacques Ellul. Although Ellul has written extensively about technological society, the early chapters of his book by that name are particularly pertinent for our purposes.

Ellul begins his study by offering a simple definition of technique, a definition based on his sociological investigation of the phenomenon: "The term *technique*, as I use it, does not mean machines, technology, or this or that procedure for attaining an end. In our technological society, *technique* is *the totality of methods rationally arrived at and having absolute efficiency* (for a given stage of development) in *every* field of human activity. Its characteristics are new; the technique of the present has no common measure with that of the past."[5] It is to the development of an understanding of the newness and all-pervasive nature of technique which Ellul directs his efforts.

The human attitude toward technique is the key to Ellul's insistence that technique today is totally different from that of the past. This is so because, rather than talk about technology alone--the nature of which does not change from age to age--he is interested in "the characteristics of the relation between the technical phenomenon and society" (63).

The first characteristic of technique resulting from the contemporary relationship between technique and society is, not surprisingly, the absence of the limits put on technique by all traditional societies, and more especially the limitations imposed by the Church's demand that each new technique be subject to a moral judgment. To this characteristic, Ellul adds two more: rationality and artificiality. These are relatively well-known and receive little attention from Ellul. By rationality he means the reduction or leveling down of everything to the schema of logic. By artificiality he suggests that technique either destroys, eliminates, or subordinates nature. Besides these, Ellul offers five other characteristics which he feels are of great importance, more important than the three already mentioned insofar as they are often overlooked or misunderstood.

The first is the automatism of technical choice. Automatism has two aspects. On the one hand, "inside the technical circle, the choice among methods, mechanisms, organization, and formulations is carried out automatically" (82). On the other, "there is no choice possible between technical means and nontechnical means based on imagination, individual qualities, or tradition" (84).

The cause of this characteristic is our renunciation of control
over technique, our preference not to lift a finger, our acceptance
of the premise that the system is the solution.

Self-augmentation is the second new characteristic. This refers to the fact that technical progress is the result of a continued growth of scientific data, thanks to the work of a multitude
of technicians. "What is decisive," writes Ellul, "is the anonymous accretion of conditions for the leap ahead" (86). Added to
this is the fact that technical development poses technical problems. But such a situation, especially in light of comments made
in the paragraph above, is the function of another factor, human
commitment. As Ellul sees it, "modern men are so enthusiastic a-
bout technique, so assured of its superiority, so immersed in the
technical milieu, that without exception they are oriented toward
technical progress" (85). The result of this situation is that
humans act less and less except according to the nature of a re-
cording mechanism, and that technique loses all finality.

The third characteristic of technique is monism. Put simply,
in the words of Ellul, "the technical phenomenon, embracing all
the separate techniques, forms a whole" (94). Correlated to this
is the impossibility of analyzing elements out of the ensemble.
Therefore, the question of morality becomes superfluous, while the
distinction between technique and use is rendered nonsensical.
"There is no purpose or plan being progressively realized. There
is not even a tendency towards human ends. We are dealing with a
phenomenon blind to the future, in a domain of integral causality"
(97).

Technical universalism, the fourth characteristic of technique,
refers to the fact that technique supplants existing civilizations.
"Technique is the same in all latitudes and hence acts to make different civilizations uniform" (117). More than that, Ellul believes
that technique *is* a civilization. "*Technical civilization* means
that our civilization is constructed *by* technique (makes part of
civilization only what belongs to technique), *for* technique (in
that everything in this civilization must serve a technical end),
and *is* exclusively technique (in that it excludes whatever is not
technique or reduces it to technical form)" (128).

The last, and possibly the most important, characteristic of
technique today is autonomy. Benefiting from the insights of F. W.
Taylor, Ellul writes, "The complete separation of the goal from
the mechanism, the limitation of the problem to the means and the
refusal to interfere in any way with efficiency: all this is clearly

expressed by Taylor and lies at the base of technical autonomy"
(133). Technique is not determined except technically. It is determined neither by economic and political considerations nor by
moral and ethical judgments. Where it cannot assert this power,
as over physical laws, it dominates and subordinates.

As such, autonomy has a devastating effect. "It is common-
place to say that the machine replaces the human being. But it
replaces him to a greater degree than has been believed" (135).
This replacement occurs inevitably. First of all, it is the fulfillment of the ideal notion that we should be free of toil. But,
further, it is in faithfulness to itself that technique replaces
the human--for reasons of efficiency. "Technique must reduce man
to a technical animal, the king of the slaves of technique" (138).

If the above can be called a first consequence of technical
autonomy, there is also a second. "The second consequence of
technical autonomy is that it renders technique at once sacrilegious
and sacred" (141). As sacrilegious, technique destroys what was
held to be mysterious. "It has a single role: to strip off exter-
nals, to bring everything to light and by rational use to transform
everything into means" (142). This singular role is based on a
particular view of the world. "Technique advocates the entire re-
making of life and its framework because they have been badly
made" (142-143). But some sense of mystery is needed by man. "He
therefore transfers his sense of the sacred to the very thing which
has destroyed its former object: to technique itself" (143). For
Marxist and capitalist alike, in Ellul's estimation, technique is
sacred.

What then is technological society? Technological society is
the result of humanity's attempt to remake the world. It is based
on that which can be rationally controlled, mathematically quanti-
fied. Its scope is limited to efficient ordering, concerned neither
with ends nor with the moral dimensions of means. It is a society
which sprang up once Christianity had lost its hold on western
civilization, subsuming the traditional religious attitudes under
its drive toward the one best means.

The being inhabiting this technological society has been overwhelmed by what the technical phenomenon has been able to accomplish.
In light of these accomplishments, technique is freely chosen and
allowed to follow its own logic of development. This being has
thus benefited tremendously from the technical gadgets that surround
him, but has surrendered his responsibility for the world in the
process. Stripped of traditional values, the inhabitant of

technological society endows technique with the aura of sacredness. Technological man is idolatrous in relation to technique while his religion has become but one technique among many.

It would be foolish to deny that this presentation of Ellul has not been tendentious to a degree. Signposts need to be erected, otherwise the conclusions would appear too artificial. This caution--or apology, if you will--having been noted, we proceed to a consideration of the following four points which have emerged as significant in my own interpretation of Ellul's work: First, Ellul indicates that the rise of technological society coincided with the corruption of the Christian faith. Second, he puts stress on the Promethean character of the new age. Third, he insists on the unquestioning attachment that has been forged between tool and tool-user. Fourth, Ellul shows an awareness of the reductionism or leveling down of nature, society, and the individual that has taken place.

Ellul views technology as, first and foremost, a religious problem. Of course there are considerable economic, political, and social problems as well, but what Ellul affirms is that these are derivative. One would not expect other than a religious answer at this point. In fact, I find in the works of Ellul hints of a theology of culture relevant to a technological society. To look for these hints would involve more space than is presently available. But to suggest the directions for a Christian response to technology--my purpose here--I would like to elaborate on the four points listed above.

I. *The demise of Christian faith and the birth of the technological age.* It is important to stress that all hope for a rebirth of Christianity has not been ruled out by Ellul. Though there may be no chance for a Christian reawakening based on the model proposed by Jacques Maritain or that of the existentialists, nowhere does it appear that, in principle, such a reawakening is impossible. If anything, Ellul's comments elsewhere rightly lead one to believe that the contemporary protest against Christianity is based more on misrepresentation and misunderstanding than on sound philosophical or scientific bases. After all, what was left of Christianity at the time of the industrial revolution was but a hardened shell, a shell that may not indicate death but metamorphosis.

This is by no means intended to be a mere reiteration of the quip that Christianity has not failed because it has not yet been tried. The challenge implied in the quip is a challenge for all

ages. Here it is more a plea that Christianity deal with the world
for reasons other than the fact that it is forced to do so. Put
another way, it seems to be time for Christianity to take stock of
its resources and traditions and to realize that God did not create
the world so that we would have something to abandon or so that
we could occupy ourselves with something worthwhile till the last
trumpet sounds. God did not even create the world, it seems reasonable to assert, so that in it humanity would discover its true
destiny as some future goal. Christianity is not a religion
stretched between an *already* and a *not-yet* as much as it is good
news for here and now. Emphasizing that fact anticipates any protest against Christianity as well as attempts to render Christianity contemporary by reinterpreting it in light of some immanentist
soteriology, Marxist or otherwise. As important as the theologies
of hope and their offspring are, much more has to be done to high-
light the genuinely world-confronting, world-transforming character
of Christian faith.

     II. *Prometheanism*. The Promethean character of the technical
revolution is scarcely Ellul's discovery. Inclusion of this insight is significant, however, to the present undertaking. The
technical revolution seems to have taught, in a very short time,
what Christianity has struggled with for centuries, that is, that
humanity is responsible for the world. Human beings must assume
an active role in the world. Furthermore, this role cannot be
that of a guarantor of the status quo, but of a transformer of it,
that continually molds the world into a more suitable dwelling
place.

     The Promethean character has also taught us what we are capable
of once our energies are released upon the world. Mechanization
and computerization are considerable advances. The weight of technologies is overwhelming; the expanse of their influence is incal-
culable.

     Unfortunately, this Prometheanism includes the attitude that
when one responds to the world one does so by stealing power that
rightfully belongs to God. He strips responsibility from God and
burdens himself with it. God formed the world and, in the aftermath of some mishap, reformed it. The Promethean agenda is a coun-
ter-reformation, victimized by the pitfalls of all counter-reforma-
tions.

     From a Christian point of view, it is possible to redefine
the human project. It is as co-creator that the person must assume
responsibility for the world. He must be about the work of hu-
manizing what is not fully human in complete awareness that he is

the primary object of this work. That is what is meant when humanity is understood as created in the image and likeness of God. This entails the recognition that the human project is not directed toward the realizable so much as it is an attempt to begin again in view of the wholly other. Humanity will, thereby, stumble upon the newness that is its function as *imago Dei* and the world's as *theatrum Dei gloriae.* Such an understanding does not contradict the directionless nature of technique, but it does overturn its endless dehumanization.

III. *Idolatry.* The idolatrous attachment to technique should not be at all surprising. Humanity is constantly tempted to accept as final that which has proven to be of great benefit, especially if it has granted some semblance of self-sufficiency. The human person is a creature of hope, of aspiration, and often takes that which fulfills significant aspects of this hope as hope fulfilled in its entirety. This is what has been done, according to Ellul, in regard to technique. And not even Christians were spared this blindness.

The freedom that was won, thanks to this new-found power, was expropriated by that very power. Having assumed responsibility for the world, humanity all too soon reneged on that responsibility. Intent on transforming the world, humanity itself was transformed-- into a slave. By the same token, technique became something new. Understood as more than efficient means, it became less than efficient. Tools were forced to produce salvation first--in the form of profit, prestige, power, and pleasure--and efficiency second.

If Christianity were to recover its iconoclastic thrust, it would be in a position to bring about an awareness of this situation. It could aid in the realization that if human beings have been given responsibility for the world, a soteriological worldview, whether other-worldly or immanental, would be superfluous. Such iconoclasm could direct attention toward an Other world and this would free technique from its divine duties. Rather, technique would be what humanity is continually equipped with to begin to transform the world at those points where an image of this Other world graciously appears.

IV. *Radical Immanentism.* In view of the leveling down that has occurred, we should be quick to remind ourselves that, thanks to the ethic of radical immanentism, it is no longer possible to conceive of a god who is merely the prime mover, a god who easily becomes a vestigial appendage of the universe. Equally, we must realize that science has made great discoveries because it did

reduce its field of vision to the experimentally recreatable. If
our culture is based on an abhorrence of nature, it is nevertheless
true that we have come very close to nature, understanding many of
its baffling mysteries. Somewhere in this reductive view, however,
lies the same debilitating tendency that we noticed in regard to
technological idolatry.

We have defined technique too narrowly. We have substituted
realization for fullness. Technique is, after all, art, a product
of the human imagination. It is only recently that we have con-
fined technique to the narrow limits outlined by Ellul. The impressive results of technology seem to have caused a narrowing of
our field of vision, narrowing down the human in the process.

Our technological society has shown us that the human is a
technique, that is, an art. But if technique is art, it can no
longer be defined as the imitation of nature, nor can humanization
be limited to the process of realizing or actualizing the full potential of an essential human nature. Rather, we are what we make
of ourselves in light of the fullness of a God who comes.

The mention of art and imagination brings the present argument
to the point where positive, concrete suggestions for a Christian
response to technological society can be made. As I have argued
elsewhere, the trouble with technological society stems directly
from a reductionistic application of the human imagination, a limitation of the imagination to one or the other of its many functions.
I argued, further, that hope for technology lies in the direction
of a full utilization of the imagination, which utilization broaches
the religious question--but in the name of what?[6]

Essential to this argument was the scientifically established
data concerning altered states of consciousness,[7] as well as the
technology which has been developed for inducing these states.[8]
What Christianity has to offer is the wisdom of its mystical tradition. Let me make quite clear what I am suggesting: Science
and technology offer a more and more precise way of explaining and
stimulating human imaginative activity. The western mystical
tradition offers a response to the religious question which avoids
both technological idolatry and primitivistic Luddism.

The western mystical tradition, true to the secularizing tendency of the Judeo-Christian tradition, has never shunned involvement in the world. Theologians like Gabriel Vahanian and philosophers like Ernst Bloch have shown the powerful social effects that
mysticism has had, effects highlighting the inherent utopianism
of this tradition. In the same vein, historians of technology have

begun to uncover the important technological advances contributed
by western monasticism, contributions explainable as attempts to
make concrete the vision of the coming kingdom.

Nothing definitive has been written concerning the relationship
between mysticism and technology. I sense though that there is a
close one and feel urged to offer the following observations.
Mysticism, the attempt to stretch the human imagination to its
limits, can provide technology with a much-needed critical edge, as
well as with that creative thrust which would stimulate the development of those techniques necessary for our continued stewardship
of creation. Advanced technology, on the other hand, can provide
Christians with the information necessary to refine mystical techniques, thus making the fruits of mysticism just mentioned more
widely available, more effective. The connection is certainly not
automatic and the relationship must remain dialectical, but the
suggestion does seem to have some merit. It addresses technological
society in its own terms.

Further reflections on the four corollaries to Ellul seem appropriate here:

(1) A mysticism of technology recognizes God as radically im-
manent, "closer to us than we are to ourselves." It also provides
for a fuller understanding of the human, insofar as it is the human
imagination, exercised to its fullest, which provides the design for
technological society. And it takes seriously the creative effect
that technology has upon the human.

(2) A mysticism of technology makes clear the otherness of God
rather than of technique. It thereby places responsibility for the
world in the hands of humanity, and not in technique. Technique for
the sake of technique is shown in all its foolishness. Even, and
especially, the mystical techniques receive their proper emphasis--
as *means*.

(3) A mysticism of technology allows for exercising what seems
to be the god-like powers of technology without Promethean guilt.
It is with God as creator that humanity tends to the world, the more
effectively the more it is open to God.

(4) As such, a mysticism of technology does seem to offer new
life to Christianity--not a new Christian culture, to be sure, but
one in which Christians can play a significant, creative role.

The pedagogical implications of the foregoing seem obvious to
me--and not at all radical. The implications take advantage of
much good that is already available. What is implied is the need
for education in mysticism. Such education would include developing

an awareness of the long and prized tradition of Christian mysticism. It would also include an emphasis on the world-confronting,
world-transforming aspect of this tradition. Further, there would
necessarily have to be developed an appreciation for and facility
with mental techniques which have been shown to be of significant
value in stimulating the creative work of the imagination, recognizing God, the wholly other, as the source of this creativity.
All of this would be directed by an awareness of the nature of the
cultural context within which we live. The final purpose would be
to imagine and make concrete a world which was truly a prolepsis
of the kingdom of God.

     Our technological society, a society whose legacy is the fail-
ure of Christianity, has released energies which have yet to be
fully comprehended. If what I have presented is at all accurate,
these energies have not shown themselves inimical to Christianity.
What I suggest is that we have closed our eyes to these energies
at precisely those points where intersection with Christian faith
might occur. In this sense, if our society says "No" to Christianity, it says "No" to its technological orientation as well. If
our society is post-Christian, it is half-heartedly technological
also. And if it is half-heartedly technological, it is so to the
degree that it is idolatrous.

     These suggestions are tentative, to be sure. But the world
is a world in the making and God a gracious God. Tentativeness is
to be expected. Christian education must make a place for the utilization of the techniques of creativity which allow for the development of a critique of technique. In this way creative men and
women, who appreciate the really new because they have experienced
the wholly other, can begin to take stock of our technologies and
to strive to make our technological society a human society.

NOTES

[1]See Lewis Mumford, *The Myth of the Machine*, I and II (New
York: Harcourt Brace Jovanovich, 1970).

[2]See Gabriel Vahanian, *God and Utopia* (New York: Seabury
Press, 1977).

[3]See Victor Ferkiss, *Technological Man* (New York: New
American Library, 1969).

[4]Richard L. Rubenstein, *The Cunning of History* (New York: Harper and Row, 1975), p. 31.

[5]Jacques Ellul, *The Technological Society* (New York: Alfred Knopf, 1964), p. xxv. Subsequent references are noted in the text.

[6]Martin C. Kastelic, "Technology and the Human Imagination" to appear in the Summer 1980 edition of *The University of Dayton Review*.

[7]Matthias Neuman, "Towards an Integrated Theory of Imagination," *International Journal of Philosophy*, 1978, pp. 251-275.

[8]William P. Frost, "The Ethics of Religious Imagination" (unpublished manuscript) and Roberto Assagioli, *The Act of Will* (New York: Penguin Books, 1973).

HUMAN SELF-CREATION AND SELF-DEPRECIATION

George Muschalek

The following reflections will, I hope, show that *self-creation* and *self-depreciation* are concepts which literally apply to the human situation; that we find today alarming signs of a sweeping depreciation of human life, and that a theistic understanding of human freedom yields the fullest possible form of self-creation. And if we can overcome a mistaken understanding of it, we must say that today we need more, not less, self-creation.

Human Depreciation

Depreciation of the Human World

For more than ten years we have been aware of a deep deterioration of our conditions of life, more exactly of the human environment. The United States has discovered, earlier than Europe, that the world's technological culture with its accelerated pace has revealed a life of its own which turns out to be hostile towards its creators. Water is poisoned; nature is being replaced to a frightening degree by concrete. What is coming down from the skies is, at times, no longer gentle, refreshing, and life-giving rain, but liquid acid. Man-made chemicals slowly destroy the ozone layer so that in the future the inhabitants of the earth may be exposed to deadly heat or cold. It is as if nature has taken revenge for the injuries inflicted upon her.

We used to call that deterioration *pollution* of the human environment--an innocent word as seen from today. What is polluted just seems to need a good wash, and the problem would be solved. Our problem today though is far more serious. Things are affected more deeply. We have to speak of a loss of value, of a depreciation of human life. A nature which is mutilated and sick, which can barely maintain the balance of its own life, has diminished in value for humans. Nature has not only disappeared, here and there, so that it will be missed, it has turned against humans like a sore beast of the wilderness.

Our world is no longer just polluted. It has undergone a depreciation. In the last three years or so, we could hear voices which sounded deeply worried. There were not only the grim prophetic warnings of the Club of Rome, as recently as 1979, but also

more restrained assessments of the situation which made it clear
that the glowing optimism of progress into an ever brighter future
of mankind had become muted. This is the view of competent sci-
entists, with theology lagging slightly behind. Pessimistic voices
ask whether we regress at an anxious pace, instead of progressing
continuously.

In what does human depreciation consist? Where is human depreciation rooted? Is it to be found in the deterioration of the
human environment--of air, water, landscape--or does it consist of
the lack of an adequate living standard? Or are those two dimen-
sions--environment and possessions--areas which, on the one hand,
are influencing human life deeply, shaping or even destroying it,
but, on the other hand, are merely the outer field of human self-
realization, something surrounding human existence, but not identical with it? The question is whether human worth is made up primarily of impersonal realities like the air which the human being
needs vitally, but which he is not, or money without which again
humans cannot live, but which is certainly not identical with their
humanness; or whether being human is determined by values which are
not separable from it because they constitute it. Fortunately, we
still feel today that we must opt for the second part of the alternative.

Depreciation of the Human Self

If human worth is essentially determined by the fact that one
is a human being, not by the extent to which world is possessed,
it could be considered true that the present loss of the world
which humans are suffering does not really infringe upon human
integrity and happiness. The latter would be firmly grounded on
the remaining, or even increased, human worth and self-esteem. Human environment is being destroyed: it can be the occasion for a
rediscovery of the order of values--for instance, uninhibited exploitation of the world versus responsible use of it. In fact, we
have seen positive results as a consequence of our confrontation
with environmental problems and with our own poverty, as in World
War II. With the penetrating vision of a poet, Aleksandr Solzhenitsyn has described such an unexpected outcome.

We must, however, say that the loss of human worth reaches
deeper. Everyday experience points in that direction. A listlessness has spread, from which a paralyzing gloom proceeds. Sullen,
depressed faces on the streets, in the stores, in offices, in the
classrooms of schools and colleges. Listlessness everywhere. There

are fewer people who enjoy their jobs or even their free time.
Being with other people has often lost its sparkling excitement.
A great deal has been written about these and underlying problems.
In this present reflection we are interested in these things only
within a certain context, that will unfold as our examination proceeds. Therefore, my diagnostic remarks are brief, and suggestions
for therapy are missing altogether. They have been made already by
competent authorities. We are interested only in asking whether
there is a coherent process which is responsible for the loss of
human worth in so many forms.

Four observations will help to clarify the nature of this depreciation of our lives. These are chosen because they have, as
it seems, a special significance. What follows holds true for the
industrial civilization of western and eastern countries, though
with appropriate differences in color and texture, and also more
and more for countries of the Third World.

A first observation: Human life provides itself more with
quantity than quality. Many politicians stress, on either side of
the Atlantic, that the quality of life must be improved. Justified
and urgent as the objectives are, the underlying understanding of
the quality of human life still calls for examination. Quality
of life, so we are told, consists of better income, adequate housing,
healthier working conditions, better formal education, and the like.
Whoever lacks only one of these goods knows how indispensable they
are. But it is something quite different to *identify* those external
goods--even education--with the quality of human life itself. That
would mean by implication that the worth of this life is guaranteed
as soon as these requirements are met. The concept *quality of life*
is obviously meant to be appealing by reason of the fact that,
first, everything that is needed to make human life worthwhile is
being promised and, secondly, the goal has been placed within reach.
Quality of life is furnished, as we have seen, by goods which can
be produced and distributed by social planning.

Of course, these goods taken together could be called quality
of life, if it were made clear that we are talking only about a
particular segment of human life. If we do not apply this restric-
tion, we confine the worth of human existence within an area governed
more by quantitative than by qualitative principles. And in many
areas of human life quantity has replaced quality. Large numbers
impress. That is due to various reasons. Our contemporary com-
mercial world persuades us to believe this, and advertising likewise. The media follow the same principle in more ways than one.

To characterize the shift more pointedly, we have to say that
the emphasis placed on the area surrounding human existence is to
the detriment of the human being. The surrounding area, in short
the world, is the necessary realm in which humans must find themselves. Human identity is only found if commitment to other persons takes place, and if human activity is directed toward the
world. Moreover, this departure of the individual into the world
must be genuine and unselfish, not chosen as a road toward finding
one's own identity. This must be said to avoid misunderstanding
and holds true for all that we shall say about self-realization
and self-creation. Yet, today we have reached a point where it
must be made clear that the presence of the world in human life
is not, just by itself, a guarantee of a successful return of
human beings to themselves. The human person's departure into the
world--vital on all levels--may be without a return. In that case,
humans would have lost themselves.

A second guiding idea places humanity over humans. In a development which has taken centuries, mankind has placed itself,
often imperceptibly, in front of the individuals comprising it.
Mankind has won more importance than the individuals of whom it is
composed. The grand abstraction *humanity* has pressed human subjects into the background. A dislocation has taken place which
cannot be easily overestimated. Yet, only in the individual is
there freedom, responsibility, eternity, absoluteness--if indeed
absoluteness is somewhere at all in the world. The abstraction
imposes itself by magnitude, number, and duration in time computed
by centuries. Nevertheless, it is not the human subject in the true
and full sense of the word. Nor is it, for that matter, the proper
seat of human worth.

Wherever being human is realized first and foremost in humanity
instead of human individuals, a regress to more primitive cultures
has taken place. In these cultures, the humans unfold their existence fully only in the endless chain of generations, not in the
course of one individual life. The writers of the Old Testament
came to the idea of the totally completed life of the single person
relatively late. For that later period, death was more to them than
the vague disappearance of human life into an unknown nether world.
Only in an eternal fulfillment through death can the sum of human
aspirations come to rest. Lacking this, individuals remain vaguely
blended into the sequence of generations, and hope that in this
manner meaning would be realized in their lives.

A third area is that of human knowledge. We cannot deny that
we are swamped by fragments of knowledge. To begin with, we need
daily innumerable items of information to survive in our highly
sophisticated civilization. This has influenced our educational
systems, and was bound to do so. Education must offer incomparably
more data today than at the turn of the nineteenth century. The increase of educational material is, in the first place, an enrich-
ment. It is also, at times, a burden, however necessary, too heavy
to be carried by both instructors and students. A third possible
result of the ever increasing flood of information is realized when
information becomes devastating if a crucial form of knowledge can
no longer find space and time to grow, a knowledge which has to do
directly with human existence. Our forefathers called this form
of knowledge wisdom. But whatever word we choose, the content of
this kind of knowledge is indispensable if human existence takes
its fate into its own hands. By it questions both of abysmal difficulty and of great simplicity will be answered once again: what
is the human being as such? What distinguishes humans from stones
and dogs? Where do humans come from, and where are they going?
What is the right way to live, not only the most practical and
beneficial, but the truly human way? Finding answers to these questions about the human condition is dependent on special factors.
It is intimately connected with the individual's existence, the way
a person understands human life, the standard of value he accepts,
the attitude toward good and evil he adopts. Discovering this existential knowledge, as we may call it, will be then the outcome of
many, maybe very painful, decisions about life.

To be true, a human being retains innate human worth whether
its bearer has knowledge of it or not, and whether it is recognized
by others. But if humans appraise themselves wrongly, rate themselves under their true value, something is taking place which a-
mounts to a depreciation of their human existence. Human worth is
inseparable from human existence, and yet it is, on a different
level, subject to acceptance or neglect.

The fourth and final observation: Human self-determination is
more and more eroded through determination by outside factors. The
ability of the individual to determine for himself what must be
done has shrunk. Sources of wisdom can no longer be tapped, such as
the quiet observation of real human lives (not those invented for
entertainment), the consequences of other people's decisions, the
lessons of history, the understanding of the human condition displayed in literature, or the unconditional principles which are

supposed to govern human existence. As a result, we are more easily
seduced by prevailing ideas and fashions, which may concern everyday matters or ultimate questions of religion and ethics. Today,
we often read that our intellectual and religious pluralism represents progress towards heightened independence and responsibility in every individual. This situation, however, in reality over-
burdens many people, a fact which is seldom mentioned. A protective
withdrawal then takes place: if we are apprehensive of being
crushed by opposing intellectual forces, we shall instinctively
move out of the dangerous area into a safe place which is free of
confrontation, but equally free of individual decisions.

Self-Creation: A First Approach

What are the causes of this depreciation of human existence?
Many answers have been given, most of which have elements of truth,
but also stop short at crucial points. One answer is that humans
like Prometheus have reached into the realm of the gods to bring
fire to the earth in order to become independent of them. We can
safely state that our human work has developed on earth the power
of fire to an extent which no one could foresee. Is the Promethean
effort to transform the earth, beyond human proportions, the root
of the loss of human freedom and worth delineated above? More
pointedly, is the boundless will of humans to create their world
and themselves, instead of receiving themselves as creatures, the
root of human depreciation?

This answer is correct in a way, but it does not go far enough
as we shall see. We cannot deny that in many ways we are about to
create ourselves anew. We only have to think of certain educational
systems and goals as well as of new experiments in genetic biology.
Mankind is about to create itself according to its own plan.

The idea that man is the creator of his world and himself has
its origin in the modern era. At the transition from the Middle
Ages to the modern era, Nicholas of Cusa and the following generations described man a *secundus deus*, as a second god.[1] This view
of man, offered by a Christian theologian, is extraordinary. According to the Judeo-Christian tradition, God is set apart from
everything else by virtue of his creative power. The Old Testament
had in fact reserved a term for God's activity in creation to make
clear that it was his prerogative.[2] God brings things into existence, and in this he is not dependent on any condition or material
or potency.

We know that the idea of creation in the radical form can only be found in the Judeo-Christian tradition. This conception of God and world has shaped the thinking of Israel and the Christian peoples of the east and west. Today, however, the idea of creation by God has receded. Modern thinking has placed the human subject in the center. The human person is the free being who controls his own existence as well as the world. Whereas the Middle Ages saw human activity as reproducing God's designs, for us today almost no restrictions are placed on the human creation of objects, culture, and the human subject itself.

If we look directly at the nineteenth and twentieth centuries, ignoring earlier stages of development, we see it clearly. Feuerbach declared that man had to free himself from subjection to God to bring back at long last with a firm hand all the riches which he had worshipped, up there, in God. According to Marx and Engels, man creates himself through work. At the same time, the rapid development of sciences and technology apparently justified the philosophers' view: humans seemed only to have been hesitating for several millennia to reach out and take into possession the world and create it according to their plans. But sobering experiences followed, and goals had to be readjusted so that after disappointments people could still hold on to the belief that science and technology would finally solve the human problems which had been considered beyond solution for so long.

Of course, human creation of the world was restricted by the internal laws of reality which had to be obeyed. But a more serious discovery was that scientific and technological engagement with the world had distanced this world from us--despite the increase in power and control that had been achieved. The hazardous situation in which we live today is the very erosion of world in the full sense of the word. World means independence from man, originality, complementarity: it is governed by its own rules, springing from its own sources, and therefore called "nature." Only then is it a reality apart, which by its being different can create the tension which seems necessary for human realization. We know that at a breathtaking pace independent world is being replaced by man-made world. More and more we encounter only ourselves in our own products. What poets and philosophers saw long ago has come true. Humans live in an uncanny world which appears strange and forbidding although it has been made by them.[3] There is more to it than just the nostalgia of some people who yearn for nature and cannot muster their courage to make the step into the new, fully technological

age. It has rather to do with fundamental laws of human realization that it is highly questionable whether we can change this law
without transforming humans into something else.

Furthermore, it seems that the problem is not simply that one
kind of reality--the independent, self-grown world--is replaced by
another kind--the man-made world. It could probably be shown that
complete alienation from reality is a consequence of the change
that is taking place. If encountering reality also means receiving
it, then it can be seen that our attitude towards reality altogether
has changed. Producing is not encountering. Even if we personally
have not produced the many things which surround us, they have been
produced by humans and so betray the fact that in some way they
are all products of our hands. We cannot help being transformed by
the new attitude humanity has taken towards reality. A loss of
reality, though, if it is that, must have devastating consequences.

The human attempt to create the world has gone through many
stages. Philosophies of existence have come into being, from the
Christian form of Kierkegaard to the atheistic one of Sartre. A
philosophy of existence understands that only humans are capable
of putting themselves into being by freely choosing the form of
existence they want. But this description is insufficient. In the
creative human act, reality is not only molded and shaped, but something is being created which did not exist before. The free form
of existence which an individual chooses is totally new, not simply
derived from a previous design. The freedom of human self-creation
is not contradicted by the fact that humans depend on their forefathers, as is most clearly seen in their bodily existence which
certainly is not created by the individuals themselves. But the
difference between bodily and spiritual existence is sharply drawn
in the philosophies of existence. The human being as a free person,
as a moral being, does not exist before he brings himself into
existence by his free choice. In a true sense, man as a free being
with this unique form of existence creates himself.

The philosopher who has pushed the idea of human self-creation
farthest is undoubtedly Jean Paul Sartre. According to him, man
projects himself totally. There is nothing which human freedom will
find as a preexisting norm or goal. So man is totally responsible
for himself. Only the fact that he is at all, and that he is free,
is not a product of his freedom. Sartre makes it quite clear that
humans are not asked whether they want to consider their freedom
as crucial. There is no escaping freedom. Nobody is asked whether
he would create his own life. Nothing, according to Sartre, is as

obvious as the fact that we have to put ourselves into existence
through freedom.

For Sartre, the élan of self-creation finally comes to naught.
Man must create himself: that is, he must produce himself without
the help of preconditions. Such is, as we have seen, the nature of
freedom. The act of free decision is the only act in the world
which does not proceed from a potency in which it would have been
predesigned. Freedom is not nature, but spirit. Thomas Aquinas
himself characterized the free act as that which is the cause of
itself.[4] This divine creative power of human freedom has been
analyzed by Sartre more than by others.[5]

But the boundless optimism of this philosophy of freedom breaks
off abruptly. Sartre could not resolve the contradiction that man
in his unrestricted independence is constantly dependent on the
world which surrounds him. Humans are engaged in an endless pursuit
of the ideal of being totally out of themselves. They live by that
ideal and cannot be without it. But they cannot transpose that i-
deal into reality. They are ruthlessly tied to countless dependen-
cies, something which makes the ideal of boundless freedom founder.
That humans are "doomed to freedom," as Sartre says, thus finds a
deeper meaning: the most valuable reality in life, freedom, which
contains everything and lays everything open, reveals itself as a
dungeon. Freedom passes over into servitude. Sartre's freedom is
dreadfully lonely. In his philosophy, human freedom and the world
must be conceived as radically antagonistic. Then nature is experienced as being closed and forbidding. Freedom sees itself rejected by nature, and the opposition grows to the point that man
shudders and turns away. He feels nausea.[6]

Our reflection grew out of today's experience that human life
is depreciated. Searching for the cause of this loss in value, we
have found the line of modern thinking which places human existence
in the center as it had never been before. Man finally receives
recognition. He possesses divine creative power by which he produces himself. The climax of appreciation seems to have been
reached. Those philosophies, however, were developed in a period of
new loss of human value. We might assume that this contrast exists
only because the ideas of philosophers have not been heeded by humanity. If we accept this explanation, the way would already have
been shown by the philosophers, but not yet chosen by the vast majority of mankind. Sartre's philosophy, however, like similar systems,
shows that the way itself does not reach the point to which it was
hoped it would lead. It leads into nothingness, as Sartre himself
declares.

What was wrong with this understanding of human freedom if
the initial reach into the boundless realm of being and possibilities passed over into a sudden fall into nothingness? A crucial
misunderstanding of human freedom--of its independence and depend-
ence--was at the root of its failure. All the systems of human
freedom, those theoretically developed or practically lived, proceed from the fact that freedom is a reaching out to infinity.
There would not be human freedom without an awareness of, and a
claim to, infinity. It is the essence of freedom to move in a realm
of boundless possibilities. Freedom cannot accept limitations. In
a deep sense this is true and must be acknowledged by all who want
to uphold freedom. Total emancipation and the rejection of the idea
of God seem to be the inescapable consequences.

At this point, however, the systems turn over, the theoretically developed as well as the practically lived. As soon as we
assume that that most sublime of all human faculties, freedom, contains infinity within itself, or produces it out of itself, freedom
founders on the contradictions which it meets. Human freedom needs
infinity, boundlessness, or else it would not be freedom. At
the same time, freedom is creative, as we said, because it produces
its decisions out of nothing. The strange fact is that that sublime human achievement cannot be reached and retained unless freedom
is fastened to true infinity. Any merely projected infinity reveals
itself as unreal. If human freedom is severed from positively boundless reality--from real divinity, that is--it crumples and finds in
itself nothing but absence, the absence of the determinations of
which freedom boasted at the outset. The boundless realm, in which
alone freedom can move, cannot be found in human existence itself
or in the human world. Here freedom discovers only finite realities
staring at it, realities which in their finitude appear as nothingness.

We have thus reached a decisive insight which is difficult to
analyze, but easy to understand whenever it is lived. The highest
possible perfection of human existence, its divinely creative freedom, which in a true sense creates human existence, can only endure
if fed by real infinity. We are tempted to think that we could
heighten human perfection by detaching freedom from any thing or
person, especially a divine being. The opposite takes place: the
sublime realization, the subtle and fragile state of supreme perfection, is lost. It is important to realize that we are dealing
with the highest conceivable perfection of man (which cannot under
any condition be higher): we are dealing with a being which is

totally finite, and which experiences itself as such, and yet
this being is considered to be invested with infinity, this being
itself. To put it differently: a finite being is to be broadened
into infinity without ceasing to be finite, and without being
transformed into God. The latter cannot be done; if it could, there
would not be a real God. No real God can be the product of such
a transformation. We would not only lose the full idea of God by
severing freedom from the infinite; freedom itself would cease to
be the liberating fulfillment of human existence and would reveal
itself as extreme bondage. If the highest possible unity of a
finite being with infinity is sought, a theistic concept of free-
dom--a finite-infinite freedom--is the only solution.

Self-Creation: A Second Approach

What has been said so far has prepared us for a reliable understanding of self-creation. We must now look again at the problems we talked about earlier, and seek their solutions.

First, we need more, not less, self-creation. This would seem
to be in conflict with what we said about the modern idea of self-
creation being in part responsible for human depreciation. Yet, we
have also seen that, out of a misunderstanding peculiar to our
epoch, self-creation has been transformed into a human projection
toward nothingness. By this, self-creation has lost whatever of
value it possessed; namely, creating human existence out of a per-
sisting affirmation of boundless reality, so that the world in its
finite reality could be appreciated without man being precipitated
into nothingness.

We must examine briefly the legitimacy of a Christian concept
of self-creation. A totally realized existentialism is atheistic,
and we have seen reasons for that. Can the concept of a creation
of oneself be maintained where the dependence on infinite being,
God, is not severed? In no other anthropology has a full human
responsibility for the success or failure of life been so clearly
seen as in the Judeo-Christian view of man. Human beings have
been created to choose between life and death, their own life and
death. "I call heaven and earth to witness against you this day,
that I have set before you life and death, blessing and curse.
Therefore choose life, that you and your descendants may live, loving the Lord your God, obeying His voice, and cleaving to Him; for
that means life to you and length of days" (Deut. 30:19f.). It
would be reducing the significance of this text to assume that the
choice consists only between being left alive or having to face

death--in other words, to escape or not escape a death sentence.
What is proposed here to Israel is the possibility of actively
choosing and taking possession of life, their own life. This life
is, of course, Yahweh's gift to Israel. One's own life cannot,
however, be accepted like a loaf of bread. It must be accepted and
yet, at the same time, produced by the one who accepts it.[7]

It is, moreover, the theme throughout all the books of the New
Testament that human response to God's message and commitment to it
is a totally human responsibility such that no shifting the blame
to other factors is possible. Although new life and freedom are
given completely by God through Christ, they are also totally produced by human freedom.[8]

The challenge of freedom as understood by the Christian message
can be frightening. Building up human life in every respect that
truly counts is left in human hands. We have to think, first and
foremost, of the development of the human person as a free and moral subject. This reflection runs counter to the contemporary feeling that emphasis on the internal world of decisions is an illicit
withdrawal from commitment to the world and its tasks. It takes
a profound reorientation to attribute to those internal decisions
the role they really have. These decisions belong to the wide texture of human life which, through them, finally becomes good or
evil. Thus is it decided whether human life succeeds or not,
whether it finds--for others and for itself--fullness or nothingness. If we emphasize external achievements, for example on the
societal level, over against the inner decisions as to whether life
will be good or evil, we return to the idea that man completes his
existence only within the wide range of humanity as one of its unselfish components.

The modern hiatus between the world and the human inner self
cannot, I think, be bridged by an effusive commitment to the world
with its challenges, but only by a courageous reconsideration of
the primary human task: to create oneself precisely because human
existence has been so created by God.[9] To call this task primary
means that it is first in importance because it also encompasses
and engenders those activities which we usually call "praxis."

By way of conclusion, let us look back to the four modes of
human depreciation. If the external goods of life are identified
with the quality of life, the center of life shifts from those
qualities which we call human in the proper sense to those which
can be made and bought. Human life then does not succeed by compassion, faithfulness, and unselfishness. These, nevertheless,

belong in one form or another to all religious anthropologies. But
it matters that we see not only the transcendent merit of those
virtues, but also their world-immanent value, so to speak. If
the moral dimension of life is seen as deciding success or failure,
fulfillment of life--its success--is placed within the grasp of
any individual. Thus, a crucial factor for disappointment and
listlessness would be removed.

If, however, human life is made wholly dependent for its success on external "qualities," many individuals will have to face
failure. Or they are comforted at best with the meager thought
that their life will find its meaning and reward in future generations. Optimistic promises of faith in progress seem, at first
sight, to upgrade man. In reality, however, they endanger the
worth of individuals, even in those cases where everyone can enjoy
the promised goods, for then the independent worth of the human
individual is eroded.

The last two observations are intimately connected with what
we have just said. Wisdom has to reaffirm itself over against a
flood of information, if everything depends on whether the individual himself makes the right decision and thus makes life successful. Being governed from the outside can no longer be a desirable
solution. Needless to say, it may be either the totalitarian tendency of a system or the yearning of weak individuals for tutelage--
or both tendencies complementing one another--which is responsible
for a loss of self-determination.

Today we notice an alarming loss of self-esteem, self-confi-
dence, and identity. The increase of a formless anxiety, like the
use of tranquilizers, is epidemic. This particular form of anxiety
signals the loss of self-realization. Identity, self-esteem, self-
realization, even egoism, are being propagated as universal human
ideals, but subconsciously out of a therapeutic need. Humans today
seem even more essentially alienated from themselves than in Marx's
time. Human existence is slipping from our hands, and anxiety in
a form unknown even to Sigmund Freud has been the response.

The Christian message, however, is meant to give life to humans, life in an encompassing sense, which of course includes our
existence here in this world. Throughout the preceding reflections,
we have seen how great a need there is now--as always--for a renewed listening to the Christian message as well as for a renewed
effort to rephrase it so that it may pronounce its venerable truth
even to our new situation. It will, we hope, also guard us against
any distortions and over-simplifications our contemporary culture
may offer.

NOTES

[1]G. Gawlick, "Wahrheit: II. Philosophisch," in *Religion in Geschichte und Gegenwart*, Vol. VI, 3rd ed. (Tubingen: Mohr, 1962), col. 1522.

[2]W. Foerster, "ktizō," *Theological Dictionary of the New Testament*, Vol. 3 (Grand Rapids: Eerdmans, 1965), pp. 1000-1035; P. Humbert, "Emploi et portée du verbe bārā (créer) dans l'A.T.," *Theologische Zeitschrift* 3 (1947), 401-422; B. W. Anderson, "The Earth is the Lord's: An Essay on the Biblical Doctrine of Creation," *Interpretation* 9(1955), 3-20.

[3]Poets and writers have described the human condition in this light since long ago, among them Kafka in a particularly haunting way. On Kafka, see E. Heller, *The Disinherited Mind: Essays in Modern Literature and Thought* (New York: Harcourt, 1975), pp. 199-231.

[4]"Liber enim est qui sui causa est": "Free is he who is the cause of himself" (*Summa contra Gentiles*, lib. III, cap. 112, Adhuc).

[5]Interestingly enough, Sartre characterizes in the negative the same creative human power Thomas Aquinas defined: "l'homme est condamné à être libre" (*L'Existentialisme est un humanism* (Parish: Nagel, 1946), p. 37. See J. Streller, *Jean-Paul Sartre: To Freedom Condemned* (New York: Philosophical Library, 1960).

[6]See J. P. Sartre, *Nausea* (Paris: Gallimard, 1938), pp. 178-190.

[7]I have discussed these questions in *Tat Gottes und Selbstverwirklichung des Menschen* (Freiburg: Herder, 1973).

[8]The transcendental paradox of God and man is unavoidable: Whatever man produces is given him by God. This applies first and foremost to freedom itself: it is given to man by God, and in the same act freely achieved, or brought into existence, by man. This essential view of human existence has formed Christian self-understanding. To be true, it has often been reduced to simplified everyday understanding of either God's sovereignty alone or human responsibility alone, often with appalling consequences. If God is seen as giving or withholding life, leaving humans passive, his followers will be tempted to subject everyone to his rule, be it in violent conversion or in an authoritarian inner-ecclesiastical government which acts in the name of God without always remembering that only God himself knows "the secrets of the heart" and can act upon humans without reducing their freedom and responsibility. If, on the other hand, it is essentially human wit and endeavor which are supposed to bring about a fully human life, the design of that life will fall immensely short of God's original scope, and will at the end result in a similar threat to human freedom and realization. But despite all practical distortions, the idea of God-given self-creation has remained a sign-post throughout history and often found in systematic thinking a precise expression.

[9]Human self-creation cannot therefore be, as is sometimes stated, a straightforward listening to and obedient acceptance of contemporary culture, bringing it close to, or equating it with, divine revelation. A critical attitude, so crucial in modern understanding of human responsibility, must not only be directed to particular social facts or structures, but also, whenever necessary, to the tendencies of the culture within which we live, and out of which social decisions are born.

TILLICH'S PRINCIPLE OF CORRELATION:

A METHOD FOR ALL SEASONS

Robert Kress

"The method of correlation shows, at every point of Christian
thought, the interdependence between the ultimate questions to
which philosophy (as well as pre-philosophical thinking) is driven
and the answers given in the Christian message."[1] This principle
of correlation is one of the many contributions to theology for
which Paul Tillich is famous, although, as L. Gordon Tait points
out, "Tillich knows that there are weaknesses in his own method of
correlation; further, he is aware that he has not invented a new
method. Indeed, correlation is very likely as old as theology
itself."[2] Tillich himself says, "Systematic Theology uses the
method of correlation. It has always done so, sometimes more, sometimes less, consciously, and must do so consciously and outspokenly,
especially if the apologetic point of view is to prevail."[3]

For Tillich, "theology is the methodical interpretation of the
contents of the Christian faith" (ST, I, 15; II, 60). Theology
is the cognitive dimension of "religion [which] is directedness toward the unconditional, and culture is directedness toward the conditioned forms and their unity."[4] Tillich never tired of emphasizing
that religion is the substance of culture, culture the form of religion. For religion is not a "functional speciality" (*sit verbo
venia*) of the human being, but "the dimension of depth in all the
functions."[5]

Thus, it is important to note that for Tillich the principle
of correlation belongs not only to the heart of the theological
enterprise, but also to the very essence of Christianity. Not only
Tillich's theology, but also his life was correlational, lived as
he often explained, autobiographically, *On the Boundary*.[6] However,
for him the boundary is less the symbol of separation and more the
symbol of unity, at least of the ontological longing for unity.
As Fernand Chapey has noted, "Tillich's fundamental vocation lay
therein, to unite what was divided . . . . Tillich's entire thought
was dominated by the compulsion for unity."[7] Tillich himself says,
"In spite of the fact that during most of my adult life I have been
a teacher of Systematic Theology, the problem of religion and culture has always been in the center of my interest. Most of my

writings--including the two volumes of Systematic Theology--try
to define the way in which Christianity is related to the secular
culture."[8] Why Tillich began this statement with "in spite of" is
not clear. "Because" would have been much more appropriate since
Systematic Theology is precisely the mediation of the religious
tradition to the secular culture.

It was not just his personal experience which led Tillich to
urge the principle of correlation. For him Christianity and culture were correlational from the very beginning, although not without a struggle. Thus, at its very beginning the Greek philosophical
"doctrine of inspiration gave Christianity . . . a chance to enter
the world. . . . Long before Christianity the idea of inspiration
was developed in these Greek schools."[9] Thus, the time of Christ's
birth, and Christianity's, is not merely *chronos*. It is a *kairos*,
a *kairos*, we might say, of correlation.

Not only historically, but also essentially Christian theology
is correlational for it is both apologetic, an "answering theology"
(ST, I, 31), and "pedagogical" (I, 6; II, 13), as St. Paul indicates:
"I am in labor again until Christ be formed (*morphothe*) in you"
(Gal 4:19). For Tillich the connection between theology's pedagogical function and correlation is explicit. "The problem of the
Church School is more than the problem of a particular educational
aim. It is the problem of the relation of Christianity and culture
generally and Christianity and education especially. The problem
is infinite and must be solved again in every generation."[10]

Because of the influence of Ritschl and Harnack, our understanding of "Hellenization" has been unduly focussed on metaphysical
and cosmological theories of Christology and soteriology. However,
Tillich would certainly agree with Werner Jaeger: "That which we,
usually and rather vaguely, describe as the Hellenizing of the
Christian religion I would prefer to understand more concretely as
the reception of the Greek paideia by the Christian religion and
its transformation into the Paideia Christi."[11] Indeed, it was
through Hellenistic cultural forms that Christianity was able to
give birth to Christ "from Jerusalem . . . to the ends of the
earth" (Acts 1:8). Already in 1923 Tillich had noted his awareness
of "the very close connection between" his philosophical-theological
studies and "our current age and '*Geistelsage*' (spiritual condition)," for "every age has the task of creating anew the eternal
meaning of all ages from its [own] life and its [own] words."[12]
Tillich's principle of correlation must be understood not only as
a theoretical, speculative, but also a practical, pedagogical method.

Clearly, then, Tillich is right when he says that correlation
is as old as theology itself--at least for the Judeo-Christian
tradition. The only choice one has is not whether, but what kind
of correlationship one wishes to have between the religious tradition and the general culture. The New Testament itself knows a
negative correlation, whether the hostility of James (4:13-5:6) or
the indifference of Paul (1 Cor 7:31). A negative "paideia" can
be traced throughout Christian history. From Tertullian's out-
burst--

> What indeed has Athens to do with Jerusalem? What
> concord is there between the Academy and the Church?
> Away with all attempts to produce a mottled Christ-
> ianity of Stoic, Platonic and dialectic composition.
> We want no curious disputation after possessing Jesus
> Christ, no research after enjoying the gospel. With
> our faith we desire no further belief[13]--

through medieval Catharism and reformational enthusiasm, and beyond
Karl Barth's "No" to the heated imminent apocalyptic and millenarian
expectations of contemporary Fundamentalism, one solution to the
problem of Christianity's relationship to the world has been the
simple repudiation of the latter. However there are also Biblical
roots for the positive correlationship. Although tentatively, the
Christian "salvation-answer" (Acts 4:12) did seek a positive relationship with the greater culture, as Peter's experience indicates
(Acts 10:14, 34-37; 11:3, Gal 2:11). The direct proportion between
this positive correlationship and Christianity's increasing awareness of its universalism[14] is very important for our conclusion.
Not all positive correlation is immediately successful, as Paul's
experience in Athens illustrates. This does not, however, justify
the negative and specious conclusions of Lucien Cerfaux.[15] Classical theologians like Clement of Alexandria, Origen (for all his
rigorism), Albert the Great, Thomas Aquinas,[16] as well as contem-
poraries like Maurice Blondel and Karl Rahner illustrate the truth
of Tillich's contention that theology is correlational in its very
essence. Hans Georg Gadamer's remarks describe the status of
Christianity in today's pluralist society: "The hermeneutical problem only emerges clearly when there is no powerful tradition present
to absorb one's own attitude into itself and when one is aware of
confronting an alien tradition to which he has never belonged or
one he no longer unquestioningly accepts."[17] Christianity's definition of reality has lost its "immediate plausibility and objectivity." It is no longer simply "taken for granted."[18] Hence theology
must once again analyze the culture to see how the revealed answer

(now the tradition) can be made effective today. The only other
alternative would be the "negative correlation" of the Barthian
"No"[19] whose logical outcome would be a solipsism wholly inconsis-
tent with the biblical God who acts in history. It would reduce
all history to *chronos*. However, positive correlational theology
is aware that every culture is a divinely given *kairos*.

Hence, now as then, "systematic theology has to show that the
religious symbols are answers to this question . . . implied in
man's very existence, . . . [namely] man's predicament." "Existentialism analyzes, . . . formulates the question in all directions
and in every dimension of man's being."[20] This "analysis of the
human situation employs materials made available by man's creative
self-interpretation in all realms of culture. Philosophy, poetry,
drama, the novel, therapeutic psychology, and sociology" (ST, I,
63).

Tillich insists that only thus can theology surpass those "inadequate methods," which impede "any possible effect of theology on
the secular world," with the result that "traditional answers become unintelligible, and the actual questions remain unanswered."
He names these methods supranaturalistic, naturalistic (humanistic), and dualistic. The last is most like correlation, but is
rejected by Tillich because it contains "self-contradictory expressions" like "natural revelation" and "arguments for the existence of God." This "natural theology," as he also calls it, will
continue to fascinate "great philosophers and theologians" because
it "realizes that there must be a positive relation between man's
spirit and God's spirit in spite of the infinite gap . . . ." But
it has become "a mixture of truth and falsehood" (ST, I, 64-66).
Whether Tillich's appreciation of this natural theology is consistent in itself and in regard to his principle of correlation is
not at all clear, but also beyond the scope of this investigation.
Suffice it to say that Tillich's Lutheran patrimony of *natura humana
totaliter corrupta* and "reason as harlot" is more discernible here
than elsewhere.

What Tillich terms "naturalistic," Roman Catholics will recognize as the complex of positions condemned as modernism. For it
"the contents of the Christian faith were explained as creations
of man's religious self-realization in the progressive process of
religious history. Questions and answers were put on the same level
of human creativity" (ST, I, 65). Although Tillich is continually
accused of this error himself, he is not guilty.

What Tillich calls the supranaturalistic method has been his
most persistent critic and opponent. For it "the Christian message [is] a sum of revealed truths which have fallen into the human situation like strange bodies from a strange world. . . .
These truths create a new situation before they can be received.
Man must become something else than human in order to receive divinity; . . . human receptivity is completely overlooked. But man
cannot receive answers to questions he has never asked" (ST, I,
64-65). Tillich correctly finds in this method the traits of the
classical docetic-monophysitic mind. Tillich regards his method
of correlation "as an attempt to overcome the conflict between
these types of theology," one called "dialectical in Europe, neo-
orthodox in America, the other liberal in Europe (and America) and
sometimes humanist in America."[21]

Tillich's popularity as preacher, teacher, and author cannot
be explained apart from the attraction exerted by his method.[22]
However, not all have responded affirmatively. Indeed, recently
another University of Chicago theologian, David Tracy, has
demurred:

> The fact is that Tillich's method does not call for
> a critical correlation of the results of one's inves-
> tigations of the "situation" and the "message."
> Rather, his method affirms the need for a correla-
> tion of the "questions" expressed in the "situation"
> with the "answers" provided by the Christian "mes-
> sage." Such a correlation, in fact, is one between
> "questions" from one source and "answers" from the
> other. . . . One cannot but find unacceptable this
> formulation of the theological task of correlation.
> For if the "situation" is to be taken with full
> seriousness, then its answers to its own questions
> must also be investigated critically. Tillich's
> method cannot really allow this.
>
>   A classical example of this difficulty can be
> found in Tillich's famous dictum, "Existentialism is
> the good luck of Christian theology." . . . No one
> (not even a 'Christian theologian') can decide that
> only *the questions* articulated by a particular form
> of contemporary thought are of real theological in-
> terest. . . .
>
>   Tillich's method does not actually correlate;
> it juxtaposes questions from the "situation" with
> answers from the "messages."[23]

What of this criticism? First of all, Tillich does not limit
the question to "a particular form of contemporary thought."
Quite otherwise. "The Existentialism of the twentieth century is
not a special philosophy . . . of a few thinkers, but it is the
mirror of the situation of the Western world, . . . the anxiety of

our period as the special actualization of man's basic anxiety, . . . the awareness of his finitude."[24] Even if Tillich's factual appreciation of existentialism were to be awry, he would still not be liable to Tracy's accusation. Furthermore, given Tillich's expansive investigations of philosophy and religion, it is at best ingenuous to accuse him of not having allowed "full serious-ness" to the "situation" and "its answers to its own questions." What is really at play here is Tracy's own imprecision about the role played by the faith of the "theologian qua theologian" and his attempt to replace the traditional loyalty of the theologian to his tradition with a "fundamental ethical commitment, . . . [a] fundamental loyalty to that morality of scientific knowledge which he shares with his colleagues, . . . that community of sci-entific inquiry."[25]

How one is to avoid schizophrenia (can one existentially re-gard all possible options with the same "scientific" objectivity?), one is not told. Nor how, in the midst of the knowledge explosion, the "gnoseologically concupiscent" like us, who have all become *rudes*,[26] are to secure any firm perspective or standpoint.[27] It is not at all clear that, in his attempt to avoid what Tillich terms "supranaturalism," Tracy has not fallen prey to the "naturalism" of dogmatic secularism. Avery Dulles correctly notes, "As a revision-ist, Tracy is quite prepared to challenge the reigning models of theology, but he seems less prepared to call into question certain popular conceptions of science."[28] Further, Peter Berger notes "that the 'corrections' are hardly mutual. It is Christianity that must be 'corrected,' and it is the modern spirit that serves as the cognitive instrument for this operation."[29] Tracy's defense of his position is not convincing. His explicit reluctance about Tillich's "questions from one source and answers from another" ren-ders him liable to suspicions of reductionism. The vagueness of Tillich's understanding of revelation is well known and has prompted barrages of reductionist accusations. Nevertheless, Tillich insists that "the answers . . . of the Christian message . . . are contained in revelatory events . . . [and] cannot be derived from the ques-tions . . . from an analysis of human existence. They are spoken *to* human existence from beyond it" (ST, I, 64). In contrast, Tracy contends that the theologian is "obliged to explicate how and why the existential meanings proper to Christian self-understanding are present in common human experience" (*Rage*, p. 46). Unfortunately, this "common human experience" is remitted to clearly non-scientific vagueness. Neither does Tracy explain why it should be the norm of

the Christian, nor how, in such a view, anything specifically, to
say nothing of specially Christian remains.

In truth, Tracy seems much more liable than Tillich to the
Barthian accusation "that any kind of divine-human correlation
makes God partly dependent on man." Be that as it may, Tillich
correctly contends that "although God in his abysmal nature is in
no way dependent on man, God in his self-manifestation to man is
dependent on the way man receives his manifestation" (ST, I, 61).
As Tillich further insists, "in respect to content the Christian
answers are dependent on the revelatory events in which they appear; in respect to form they are dependent on the structure of
the questions which they answer." Indeed, "God is the answer to
the question implied in human finitude" (ST, I, 64). Tillich does
not say that God can answer only what man can ask. He says, rather,
that whatever man can ask can be answered only by God.

Thus J. Heywood Thomas' appraisal is wrong:

> It could even be said that he allows his conception
> of philosophy to determine the nature of theology.
> No amount of protesting that the content of the theo-
> logical answer is given in revelation can remove the
> offence of regarding theology as having merely the
> value of providing us with the answers to *our* questions
> instead of being the light that lightens our feet so
> that even the question is given.[30]

First of all, is it really theology which should provide this
"light"? Is it not, rather, revelation or grace or whatever one
might choose to call it? But theology? Certainly, theology is
light. But it is light from the Light (a sort of *lumen illuminatum
illuminans*). Second, what kind of questions other than ours should
we want to be answered? Answers to other people's questions can,
of course, become our answers--if we are made privy to the questions.
But then, whatever their origin, these questions have become ours.
Why "merely"? For theology to surpass this "merely" (given that it
answers the question which we are by our very being, it can hardly
be a "merely" in any case), it would have to be the message itself.
But, for Tillich the task of theology is "mediation . . . between
the mystery which is theos and the understanding which is logos."[31]
Thomas' assertion that his objection "has been argued by more than
one Catholic critic" brings no serious support to his argument.
For it is obvious that Catholic theologians are not immune to at
least moderate Barthianism.

Furthermore, even for Tillich the questions are not purely
"naturalistic" or "humanistic," although here as elsewhere he is
not as unambiguous as we might desire. However, Tillich does say,

"Symbolically speaking, God answers man's questions, and under the
impact of God's answers man asks them" (ST, I, 61). Likewise, it
must be repeatedly emphasized, Tillich does not correlate as a
neutral, uninterested, "scientifically objective" observer, as if
from the outside looking in. By virtue of his *Sitz-im-Leben*, he
can write, "The substance of my religion is and remains Lutheran."[32]
"The Church has always been my home."[33] Hence, the questions he
asks are already illuminated by the "divine self-manifestation. .
. . A symptom of both the essential unity and the existential
separation of man from his infinity is his ability to ask about the
infinite to which he belongs" (ST, I, 61). The unconditioned and
conditioned stand in mutuality, a circle. The absence of reference
to "under the impact of God's answers man asks them" from even fa-
vorable commentaries on Tillich's principle of correlation is per-
plexing.

Even James Luther Adams "is frequently left wondering, is this
supposed to be Christian doctrine, or is this Tillichian philosophy,
or has Tillich read his philosophy into the Christian terms?"[34]
One wonders why "into" and not "out of." In any case, one could
respond to Adams, "Yes." One is even more perplexed by Adams'
footnote: "This question is the more pressing when we consider
that Tillich says that philosophical theology is based on the
Christian kerygma." Not that this statement of Tillich's is unprob-
lematic. In the article to which Adams refers, Tillich says that
"the problem . . . of the relation between philosophy and theology
is not easy to [solve]. Nevertheless, it must be attempted in
every generation as long as theology exists, for the question of
the relation of philosophy and theology is the question of the nature of theology itself."[35] What we may conclude from all this is
that for Tillich the world is ontologically so structured that the
unconditioned and conditioned are fundamentally congenial. This
congeniality is due to the unconditioned and remains the case even
in the conditioned's fallen state and tragic predicament. The fall
is, thus, not nearly as tragic as an utterly abstract, unreal speculation might wish it, for from the congenial unconditioned comes
that "New Being in Jesus as the Christ . . . according to Paul's
constructive doctrine of the New Creation in Christ which included
the prophetic-eschatological message of the new eon!" (ST, I, 50-
51). Tillich can say this because, for all their reluctance about
the God-world relationship, "against the Extra-Calvinisticum, . . .
the Lutherans asserted the Infra-Lutheranum; namely, the view that
the finite *is* capable of the infinite, and consequently that in

Christ there is a mutual indwelling of the two natures."[36] Consequently, "in spite of the theonomous union between religion and culture, these two do not lie on the same level. Religion is the
depth-dimension of culture, and theology points to this dimension
not only in philosophy, but also in art and politics (which makes
neither of them a theological discipline). . . . Unity does not
exclude definitory [sic] distinction. And this distinction between
the two becomes important even if the unity is real only in a frag-
mentary way."[37]

It is, of course, unity between God and man--apparently of any
kind and any degree--about which Barthians are so squeamish: hence
their squeamishness about Tillich's correlation. Alexander J.
McKelway's doctoral dissertation, prefaced by Karl Barth, illustrates this strikingly. First, he asks, "Has God's revelation
ever come in any other way except through the breaking of the idols
men raise to their own subjectivity?" Then he asserts that "Tillich
argues that such destruction destroys man."[38] Only if subjectivity
is equated with idols, as McKelway apparently thinks. Tillich does
not, for his objection to the supranaturalistic view is not that
it destroys idols--certainly one of Tillich's own favorite themes--
but that it destroys the human in order to make it capable of receiving divinity (ST, I, 65). McKelway goes on to explain as if
somehow or other to refute correlation: "The absolute necessity of
the inviolate objectivity of God's revelation is required and determined by that revelation itself." (267). Tillich would hardly
doubt that. He might well wonder, however, what kind of contrast
is implied in McKelway's assertion. Could God really be interested
in providing a violated, subjectivistic revelation? Of course,
McKelway wonders whether "the integrity of the Christian message is
maintained in the method of correlation when its form is dependent
upon the question of man" (47).

Again it must be pointed out that the integrity of the Christian message is not threatened by the method of correlation. Theology mediates between the message, which is and remains the answer,
and the existential questions which it discerns in human existence.
Theology may mediate well or poorly, but the method of correlation
as such does not imperil the integrity of the Christian message as
such. McKelway also wonders "whether or not the method of correlation does not undermine this defense [of the freedom of God]"
(48). Of course, what this really means is that "we [McKelway]
resist the current attempt . . . to demonstrate a *useful* 'correspondence' between the ontology and theological method and

hermeneutics. . . . Does not theology involve itself in a contradiction when it looks either to natural science or to philosophy
for an epistemology adequate for the special kind of knowledge
(faith) peculiar to its own 'subject' (God)" (267)? If one
expects thus to comprehend God scientifically and philosophically,
yes. If one seeks a means whereby one can best share one's understanding of God, however received, no. We must again note that
the pedagogical dimension of Tillich's correlation is completely
ignored. As we might expect, McKelway also takes umbrage at
Tillich's assertion that "since there is no revelation unless
there is someone who receives it as revelation, the act of reception is part of the event itself" (49). Once again the fear of too
much (any?) unity or communion between God and man is explicit.
Thus, McKelway is displeased with Tillich's understanding of the
word of God and revelation, for it is too suffused with the classical Greek sense of "logos [as] the rational structure of the
ground of being" (87). Consequently, McKelway tends to find
revelation as general situation (the rational structure of being
itself) and revelation as event (God does something; God has
"spoken" to man in Jesus Christ) mutually exclusive rather than
mutually congenial and complementary (89). One can certainly ask
whose understanding of God more severely limits the revealing
power of God--Tillich's correlational or McKelway's Barthian abysmal?

    An interesting counterpart to the Barthian objection to Til-
lich's approach asserts that Tillich unduly limits philosophy.
David Tracy's criticism, examined above, implies this, but he is
not alone. Carl J. Armbruster remarks, "Tillich's unabashed reliance upon ontology has made him the hope and despair of his fellow theologians," but then cites William L. Rowe, who "concludes
that Tillich's ontology is not valid because it is meaningful only when understood in quasi-psychological terms."[39] The irrele-
vance of this evaluation has been pointed out by Peter Berger.[40]
In any case, it would not endanger Tillich's method of correlation
in principle. Armbruster also cites Pierre Barthel who "shows how
Tillich's correlation of human questions and revelatory symbols is
achieved by reducing both to the lowest common ontological denom-
inator" (310). One can only wonder how ontologically low the
question of the meaning of life and being is. Armbruster continues:
"Does the method of correlation require ontological categories?
And, more fundamentally, is the method of correlation completely
adequate" (290)? Tillich never claimed perfection. In fact,

he insisted: "The method of correlation is not safe from distortion; no theological method is. . . . No method is guaranty against such failures" (ST, II, 16). Furthermore, one can hardly imagine that Armbruster would delight in being charged with providing a "completely adequate" method, whether through invention or retrieval.[41] Elsewhere he elaborates:

> However, it is questionable if the method of correlation necessarily demands an ontological analysis of the human situation. Moreover, the very question-answer structure of the method is limited. Certainly theology must speak intelligibly to man, but revelation far outstrips the range of human questions (296).

In response to these statements one would want to ask several counter-questions. Why not an ontological analysis? What could one possibly gain from omitting it? How could one even begin to achieve any unity at all within the multiplicity of human questioners and questions? Would not the absence of ontological analysis be a limiting of the Christian message's answer--at least insofar as precisely *human* beings are to receive it? So Thomas O'Meara insists:

> As apologetic rather than kerygmatic theology, answering the contemporary situation, Tillich's theology must speak to man in both existential (from the ontological analysis of human existence related to Being) and existentiell (what affects man personally in his concrete life) terms. The method and structure of theology is both ontological and man-centered. . . . These threats (to man's fallen existence) are not only ontological and social but moral.[42]

That the question-answer structure is limited is a quite acceptable assertion--and equally insignificant. At best, such a statement simply describes the basic human situation. At less than best, it deceptively avoids the problem of theological methodology by giving the appearance that some other approach escapes limitation. At less than best, it deceptively avoids the problem of theological methodology by giving the appearance that some other approach escapes limitation.

Most distressing, however, is Armbruster's third sentence in the citation above. Without an analysis of the questioning human being, how could Armbruster know that "revelation far outstrips the range of human questions?" How could he even speak of revelation--in contrast to what would be revelation and not (merely) something else? Furthermore, Armbruster simply disregards the pedagogical and apologetical dimensions of Tillich's theological

correlating. In any case, what would theology do with the presumed
revelation, if it had not bothered to analyze the human situation-
question, to which the divine revelation is supposed to be the
answer.

Hence, I do not find compelling Armbruster's assertion that
"the most serious charge itself is that he 'ontologizes' the
Christian mysteries, that is, he reduces them to purely philosophical principles" (294). For support, Armbruster invokes George
Tavard and Avery Dulles. In regard to "speculative theology" in
general, Dulles remarks that "one must be on guard against trying
to squeeze divine revelation into any man-made framework of metaphysical speculation." In regard to Tillich in particular, he continues:

> But he does not sufficiently purify his philosoph-
> ical categories in the light of the revealed mes-
> sage. Instead, he lets the exigencies of his philo-
> sophical system determine in advance what God's rev-
> elation can and cannot be. The biblical message is
> reduced to the dimensions of an all-too-human phi-
> losophy. Because of this initial error in method,
> Tillich's efforts to translate . . . biblical reli-
> gion into a sophisticated theological scheme are
> vitiated at the source.

That is the temptation of any theological method which surpasses
what Dulles terms the "radical biblicist in his unwillingness to
depart from the letter of the Bible."[43] Thus it is clearly the
temptation of the method of correlation in general and Tillich's
in particular.

However, neither temptation nor failure in execution invali-
dates the method in principle. Nor is it clear that it is precisely
the method of correlation that leads to that doctrinal deficiency
which evokes Dulles' criticism. Noteworthy is the fact that Dulles
reacts as a Roman Catholic theologian to Tillich as a Lutheran
theologian. It is to be conceded, of course, that Tillich's philosophical positions may induce him to "deform" the Christian message
either in itself or in regard to some other understanding, such as
Dulles'. However, it seems to me that another possibility is always overlooked.

For this reason I have mentioned the ecclesial affiliations
of Tillich and Dulles. Is it not possible that "before" and apart
from all ontological analysis and subsequent theological correlation
of existential question and revealed message-tradition-answer,
Dulles would find Tillich's interpretation of the Christian message
at least partly unacceptable. For example, would not Dulles also

find Barth's interpretation of the Christian message wanting? But would this be on the basis of a philosophical-cultural correlation? Certainly not on Barth's own terms, although it must be emphasized again that no theology can refuse to correlate. The option remains not whether, but how. My point here is that, since Dulles can take exception to the theology of both the correlational Tillich and the anti-correlational Barth, there may be some ground other than the method of correlation itself that is responsible for the dis-agreement--and not just particular philosophical tenets espoused by Tillich. However important they may be, they are not as impor-tant as the religious tradition within which Tillich theologizes.[44] Is not the difference between this particular tradition and Dulles', for example, much more important than philosophical or methodo-logical differences? Thus, for critics like Dulles or even Tavard, Tillich's "initial error" may well lie in the particular tradition of the Christian message made available to him by his Church and his own personal appropriation of that message-tradition rather than in his "method."

One need only recall Tillich's statement that "the substance of [his] religion is and remains Lutheran," and his explication that "it embodies the consciousness of the corruption of exis-tence."[45] This Lutheran fascination with the corruption of human nature clearly compromises both the principle and practice of cor-relation, for it denatures human nature which is one of the two partners to be correlated. This denaturing can be of greater or lesser intensity, but in any case it skewers the equation of divine answer and human question.[46] It is not correct to attribute this denaturing fascination solely to his personal passion or his phil-osophical preceptors. Tillich may indeed "start with an unsound philosophy of man,"[47] as Eugene Kane would have it, but this "philosophy" is provided him by his particular Christian Church-tradition. In this tradition there are other attitudes which would induce him to correlate in a manner unacceptable to Dulles--and those of other theological persuasions and ecclesial memberships--and which may well be part of his Christian tradition and not the consequences of precisely his ontological and correlational enter-prise. I think of such elements as his diffidence in regard to the *analogia entis* and the sacramental economy and the consequent overwhelming fear of idolization, his evaluation of natural theol-ogy and the proofs for the existence of God, his heightened fear of heteronomy, and the extreme elasticity of his *Protestant* (not philosophical, not Schellingian) *principle*.[48] Let one more example

suffice. Roman Catholic critics often perceive Tillich's Christology to be monophysitic, Docetic, Nestorian, and adoptianistic.
But Roman Catholic theologians have always been wary of the ade-
quacy of Luther's Christology.[49] May it not be, then, that the
inadequacy they perceive in Tillich's Christology is rooted more
in his "Lutheran reception" than in his "philosophical system" and
his "man-made framework of metaphysical speculation." Even if but
partly, the "initial error" would not be the method, but the received tradition. Long before Tillich met Schelling's philosophy,
he had met the Lutheran tradition with its confessional, theological, and spiritual *Denkformen* (forms of thought) and *Denkvollzugs-
formen* (intellectual styles of performance).[50]

  Although Tillich's principle or method of correlation successfully resists theoretical attacks, his practical performance
may not be as successful. As we have just seen, his Lutheran
tradition is not unconditionally congenial to the correlational
enterprise.[51] Although Luther (and Lutheranism) is famous for the
correlational *simul justus et peccator*, he is more famous for his
personal *Einseitigkeit* (excessive one-sidedness) and his doctrinal
sola's (scripture alone, grace alone, faith alone).[52] The latter
are not only questionable in themselves, but also compelling illustrations of the Lutheran *Denkvollzugsform*, a style of intellectual
performance which is decidedly one-sided. Otto Hermann Pesch describes it as *existential* (more properly *existentiell*) in contrast
to the balanced *sapiential* style of Thomas Aquinas. At the conclusion of this paper I shall indicate how, in the Roman Catholic
tradition, Karl Rahner is enabled to achieve a greater balance
and thus avoid in his own correlational theology some of the
Anfechtung (vexatious testing and temptation) which Tillich suffers
precisely from his own tradition.

  However, Tillich's principle and practice of correlation *must*
be regarded as the considerable achievement which it in fact is--
even though it is, as Tillich admits, as old as theology itself--
and the reasons are these. Tillich is justly famed because he made
explicit what was implicit in the Protestant tradition, namely the
principle and practice of theological and ecclesial correlation.
His achievement is all the more impressive not simply because he
was able to provide the implicit practice with an explicit theory.
To do this he also had to overcome the explicit theoretical denial
in principle. This theoretical denial of correlation is certainly
abetted by the Lutheran *sola's* and, more significantly, by Luther's
two-kingdom doctrine, which Tillich, of course, could not accept.[53]

No matter how diligent--and tortured--the theological defenses of this principle have been,[54] its consequences for ecclesial and civil society and for Christian and cultural praxis have been and remain baneful. Though unintended, the doctrine nevertheless allowed a divorce in the reality of the one creation. Consequently, there was not only parallelism between the worldly and spiritual kingdoms, there was dualism. And this "ontological" dualism was not able to be bridged by Christians' "using" it in their everyday *existentiell* vocations. In contrast to Luther, for whom the world is merely the occasion of the Christian's believing and living (thus a correlation which is only "vocational"), there is for Tillich both an ontology and a theology of culture.[55] However, one can and must still wonder about the toll exacted by this aspect of the Lutheran tradition on Tillich and his principle of correlation, especially its practice. Similarly, the "Lutheran equation of *traditio* with *abusus*"[56] is hardly conducive to a correlational attitude and *Denkvollzugsform*. In the same vein are Luther's impatience with, if not despair of, fallible finite history[57] and his yearning for the end.[58] Finally, in spite of the Lutheran difficulty with the universal salvific will of God and the free will of human beings,[59] Tillich's correlational theology is clearly more responsive to the "catholic and apostolic" tradition/church than the Christomonism[60] and hypertheism[61] of others. Thus, it is worth repeating that dissatisfaction with Tillich's principle of correlation may *not* have its proper source precisely in the principle itself, but in the differing philosophical perceptions and especially in the different ecclesial traditions of the dissatisfied.

However, one obscurity, if not inconsistency, in Tillich's explanation of the principle does make him (and it) vulnerable. That is the mutual dependence between question and answer (ST, I, 64). Although there is a dependence, Tillich insists that "it is impossible to derive the answer from the question or the question from the answer. . . . It is equally wrong to derive the question implied in human existence from the revelatory answer. This is impossible because the revelatory answer is meaningless if there is no question to which it is the answer" (ST, II, 13). However, this "because" could be compelling only if there would be no difference whatsoever between the answerer and the questioner. Furthermore, it is not at all clear how this is to be reconciled with his assertion that "symbolically speaking, God answers man's questions, and under the impact of God's answers man asks them" (ST, I, 61).

Earlier Tillich had been even more emphatic:

> And, vice versa, the content of the question is de-
> termined through the content of the answer. No one
> can posit questions concerning God, revelation, the
> Christ, etc., if he is not already in possession of
> a certain [i.e., some kind of] answer. We can say,
> therefore, that questions relating to the ultimately
> valid concerns of man bear the content of the answers
> in themselves and the answers are stamped with the
> form of the questions. . . . Ultimately the philosoph-
> ical form of the question is positively related to
> the content of the theological answer. Thus question
> and answer are not alien to each other.[62]

This passage comes from a 1946 lecture, published the following year. Volume I of *Systematic Theology* was published in 1951
and Volume II in 1957. How can one not assume that the later, less
correlational, more "Barthian" separation of question and answer
stems from the defense of correlation which Tillich felt compelled
to provide against accusations like those of McKelway and Thomas
discussed above? However, Tillich would have done better on all
counts, it seems to me, to have stood his ground. **His** earlier position admittedly enjoys--or suffers--a certain ambivalence. It
has usually evoked complaints of reductionism--lowering the divine
to the human. However, it is equally patient of an explanation
which might be called "elevationism"--the raising of the human to
the divine. He could thus escape the western (especially August-
inian-Lutheran-Jansenist preoccupation with sin and redemption
whereby ontology tends to be equated with hamartiology) and enjoy
eastern theology's *theiosis*.[63] That this eastern emphasis on the
"divinization of man" as the purpose and effect of God's revelation
and communication of himself to the non-godly should be congenial
to Tillich, in spite of his Lutheran background, is indicated by
Tillich's insistence that

> this [the complex of theology, questions implied in
> human existence, and the answers implied in divine
> self-manifestation] is a circle which drives man to a
> point where question and answer are not separated.
> This point, however, is not a moment in time. It
> belongs to man's essential being, to the unity of
> his finitude with the infinity in which he was cre-
> ated . . . and from which he is separated (ST, I, 61).

It is at this point, it seems to me, that Tillich's correlating
theology runs into its most serious difficulty--precisely because
of his Lutheran patrimony and its dim view of human nature, especially fallen human nature. Certainly Tillich avoids the "abyssism"
of Karl Barth. Tillich also surpasses the minimalism of Emil
Brunner's *Anknüpfungspunkte* (contact points between the world and

the revealing God). But Tillich does not certainly provide an adequate explanation of the communion of (we could say, the balance between) the answering God and the questioning man. Hence, in theory and practice his principle of correlation needs support. Insofar as Karl Rahner's entire theological enterprise has been dedicated to showing that the *theo*logical--which is the *onto*logical --circle is not vicious but gracious, we may legitimately seek correlational insight from him.

In general, a greater affinity has been noted between Tillichian and Catholic theologies.[64] In particular, George Lindbeck has noted that Rahner is a "man who in comprehensiveness and sheer intellectual quality can, alone among contemporary Catholics, be ranged alongside of Barth and Tillich, and who in terms of balance is perhaps the greatest of the three." And John Macquarrie, also, notes Rahner's balance when he says, "Among contemporary theologians, I have found Karl Rahner the most helpful. . . . He handles in a masterful way those tensions which constitute the peculiar dialectic of theology . . . : faith and reason, tradition and novelty, authority and freedom, and so on."[65] I include these two evaluations by non-Roman Catholic theologians not to transform this paper into a paean of Karl Rahner, but because they indicate that in his theology there is present that balance necessary for the adequate performance of the principle of correlation. In pursuit of Lindbeck's comparison, it may not be inappropriate to suggest that Rahner's greater balance is rooted in his Catholic tradition, with both upper and lower case *c*'s. This Catholic tradition has always emphasized the both/and in contrast to the Protestant "solely" and either/or. Thus, for example, Rahner speaks of the "Catholic and."[66] More specifically, this Rahnerian balance is rooted in his Thomastic philosophy[67] and theology as well as in his Ignatian spirituality.[68]

Like Tillich, Rahner emphasizes that all systematic theology (1) is essentially apologetic,[69] (2) must correlate with contemporary culture,[70] (3) is unavoidably philosophical or ontological,[71] and (4) is primarily not for the "contemplation of truth [but] the salvation of man."[72] The similarity (not identity!) in their approaches is also suggested by the similarity of reproaches made by their opponents. For example, Rahner can report:

> A German bishop once said that God can certainly give
> the human being more answers than he has asked. . . .
> Now, I would say that, as a practical guide, what the
> bishop says is certainly correct. But, fundamentally,

> such a view is nevertheless not right. If,
> from the very beginning, through what we call
> grace, the self-communication of God and Holy
> Spirit, God is in and lives in the innermost
> center of my existence and comes to me, not from
> without, but from the very center of my existence,
> then all that is already a revealed theology
> that is fundamentally and radically present [in
> human beings]. Certainly nothing further in the
> way of answers could be added to this [revelation].
> Obviously, of course, this does not mean that any
> single individual as such would be able to objectify
> and verbalize this revelation, which is truly present
> in him, apart from the whole of revelation history.[73]

How Rahner's theology of the supernatural existential is able
to elucidate Tillich's "circle . . . where question and answer
are not separated" (ST, I, 61) is thus at least intimated. It
must be emphasized that Rahner's supernatural existential is neither a self-contained theological entity nor a speculative theorem
of philosophical idealism, but a "conclusion" deduced from the revealed universal salvific will of God, whereby "he wants everyone
to be saved and reach full knowledge of the truth" (1 Tim 2:4).
This verse, which is the single most important scripture in all of
Rahner's theology,[74] is the reason that there can be a correlational theology, for it is also the source of Rahner's *Heilsoptimismus*
(optimism about salvation). Not transcendental philosophical speculation and deduction,[75] but apostolic faith in the revealed universal saving will of God leads Rahner to the theory of the supernatural existential. In turn, this enables him to develop the theory
of the anonymous Christian, which is not an insulting exercise in
ecclesial and theological fascism, as some erroneously assert,[76]
but the attempt to understand the ontological transcendental correlation of the divine and the human so that their historical,
cultural correlation can be better appreciated and practiced.

What Tillich calls correlation is basically what Rahner calls
transcendental reflection. They are theological methods. They
do not impose speculative limits on God. They do attempt conceptual clarifications of the correlation of God and world as revealed
in the Judeo-Christian tradition. Thus, according to Rahner,

> what was first and most strictly ordained by God is
> the permanent supernatural existential of grace, the
> proffered self-communication of God, and hence a
> transcendental condition of man. The self-communica-
> tion of God in grace (by virtue of the universal
> salvific will of God) is undoubtedly a "transcen-
> dental" existential of man. But it has its proper
> being in the history of salvation and revelation (in-
> dividual and collective) and this is the medium

through which it is accomplished and comes to
us. It is precisely the task of a transcendental
theology to show that the metaphysical essence of
a reality and its history (and hence grace as an
existential and salvation-history) are not simply
juxtaposed but condition each other.[77]

This theological correlation and transcendental reflection
are more important today than ever. Not only because the correlational attitude and approach more adequately correspond to the
way be-ing be-s.[78] Not only because, as Tillich contends, the
very sentence which denies correlation assumes the truth it wants
to deny.[79]

It is, rather, more important because of the contemporary situation of the Christian Church(es). It is interesting that near
the end of their careers both Tillich and Rahner became more and
more interested in non-Christian religions and their relationship
to Christianity. Indeed, the title of one of Tillich's last works,
Christianity and the Encounter of the World Religions, could readily serve as the subtitle for their latter years. This is also in
keeping with the New Testament phenomenon we noted earlier, namely
that positive theological ecclesial correlation goes hand in hand
with increasing awareness of Christian universalism. Thus, neither
Tillich nor Rahner is led to either the abandonment of his own
religious tradition or the syncretistic mixture of a new, abstract
universal religion. Rather, they are both urged "to penetrate into
the depth of one's own religion" to see how it answers "the question of the ultimate meaning of life."[80]

The contemporary urgency of this need for penetration and correlation in Christianity's encounter with the world's religions has
most recently been emphasized in Karl Rahner's contention that
the Roman Catholic Church has entered a new epoch. In this third
epoch (the other two were Jewish Christianity and Hellenistic-
European Christianity), the Church has made "the transition [from]
the Western Church, . . . a break which has occurred only once before, that is, in the transition from Jewish to Gentile Christianity. . . . [This] third is the period to which the sphere of the
Church's life is in fact the entire world. These three periods
signify three essential and different basic situations for Christianity and its preaching."[81]

My contention here is not just that the theological methods
of Tillich's correlation and Rahner's transcendental reflection
have successfully resisted refutation. Nor is it simply that they
have shown themselves to be most consistent with the ontology and

revelation of the Judeo-Christian tradition. It is, rather, that
in principle and practice they have demonstrated that they are most
apt to mediate theologically the revealed saving answer of God to
the ontological, cultural question which is man.[82] Finally, the
greater balance of Rahner's theology enables theological correlation to be even more secure in principle and effective in practice.
Thus nature and grace are seen to be not merely compatible, but
truly congenial. After all, even the Tertullian who could wonder
"what do Athens and Jerusalem have in common?" could also proclaim
the *"testimonium animae naturaliter Christianae"* ("the testimony
of the naturally Christian soul," *Apologeticum* 17:6). We may,
then, certainly agree with Paul Tillich, exulting that *"against*
Pascal [we] say: The God of Abraham, Isaac and Jacob and the God
of the philosophers is the same God."[83] For, as Karl Rahner explains, "because the salvific will wills a salvation which is God
himself, he has made a creature to attain it."[84]

NOTES

[1]Paul Tillich, *The Protestant Era* (Chicago: University of
Chicago Press, 1957), p. xxii.

[2]L. Gordon Tait, *The Promise of Tillich* (New York: Lippincott, 1971), p. 46.

[3]*Systematic Theology* (Chicago: University of Chicago Press,
1967), I, p. 60. (Henceforth abbreviated ST with volume and
page numbers--e.g., ST, I, 60--and included in the text).

[4]Tillich, *What is Religion?* (New York: Harper & Row, 1969),
p. 15.

[5]Tillich, "die Dimension der Tiefe in allen Funktionen," in
Religion als eine Funktion des Menschlichen Geistes? in *Gesammelte
Werke,* ed. Renate Ahlbrecht (Stuttgart: Evangelisches Verlagswerk,
1964), V, p. 39.

[6]As the separate revision of Part I of *The Interpretation of
History* is entitled (New York: Scribner's 1964). The same theme
is also developed in his "Autobiographical Reflections" in *The
Theology of Paul Tillich,* ed. C. Kegley and R. Bretall (New York:
MacMillan, 1961), pp. 3-21, and also in his *My Search for Absolutes*
(New York: Simon and Schuster, 1967), pp. 23-54.

[7]F. Chapey, "Paul Tillich," in *Bilanz der theologie im 20.
Jahrhundert: Bahnbrechende Theologen,* ed. H. Vorgrimler and R.
Vander Gucht (Freiburg: Herder, 1970), pp. 44-50, 63.

[8]Tillich, *Theology of Culture* (New York: Oxford University
Press, 1964), p. v.

[9]Tillich, *A History of Christian Thought* (New York: Simon and Schuster, 1968), pp. 4-5.

[10]*Theology of Culture*, pp. 156-57.

[11]W. Jaeger, "Paideia Christi," in *Zeitschrift für Neutestamentliche Wissenschaft* 50 (1950), 2.

[12]*Gesammelte Werke*, VII, p. 240.   Even more detailed: "History and Christology belong together as question and answer.   Therefore we want to proceed in the following manner: we shall first develop the historical and philosophical question in order to be able to demonstrate the meaning of the Christological answer." P. Tillich, *Religiöse Verwirklichung* (Berlin: Furche, 1930), p. 111.   Tillich's development of the principle of correlation is detailed by John Clayton, "Questioning, Answering, and Tillich's Concept of Correlation," in *Kairos and Logos*, ed. J. J. Carey (Cambridge: The American Paul Tillich Society, 1978), pp. 135-157.

[13]Tertullian, *De Praescriptione Haereticorum*, 7, cited by J. Quasten, *Patrology* (Ultrecht: Spectrum, 1953), II, pp. 320-21.

[14]See F. Schupp, *Glaube-Kultur-Symbol* (Düsseldorf: Patmos, 1974), pp. 31-33, 38.

[15]L. Cerfaux, *L'Eglise des Corinthiens* (Paris: Cerf, 1946), pp. 24-25, and *Le Christ dans la theologie de saint Paul*, 2nd ed. (Paris: Cerf, 1954), pp. 120-124.

[16]Inspiration and modelling for genuine correlating can be found in St. Thomas Aquinas' middle course between Biblicist Angelism and Averroistic Philosophism, as has been exquisitely shown by J. Pieper in *Scholasticism* (New York: McGraw Hill, 1964), pp. 118-136, and in his *Guide to Thomas Aquinas* (New York: Pantheon, 1962), pp. 21-23, where he cites L. B. Geiger, "Il [Thomas] n'a pas choici," and also pp. 43-54.

[17]*Philosophical Hermeneutics* (Berkeley: University of California Press, 1977), p. 46.

[18]P. Berger, *Facing Up to Modernity* (New York: Basic Books, 1977), pp. 173-179.

[19]That such a stance is ultimately impossible, indeed self-contradictory, is emphasized by Tillich.   "And the famous 'No' of Karl Barth against any kind of natural theology, even of man's ability to ask the question of God, in the last is a self-deception, as the use of human language in speaking of revelation shows" (ST, II, p. 14).   This is developed in *Gesammelte Werke*, XII, pp. 187-193 and 324-26.

[20]*Theology of Culture*, pp. 125,174.

[21]*The Protestant Era*, p. xxii.

[22]See J. J. Carey, "Introduction," in *Kairos and Logos* (Cambridge: The North American Paul Tillich Society, 1978), pp. 7-8.

[23]David Tracy, *Blessed Rage for Order* (New York: Seabury, 1975), p. 46.

[24]*Theology of Culture*, p. 174.

[25]Tracy, pp. 7-8. See also his "Response to Professor Connelly," *Proceedings of the Twenty-ninth Annual Convention, The Catholic Theological Society of America* (Bronx: Manhattan College, 1974), pp. 67-76.

[26]As we are regularly reminded by Karl Rahner, *Grundkurs des Glaubens* (Freiburg: Herder, 1977), pp. 13-34; *Zur Reform des Theologiestudiums* (Freiburg: Herder, 1969), pp. 54-76.

[27]See, citing Isaiah 7:9, J. Ratzinger, *Einführung in das Christentum* (Munich: Kösel, 1968), pp. 43-48.

[28]A. Dulles, "Method in Fundamental Theology," *Theological Studies* 37 (June 1979), 306.

[29]"Secular Theology and the Supernatural," *Theological Studies,* 38 (March 1977), 49. Tracy's response is in *Theological Studies,* 39 (September 1978), 502-507.

[30]J. Heywood Thomas, *Paul Tillich* (Atlanta: John Knox, 1965), p. 9.

[31]*The Protestant Era*, p. ix.

[32]*On the Boundary*, p. 59.

[33]Tillich, *The Interpretation of History* (New York: Scribner's, 1936), p. 54.

[34]J. L. Adams, *Paul Tillich's Philosophy of Culture, Science and Religion* (New York: Schocken, 1970), p. 260.

[35]*The Protestant Era*, p. 83.

[36]"Autobiographical Reflections," in Kegley and Bretall, p. 5.

[37]Tillich, "Reply to Interpretation and Critics," in Kegley and Bretall, p. 337.

[38]Alexander McKelway, *The Systematic Theology of Paul Tillich* (New York: Dell, 1964), p. 267. Further references are in the text.

[39]C. Armbruster, *The Vision of Paul Tillich* (New York: Sheed and Ward, 1967), pp. 290, 301-310. G. Weigel likewise notes the philosophical dimension of Tillich's thought, but has considerable reservations about his philosophy, wondering whether, at least in some respects, it may be "not ontology, but its betrayal." See G. Weigel, "Tillich's Theological Significance," in *Paul Tillich in Catholic Thought*, ed. Thomas O'Meara and Conrad Weisser (New York: Doubleday, 1969), p. 48. Wayne Mahan's attempt to expose the principle of correlation as destructive also founders because *he*--not Tillich--does not understand the philosophical dimension of all theology. See his *Tillich's System* (San Antonio: Trinity University Press, 1974). The anecdotal account of Ved Mehta, *The New Theologian* (Harmondsworth: Penguin, 1965), pp. 53-65, provides an entertaining sparring match between Tillich and his philosophical opponents. Further references to Armbruster are noted in the text.

[40]*Facing Up to Modernity*, pp. 163-167.

[41]Nor, for example, J. K. S. Reid, who asks reproachfully,
"Is the correlation of existential and theological answer really
so exact? . . . In other words, correlation is not the whole
story." Indeed it is not, but for reasons other than Reid would
accept. And, in any case, which theological *method* can claim
to be the whole story? See his *Christian Apologetics* (Grand
Rapids: Eerdmans, 1970), p. 200.

[42]T. F. O'Meara, *Paul Tillich's Theology of God* (Dubuque:
Listening Press, 1970), pp. 64-65.

[43]Dulles, "Paul Tillich and the Bible," in *Paul Tillich in
Catholic Thought*, pp. 178-79. In this context Tavard's Barthianism
is self-refuting. Hence we shall omit addressing his comments.

[44]Tillich is aware of the crucial importance of tradition, for
"even the Reformers were dependent on the Roman tradition against
which they protested" (ST, I, 36). "The principle of tradition in
the Church stems from the fact that the nature of the churches and
the character of their life are determined by their function in
the New Being as it has appeared in Jesus as the Christ and that
the tradition is the link between this foundation and every new
generation" (ST, III, 184). See also his "Problem of Theological
Method," in *Four Existentialist Theologians*, ed. Will Herberg
(New York: Doubleday, 1958), p. 246.

[45]See the passages in notes 32, 33.

[46]See Max Lackmann, *Vom Geheimmis der Schöpfung* (Stuttgart:
Evangelisches Verlagswerk, 1952), pp. 320-67. Also J. Witte,
De Theologia Protestantium (Rome: PUG, 1968), pp. 57-71, 77.

[47]Eugene Kane, *Three Christological Positions in Contemporary
American Protestantism* (Rome: PUG Dissertation excerpts, 1959),
p. 56.

[48]For example, Tillich responds to G. Weigel: "Nevertheless,
I believe you are right when you say that my understanding of
analogia entis is more negative-protesting than positive-affirming.
I am more worried about the idolic character of traditional theology
and popular beliefs about God than you are." See G. Weigel, "The
Theological Significance of Paul Tillich," *Gregorianum*, 37
(1956), 54.

[49]See Y. Congar, *Le Christ, Marie et l'Eglise* (Bruges: Des-
clee, 1952); Richard Stauffer, *Luther As Seen by Catholics* (Atlanta:
John Knox, 1967); O. H. Pesch, *Twenty Years of Catholic Luther
Research* (Geneva: Lutheran World, 1966).

[50]See Pesch, *Die Theologie der Rechtfertigung bei Martin Luther
und Thomas von Aquin* (Mainz: Grünewald, 1967), pp. 935-956. Also
his "Existential and Sapiential Theology," in *Catholic Scholars
Dialogue With Luther*, ed. J. Wicks (Chicago: University of Loyola
Press, 1970), p. 65.

[51]See, for example, the remarks of J. McDonough, J. Lortz and
W. Pauck in *Luther, Erasmus and the Reformation*, ed. J. Olin (New
York: Fordham University Press, 1969), pp. 49-65, esp. pp. 50-
51, 65.

[52] "It seems clear that the *sola scriptura* has never actually worked." H. Ditmanson, "Perspectives on the Hermeneutics Debate," in *Studies in Lutheran Hermeneutics*, ed. J. Reumann (Philadelphia: Fortress, 1979), p. 104. Even P. Althaus felt compelled to write "Sola Fide Nunquam Sola," *Una Sancta*, 16 (December 1961), 227-235.

[53] See J. L. Adams, "Paul Tillich on Luther," in *Interpreters of Luther*, ed. J. Pelikan (Philadelphia: Westminster, 1968), p. 330.

[54] As, for example, K. Haendler, "Zwei-Reiche-Lehre," in *Religion und Kirche*, ed. E. Fahlbusch (Gottingen: Vandenhoeck & Ruprecht, 1971), IV, pp. 277-79.

[55] See H. Schwebel, "Kultur," in *Religion und Kirche*, II, pp. 272-73.

[56] J. Ratzinger, "On the Interpretation of the Tridentine Decree on Tradition," in Karl Rahner and J. Ratzinger, *Revelation and Tradition* (New York: Herder & Herder, 1965), p. 29. See also pp. 27, 60, 63.

[57] See J. Headley, *Luther's View of Church History* (New Haven: Yale University Press 1963), pp. 106, 118-24, 179, 187. Also W. Maurer, "Luthers Lehre von der Kirche: Kirche und Geschichte nach Luthers Dictata super Psalterium," in *Lutherforschung heute*, ed. V. Vajta (Berlin: Lutherisches Verlagshaus, 1958), p. 93.

[58] See N. Cohn, *The Pursuit of the Millenium*, rev. ed. (New York: Oxford University Press, 1970), p. 243.

[59] See V. Pfnür, *Einig in der Rechtfertigungslehre?* (Wiesbaden: F. Steiner, 1970), pp. 132-135.

[60] See G. Hasel, *Old Testament Theology: Basic Issues in the Current Debate* (Grand Rapids: Eerdmans, 1975), pp. 106, 111.

[61] L. Scheffczyk, *Gott-loser Gottesglaube?* (Regensburg: Habbel, 1974), pp. 190-198. He shows that Barth's fears are otiose (194) insofar as the philosophy of religion exposes the "concave structure of human reality" (197) and thus its openness to an "Inexistenz" (198) of the human and divine, the initiative being always the latter's (194).

[62] "Das Problem der theologischen Methode," in *Korrelationen*, ed. I. C. Henel (Stuttgart: Evangelisches Verlagswerk, 1975), pp. 33-34. The entire passage merits citation.

[63] See R. Hotz, *Sakramente im Wechselspiel zwischen Ost und West* (Zurich: Benziger, 1979), pp. 213-226.

[64] Various testimonies can be found throughout *Paul Tillich in Catholic Thought* and also in McKelway, pp. 32-33. Adam Siegfried, *Das neue Sein: Der Zentralbegriff der ontologischen theologie Paul Tillichs in katholischer Sicht* (Munich: Max Hueber, 1974) is able to compare post-Vatican II Catholicism with Tillich's pre-Vatican II critique and find even greater communality. See, however, J. Heywood Thomas, *Paul Tillich: An Appraisal* (Philadelphia: Westminster, 1963), p. 198, where he does not find the alleged similarity between Tillichian symbolic knowledge and Thomistic analogy compelling. How spontaneously Catholic theology correlates is clear in

H. B. Meyer, "Die Sakramente und ihre Symbolik als Antwort auf
Grundfragen menschlicher Existenz" in *Theologische Akademie*, ed.
K. Rahner and O. Semmelroth (Frankfurt: Knecht, 1966), pp.
57-78.

[65]George Lindbeck, "The Thought of Karl Rahner," *Christianity
and Crisis*, 25 (October 18, 1965), 211-15.   See also J. Macquarrie,
Principles of Christian Theology, rev. ed. (New York: Scribner's,
1977), p. vii.

[66]Karl Rahner, "Ausgeglichenheit und Mut zur Einseitigkeit,"
Foreword to D. Seeber, *Paul VI, Papst im Wiederstreit* (Freiburg:
Herder, 1971), p. 10.   This point cannot be emphasized too much.
See Hans Urs von Balthasar, *Katholisch* (Einsiedeln: Johannes,
1975).   On page 18 he speaks of "the famous Catholic 'and' which
Protestants reprimand." Herman Volk traces the Catholic "and"
back to the doctrine of creation, which enables the creature to
be really, neither identical with nor separate from God. *Gott
Alles in Allen* (Mainz: Grünewald, 1958), p. 151.   However, not
only Catholics express reserve about the Protestant *sola's*.   See,
for example, W. Stählin, *Allein: Recht und Gefahr einer polemischen
Formel* (Stuttgart: Evangelisches Verlagswerk, 1950).

[67]See my "Karl Rahner and the Christian Philosophy of St.
Thomas Aquinas," to appear in *Karl Rahner, S. J., Discoverer in
Theology*, ed. W. Kelly (Milwaukee: Marquette University Press,
1980).   In all that follows, I refer the reader to my *Karl Rahner*
which is to appear in the John Knox series "Makers of Contemporary
Theology" in early 1981.

[68]See especially K. Fischer, *Der Mensch als Geheimnis* (Freiburg: Herder, 1974).

[69]"Theology as a whole has ultimately no other purpose than
to consider how the Gospel can be preached in such a way that it
both awakens and evokes belief. . . .   Theology is the necessary
presupposition for the credible proclamation of the Gospel in a
future which has already begun, a future of scholarly and scientific
investigation and knowledge, of technology and cybernetics, of a
world wide society of humanity." Rahner, *Schriften zur Theologie*
X (Einsiedeln: Benziger, 1972), pp. 502-510.   See also *Schriften*
IX, p. 73.

[70]"In the future, theology's key partner-in-dialogue, to which
it will have to relate its 'philosophising' in the sense we have
adumbrated, will no longer be philosophy in the traditional sense
at all, but the 'unphilosophical' pluralistic sciences and the kind
of understanding of existence which they promote either directly
or indirectly.   At least in the concrete situation determined by
the cultural, intellectual, social and natural sciences, it is
science, no longer mediated by philosophy, which constitutes
theology's partner-in-dialogue." Rahner, *Schriften zur Theologie*,
VIII, p. 84.

[71]Most recently see *Schriften*, XIV, p. 15.

[72]In P. Granfield, *Theologians at Work* (New York: MacMillan,
1967), p. 43.

[73]Rahner, *Herausforderung des Christen* (Freiburg: Herder,
1975), p. 135.

[74]See H. Waldenfels, *De Sententia P. Caroli Rahner SJ circa voluntatem salvificam Dei Universalem* (Tokyo: Shingaku Kenkyu, 1962).

[75]As, for example, is charged by Hans Urs von Balthasar, *Cordula* (Einsiedeln: Johannes, 1966).   Also, in the same mood, the capricious review of Rahner, *Foundations of Christian Faith* by Leo Scheffczyk, "Christentum als Unmittelbarkeit zu Gott," *Internationale katholische Zeitschrift Communio*, 6 (1977), 444-450.

[76]For example, Hans Küng and Ernst Jüngel.   See K. Weger, *Karl Rahner* (Freiburg: Herder, 1978), pp. 99-103.

[77]Rahner, "Transcendental Theology," *Sacramentum Mundi* (New York: Herder, 1970), VI, p. 208.

[78]See my "The Church as Communio: Trinity and Incarnation as the Foundations of Ecclesiology," *The Jurist*, 36 (1976), 127-159.

[79]See note 19 above.

[80]Tillich, *Christianity and the Encounter of the World Religions* (New York: Columbia University Press, 1961), pp. 96-97.

[81]Rahner, "A Basic Interpretation of Vatican II," *Theological Studies* 40 (December 1979), 716-727, here 721, 723.   Unfortunately this article appeared too late for its insights to be incorporated into my article.   But, this much is clear: if Rahner is correct in his contention that the Church has now entered into a relationship with the whole world in a manner whose consequences are as decisive for it as were those of the primitive Church's decision for the Gentiles, then the method of correlation, ontological analysis of culture generally and of religious phenomena specifically, and philosophical theology are more important than ever.   Although Rahner's thoughts are specifically oriented to Roman Catholicism, they are clearly equally valid for Protestantism.

[82]Apparently even Hans Küng has seen the value of the principle of correlation for future Catholic and ecumenical theology, although he equally apparently thinks it is something he and E. Schillebeeckx (whom he shamelessly coopts into his own hermeneutical and methodological camp) have just discovered.   See Hans Küng, "Toward a New Consensus in Catholic (and Ecumenical) Theology," *Journal of Ecumenical Studies*, 17 (Winter 1980), 1-17.   On pages 11, 12, Küng asserts, "Thus we have arrived at the second pillar of a possible hermeneutical consensus in Catholic theology," in which "theology has to establish a critical correlation between traditional Christian experience and contemporary experience."   Later Küng allows that this "critical correlation" might have to be "transformed into critical confrontation" (p. 17).   This is all well and good, but to find in 1979 the assertion "thus we have arrived at" in the mouth of one who prides himself on being an historically adept theologian is at least unseemly.

[83]Tillich, *Biblical Religion and the Search for Ultimate Reality* (Chicago: University of Chicago Press, 1955), p. 85.

[84]Rahner, "Salvation," *Encyclopedia of Theology* (New York: Seabury, 1975), p. 1504.

PART TWO

Scripture,

Tradition,

and

Wholeness

FREUD AND ST. PAUL: A DIALOGUE ON RELIGION AND CULTURE

James J. Forsyth

In the dialogue between Freudian psychology and Christian theology, at least three possible readings of Freudian theory can be discerned. As a psychology of religion which interprets religion as a regressive illusion and an obsessional neurosis, Freudian theory has predictably drawn a defensive and apologetic response from Christian scholars. On the other hand, as a theory of neurosis, Freudian theory has provided a basis for the work of the pastoral psychologist in identifying neurotic distortions of the Christian life, and thereby distinguishing between authentic and inauthentic expressions of Christian faith. Mutual fascination and dialogue, however, can only be explained in terms of a common preoccupation or focus of concern. In the case of Christian theology and Freudian theory, that common concern, I believe, runs deeper than the attempt to account for neurotic distortions of the Christian life; for at a third and more profound level, namely, the level of psychological anthropology in dialogue with theological anthropology, both Freudian and Christian thought are concerned with the fundamental question: Can life prevail over death? It is at this level that a convergence of Freudian theory and Christian theology is discernible, for in locating the source of man's discontent not in the subject-object duality of the individual and society, but in the duality to be found in human nature itself-- the "eternal struggle of Eros and the death instinct"-- Freud gives it a tragic kind of inevitability which, in this respect at least, is in accord with the Christian doctrine of sin. For both Freud and St. Paul, the basis for man's discontent is the experience of guilt. For Freud the context and occasion for this experience is man's encounter with civilization; for St. Paul it is the encounter with "the law." In comparing Freud's interpretation of the role of culture (civilization)[1] in the life of the individual with St. Paul's interpretation of the role of the law in the economy of salvation one can discern some clear implications for a theology of culture.

I. FREUD ON THE MEANING OF CULTURE

Throughout the development of his psychoanalytic theory,
Freud remained committed to a dualistic view of human nature. The
only distinction by which he could adequately account for the ob-
servable phenomena of conflict and repression was the fundamental
distinction between the life instinct (Eros) and the death instinct. "After long doubts and vacillations we have decided to
assume the existence of only two basic instincts, *Eros* and *the
destructive instincts*,"[2] he wrote. This distinction replaces an
earlier formulation based on the dualism of sex and ego instincts.
To preserve a dualistic and conflictual model, it was necessary to
discover those instincts which were truly antithetic. Consequently,
in this final formulation of the instinct theory, Eros or love is
opposed by the instinct whose aim is not self-preservation (a nar-
cissistic form of Eros) but self-destruction. Eros, moreover, is
no longer thought of as simply identical with sexual libido, and
thus sharing with the death instinct the aim of tension reduction
or homeostasis. Eros is no longer a drive which manifests the
conservative nature of instinctual life but one which, as the
antithesis of death, opposes it. In his final *Outline of Psychoanalysis* (1940), Freud speaks of Eros as an exception to the conservative character of instincts.[3]

I would suggest that it is only by understanding Eros as operating outside the conservative tendencies of instinctual life, or
"beyond the Nirvana principle," that we can understand the fundamental distinction between the death instinct as a divisive principle and Eros as a unifying principle. The function of the death
instinct is, biologically, to dissolve the unity of the multicel-
lular organism so that it returns to its inorganic state and, psychologically, to dissolve the unity between individuals through
mechanisms of self-affirmation and mastery. Eros on the other hand
is a unifying force. Biologically, it is represented by the tendency of cells to unite in order to form a living organism. Psychologically, it is operative in the sex instinct which unites two
people in psychological unity and assures the continuance of the
life of the species. The function of Eros is to "preserve living
substance and to join it into ever larger unities."[4] As such, it
is an instinct which is served by the process of culture or civilization, "whose purpose is to combine single human individuals and
after that families, then races, peoples and nations into one
great unity, the unity of mankind."[5]

Civilization, as Freud understands it, is born out of this
conflict between Eros and death: "This struggle is what all life
essentially consists of, and the evolution of civilization may
therefore be simply described as the struggle for life of the human species."[6] This is the ultimate meaning of civilization and
the repressions it carries out against the individual. In the
Freudian view, the religious and cultural systems of civilization
have as their function the regulating of interpersonal life through
the repression of human aggressiveness. By repressing the aggressive instinct which Freud called the "derivative and main representative of the death instinct,"[7] the cultural and social institutions of civilization attempt to create the conditions necessary
for the ultimate triumph of life over death. By thus repressing
the aggressive impulses--"the hostility of each against all and of
all against each"[8]--civilization serves Eros' goal of unity by repressing the divisive force of the death instinct. As Paul Ricoeur
states it, "culture comes upon the scene as the great enterprise
of making life prevail against death."[9] This enterprise is two-
fold. It consists of:

1. *The Sublimation of Sexuality*. Civilization imposes instinctual renunciation on the individual by directing the libido--
the energy of the life instinct--toward other than strictly sexual
aims, that is, toward creating ties of affection and friendship
among those who live together in civilized community. Such a community becomes possible, in Freud's view, only when men are "libid-
inally bound" to one another. Civilization, therefore, restricts
sexual love, channelling it into genital, heterosexual, and monog-
amous expressions, and directing its "desexualized" energy toward
cultural pursuits and "aim-inhibited" love or friendship. A bond
is thus established among people which runs contrary to their natural aggressive instincts.[10]

2. *The Repression of Aggressiveness*. Under the influence of
civilization, aggressiveness, which is the externalized expression
of the death instinct, is once again internalized, but this time
in the form of guilt since the energy of the repressed aggressiveness is appropriated by the superego and turned against one's own
ego. The death instinct is now experienced in the form of guilt
and the need for punishment.[11] Freud sees this inevitable "heightening of the sense of guilt"[12] as the central problem of civilization and the source of civilized man's discontent, for it means
that civilization's enterprise is ultimately self-defeating. Its
purpose is to make life prevail against death, but its existence

depends on fostering a sense of guilt in man. Progress in civilization is paid for by "a loss of happiness through heightening
the sense of guilt."[13] Civilization, therefore, is ultimately
founded on the death instinct and ends by creating the conditions
which permit death to triumph over life. In the words of Paul
Ricoeur, "civilization kills us in order to make us live."[14] In
trying to make Eros triumph over death, civilization succeeds only
in bringing man under the domination of the death instinct in the
form of guilt.

II. ST. PAUL ON THE MEANING OF THE LAW

It is at this point that the function of civilization begins
to resemble the function which St. Paul assigned to the law in
man's salvation, for, in the Freudian perspective, civilization is
the law that "was meant to lead me to life, but turned out to mean
death for me" (Romans 7:10). Freud perceived civilization as Paul
perceived the law--as an extraneous authority which promised life
but delivered death in the form of guilt.

In the seventh chapter of Romans, Paul graphically describes
the state of frustration, anxiety, and guilt he experiences in his
attempts to live a self-justifying existence through observance of
the Mosaic law. But the Mosaic law represents only one means of
self-justification. There are other types of "law," but in attempting to fulfill them, men discover another law "in their members."
The Mosaic law, therefore, becomes a prototype for all man's efforts
to live a self-authenticating existence through reliance on his
own human resources. This attempt at self-justification through
legal, religious, and moral observance leads to a psychological
state which Paul does not hesitate to describe as "death," and it
is only by transcending the law through the act and commitment of
faith that one is "delivered from this body of death."

Before this guilt-producing encounter with the law, man lives
in a state of ignorance--a stage in which he enjoys the illusion of
life because ignorant of his real situation in the absence of any
law to make him aware of the existence of sin within him. "Sin indeed was in the world before the law was given, but sin is not
counted where there is no law" (Rom. 5:13). The result of such ignorance is the illusion that one is "alive." For Paul, sin came
into the world with Adam and was therefore operative in the world
from that time, but man is not fully conscious of his sin and guilt
except through his transgressions of the law. When this happens,
the illusion of "life" gives way to the experience of "death."

"I was once alive apart from the law, but when the commandment came
sin revived and I died; the very commandment which promised life
proved to be death" (Rom. 7:9-10).

With the promulgation of the law, man becomes painfully aware
of his guilt, his inadequacy, his incompleteness. The law was good
in itself, but it served to make man aware of his basic sinfulness
through his transgressions of the law. "What then shall we say?
That the law is sin? By no means! Yet, if it had not been for the
law, I should not have known sin. I should not have known what it
is to covet if the law had not said, 'You shall not covet'" (Rom.
7:7). The ultimate effect of the law is to produce anxiety in man
because his failure to observe it makes him aware of the existential
gap between himself as he knows he should be and himself as he actually exists when he grounds his existence in his own human resources. In itself the law is just and good (Rom. 7:12), and therefore it is not the direct cause of sin, and thus death, in man.
The ultimate source of death is that basic condition of sin which
S. Lyonnet describes as "that deeply rooted egoism by which man,
since original sin, orientates everything to himself instead of
opening himself to God and to others."[15] If, therefore, Paul describes the law as the occasion of his "death," he is clearly using
the word "death" to describe the experience of guilt, anxiety, and
inner conflict which resulted from the painful awareness of his
"deeply rooted egoism" occasioned by his attempts to keep the law.
As we have seen, Freud had his own explanation of why that experience of guilt should be labeled "death."

According to Paul, the believer overcomes the "death" occasioned by the law because by grace he is liberated from the law
itself and is permitted to live "the new life of the Spirit"
(Rom. 6:6). What the believer is liberated from, however, is the
"oppression" of the law, that is, the necessity of justifying himself by observing and fulfilling the law. Thus the believer is
liberated from the law not objectively (through some kind of abro-
gation of law), for the law is still objectively valid and expresses valid moral principles to which the believer is committed
(Rom. 7:12,22), but subjectively, in that he acquires a new attitude
to the law and a new motive for observing it. This new attitude
and motive is based on the premise that God's acceptance of man is
unconditional; it is not conditional upon man's ability to keep
the law. Hence, the possibility is created of moral and religious
observance--including the love of one's neighbor--based on self-
transcending rather than self-justifying motives. This spontaneous,

self-transcending love, which the New Testament calls *agape*, is the
vital principle of the life of faith, which overcomes the "death"
occasioned by the law and makes possible that unity which is the
aim of Freud's life instinct (Eros).

Our discussion of Freud and St. Paul suggests the following
points of comparison:

1. Both are concerned with the same fundamental and essentially religious question: Can life triumph over death?

2. Both are capable only of a pessimistic answer to this
question on the basis of their respective analyses of the human
condition. For Paul, outside of the experience of grace and faith
man remains "under the law" and his attempts to authenticate his
existence through observance of the law only result in the experience of death in the form of guilt. It is that same sense of
guilt which Freud identified as the derivative and manifestation
of the death instinct and which is the inevitable fate of civilized
man. The plight of Paul's man under the law is but one instance
of the plight of civilized man in general; both had sought life
and found death.

3. Both Freud and St. Paul pronounce an apparently negative
judgment on the law (civilization) since it ends in the experience
of death in the form of guilt. It is ultimately self-defeating.
But this negative judgment is only apparently so since the law
(civilization) is seen as merely the *occasion* for man's experience
of death. Ultimately the source of death is within man himself:
for Freud in the biologically rooted death instinct and for Paul
in the *sin* which dwells in man and of which he becomes aware
through the law.

III. IMPLICATIONS FOR A THEOLOGY OF CULTURE

Given these similarities, can theology judge civilization
(culture) in the same way that St. Paul judges the law, i.e., as
the occasion and context for that experience of "death" which is
the necessary precondition for the experience of faith and life?
We have seen that both culture and the law frustrate man in his
pursuit of life and lead him in fact to the experience of death in
the form of guilt. Moreover, it should be pointed out that the
life which becomes possible for St. Paul through that freedom from
the law which comes with the experience of grace and faith, and
which has as its vital principle that self-transcending love which
the New Testament calls *agape*, is, like the Freudian Eros, essentially *interpersonal*. *Agape* is--to use Nygren's phrase--"unmotivated

love," i.e.., love which transcends the self-justifying striving
of man "under the law" and creates an interpersonal unity with
the other which is free of such self-preoccupation, and which is
consistent with that unity of living substances which is the' aim
of Eros.

This self-transcending power of interpersonal life which
resists death is precisely the meaning which Paul Ricoeur, interpreting Freud, assigns to Eros.

> If the living substance goes to death by an
> inner movement, what fights against death is
> not something internal to life, but the con-
> figuration of two mortal substances. Freud
> calls this configuration Eros: the desire of
> the other is directly implied in the emergence
> of Eros; it is always with another that the
> living substance fights against death, against
> its own death. Whereas when it acts separately,
> it pursues death through the circuitous route of
> adaptation to the natural and cultural environ-
> ment. Freud does not look for the drive for life
> in some will to live inscribed in each living
> substance: in the living substance by itself he
> finds only death.[16]

Gabriel Marcel assigns a similar meaning to the Christian notion
of "eternal life." The basis for the believer's hope in individual
immortality, he argues, is not to be found in some quality of individual life such as an immortal soul, but rather in the bonds of
love by which he transcends his individuality and becomes one with
his fellow man. It is not the individual but the bond uniting individuals that cannot be destroyed.[17] Thus, according to the Gospel
parable (Matthew 25:31-46), those who are destined to "enter into
life" are those whose love and compassion toward their neighbors
have forged such a bond of unity. Such ego-transcending oneness
constitutes life in both the Christian and Freudian sense of the
word--the life to which both the law and culture summon man in vain.

If, therefore, man's salvation means the attaining of "life"
in this sense of the word, would a theology of culture involve an
evaluation of culture which assigns to it the same kind of propae-
deutic role which Paul assigns to the law? In this case culture
would be viewed, like man's moral striving under the law, as an
area of human achievement whose limitations we must experience as
a necessary precondition for the experience of life. Such a theological interpretation of culture involves a transposing of Paul's
existential experience onto the social, cultural, and historical
plane. In the Christian perspective one must die in order to live.
For Paul this meant that the death (guilt) induced by the law is a

precondition of life. On the cultural and historical level it
would mean that the ultimate triumph of life over death cannot be
achieved apart from the death (guilt)-producing process of civilization. That process becomes the larger context for the painful
experience of one's finitude, guilt, and need for redemption which
Paul experienced at the dead end of his attempts to observe the
law. Implicit in Freud's theory of culture, perhaps, is a psychological analysis of transcendence in the sense described by Tillich
as the tendency of the finite to "point beyond itself" for, like
Paul's encounter with the law, the process of civilization brings
man to that "boundary situation" in which faith becomes possible.

    I want to suggest that this transposition of Paul's existen-
tial experience "under the law" to the cultural and historical
plane is precisely what has happened in the shift in theological
reflection from theological existentialism with its emphasis on
eschatology as vertical and existential and on salvation as personal transformation to the more future-oriented theologies of
hope and liberation which interpret eschatology as horizontal and
historical and salvation as the transcendent goal of the historical
process. Though both emphases are essential to a complete understanding of eschatological fulfillment, the shift in focus does
permit an extension of Paul's understanding of "law" to include
the historical process of civilization. That process now becomes
another instance of "law," i.e., a realm of human achievement which
promises life but delivers death. In this new theological perspective in which salvation is interpreted in terms of man's hope for
the future and his desire for liberation, man experiences his guilt
and need for redemption not only through the inadequacy of the
achievements of his moral striving under the law, but also through
the inadequacy of civilization's cultural and historical achievements. Hence, a theology of culture which, like Freud's theory of
culture, emphasizes the essential ambiguity of all cultural achievements.

    This extension and elaboration of Paul's understanding of the
law and its function begins within theological existentialism itself. For Paul, the personal transformation which results from the
experience of grace and faith requires, as a necessary precondition,
the experience of death in the form of guilt occasioned by his self-
justifying attempts to keep the law. Faith liberates him from this
realm of death and makes life possible in the form of self-transcending love or *agape*. For Paul, what the believer transcends
in the experience of faith is his guilt-producing attempts at

self-justification, so that, in a more general way, faith may be
described as the act by which man transcends all guilt-producing
efforts to live a self-justifying or self-authenticating existence
through his own human resources.

It is interesting to observe how this notion of "the law"
is elaborated by those theological existentialists who analyze
the same experience of grace and faith. What for Paul is a transition from law to grace is for Søren Kierkegaard a "leap" from the
ethical to the religious level of existence; for Karl Barth it is
a bridging of the gap between the human possibility of "religion"
and the divine possibility of grace; for Rudolf Bultmann it is a
transition from the frustrating knowledge of authentic human existence arrived at through philosophical speculation, which leaves
one powerless to realize such existence, to the transforming realization of authentic existence made possible by faith; and for
Paul Tillich it is a liberation from all estrangement-producing
attempts to find the "courage to be" in something finite (one's
self or one's world) and the discovery of that courage in the infinite ground of one's being. In this extended meaning, "law"
refers to all those self-imposed burdens by which man attempts to
justify his existence. These include all forms of moralistic striving which represent the self-consciously religious man's attempts
at self-justification (e.g., Kierkegaard's ethical man and Barth's
religious man) as well as all forms of self-actualization by which
man--religious or non-religious--attempts to authenticate his existence such as philosophical speculation (Bultmann) or strivings
toward autonomy or self-affirmation (Tillich).

In transposing this dynamic to the cultural and historical
plane, the process of civilization itself becomes the self-imposed
burden by which man tries to achieve authentic human existence.
This is consistent with the Freudian view that man creates civilization in order to carry out those repressions on himself which will
allow Eros to triumph over death. In the theologies of hope and
liberation, God becomes the power of the future which transcends
the limitations of the present, i.e., the limitations of civilization and its repressions which are painfully experienced as death
in the form of guilt. It is interesting to note, in this regard,
that just as Paul finds the ultimate source of man's experience of
"death" not in the law but in the sin which dwells in man, and just
as Freud does not ultimately attribute civilized man's guilt and
discontent to civilization's repressions but to the death instinct
in man himself, in the same way the theology of liberation does not

ultimately account for man's social and economic oppression merely
in terms of oppressive social structures but looks also to sin as
the ultimate source of oppression.

Thus the function of civilization is similar to that of the
law in that its inadequacies externalize sin as does the inadequacy
of legal observance. On the personal existential level, sin is
seen as accounting for the futility man experiences in attempting
to attain life and authenticate his existence through observance
of the law. On the cultural historical level, the presence of sin
accounts for the fact that the visible created world is "subjected
to futility" (Rom. 8:20; cf. Jerusalem Bible translation: "made
unable to attain its purpose").[18]

This shift in theological reflection to the cultural and
historical plane also highlights a conviction, common to both
Christian and Freudian thought, that "life" can only be attained
through the historical process of civilization--its repressions
and the guilt it inflicts. In spite of the theoretical difficulties
involved, Freud tried to give meaning to the historical process of
civilization. Life was not to be found by clinging to some primal
state of instinctual gratification; there was no escape from history, civilization, and the reality principle. If, in the end,
Freud remains pessimistic about the possibility of life, it is because he could find no way out of the contradiction inherent in a
civilization which, in order to promote Eros, had to inflict death
on its members in the form of guilt. If Christianity continues,
in spite of this contradiction, to hope for an ultimate triumph of
life over death, it is by reason of an assurance of faith based on
the belief in Christ's victory over death. The kingdom of God--
the triumph of Eros--represents the transcendent possibility of
civilization, a goal which transcends the possibilities of civilization and its repressions. It is, nevertheless, the end result
of that historical process. Life, therefore, in the Christian perspective also, is not to be found by clinging to the past but by
renouncing it in favour of the future. The future inevitably holds
out the prospect of "death" since civilization is a guilt-producing
process, but that death is the necessary precondition of life. The
kingdom of God--like Freudian Eros--is a concept which gives meaning to the historical process of civilization. Hence, the Christian paraphrase of Freud's definition of civilization--"a process
in the service of Eros"--would define civilization as "a process
in the service of the kingdom."

NOTES

[1]For Freud, the words culture and civilization are used inter-changeably to denote "the whole sum of achievements and regulations which distinguish our lives from those of our animal ancestors and which serve two purposes--namely to protect men against nature and to adjust their mutual arrangements." See *Civilization and its Discontents*, trans. James Strachey (New York: W. W. Norton & Co., 1971, C. 1930), p. 36.

[2]*An Outline of Psychoanalysis*, trans. James Strachey (New York: Norton and Co., 1949), p. 20.

[3]*Ibid.*, pp. 20-21. See also *Civilization and its Discontents*, p. 65, n. 2.

[4]*Civilization and its Discontents*, p. 65.

[5]*Ibid.*, p. 69.

[6]*Ibid.*

[7]*Ibid.*

[8]*Ibid.*

[9]*Freud and Philosophy* (New Haven: Yale University Press, 1970), p. 309.

[10]*Civilization and its Discontents*, pp. 58-59.

[11]*Ibid.*, pp. 70-71.

[12]*Ibid.*, p. 81.

[13]*Ibid.*

[14]*Freud and Philooophy*, p. 323.

[15]"St. Paul: Liberty and Law," *The Bridge: A Yearbook of Judaeo-Christian Studies*, IV (New York: Pantheon Books, 1961), pp. 237-38.

[16]*Freud and Philosophy*, p. 291.

[17]Gabriel Marcel, "Faith and Reality", in *The Mystery of Being*, II (Chicago: H. Regnery Co., 1965), Ch. 9.

[18]In his encyclical, Pope John Paul II uses St. Paul's phrase to point out the essential ambiguity of contemporary civilization which gives evidence of both "unprecedented progress" and its sub-jection "to futility" (see *Redemptor Hominis*, March 4, 1979, II, 8). This ambiguity of all cultural pursuits seems also to be the basis of his insistence that authentic "liberation theology" must hold out the promise of a liberation which transcends the limited possibilities of the historical, cultural process (see his address to the Third General Assembly of Latin American Bishops at Puebla, Mexico, Jan. 28, 1979, especially I: 4, 8, 9, and III: 2, 3, 6).

A CASTLE FOR THESE TIMES: *THE INTERIOR CASTLE*

Keith J. Egan

The castle is an ageless image. As Malachi Martin has re-
marked, "the Castle, as image and expression, is as old as pre-
dynastic Egypt and as modern as twentieth-century Europe."[1] On
the one hand, we may appear to be an age without our castle; yet,
on the other hand, the spiritual quest of modern culture may have
ceded near exclusive rights for its imagery to Franz Kafka's "nadir
vision of the Castle."[2] No single vision, however, communicates
adequately the meaning of any age. To our reading of Kafka's
The Castle, we are challenged to add other visions of the castle.
Although the gloom and the alienation of Kafka bespeak so much kin-
ship with our experience of contemporary culture, his vision must
be kept in tension with other insights into the experience of
reality. *The Interior Castle* of Teresa of Avila is one vision of
joy and belonging that would preserve the necessary tension between
these polarities.

Lest we lose sight of *The Interior Castle* and other writings
of the Spanish mystic of the sixteenth century (1515-1582), anniversaries remind us of her significance. Ten years had passed on
September 27, 1980 since the Roman Catholic Church declared Teresa
of Avila its first woman doctor. (Catherine of Siena was declared
doctor of the church October 4, 1970) In addition, the four-hun-
dredth anniversary of the death of St. Teresa will occur on October 4, 1982. Anniversaries are a challenge to celebrate in a new
era insights and values of the past. It is unlikely, however, that
so formidable a person and so vivid an author will ever be forgotten. However, we have in the past and may in the future read her
with a lack of understanding. A task for every age is to discover
ways of understanding the classics, writings that may not without
tragic consequences be left to superficial or careless interpretations. Yet, the temptation in recalling the visions of the past is
to filter them through glasses tinted by the limitations of prevailing culture. Teresa of Avila speaks out of the urgency of sixteenth-century Spain, an urgency like our own, that feels the need
to explore the potential for transcendence of the inner journey.
Travels to the Americas for gold in the sixteenth century and now
contemporary travels as far as the moon have produced feelings of

emptiness when there has been too little exploration of the inner
spirit. Such descriptions as Teresa's story of her journey within
is a story many yearn to hear. To benefit from her description
we must discover how to listen to it on its own terms. Stories
change inevitably in the telling and in the hearing but the original vision must not be obliterated unless one is willing to accept
false coin.

The object of this essay is a modest one--to offer the prospective reader of *The Interior Castle* from the author's experience
suggestions for approaching the text so that one may be aware of
obstacles inhibiting understanding and so that one may struggle
to understand the text as it was originally intended. Like all
the classics of the western spiritual tradition, one must come to
The Interior Castle not so much for information but to encounter
it at the level of genuine dialogue with its author. One reads
in order to enter more fully into the author's explorations. Moreover, it becomes obvious to the reader of *The Interior Castle* that
it cannot be read once only or in haste. One must return to it
often in order to listen to its messages, that cannot be absorbed
all at one time. Teresa's story of her inner journey is filled
with images that disclose many levels of experience. The serious
reader will soon develop principles for understanding Teresa on
her own ground. However, for that first encounter I share some of
my experience of this text. I do so as a beginner who expects to
be apprenticed for a long time to this gifted teacher from Avila.
I urge my readers to take to heart the wisdom I have so often heard
from my friend Ernest Larkin: Teresa of Avila is clearer than her
commentators.[3] Articles and books about Teresa should have one
purpose only--to introduce one as speedily as possible to Teresa
herself as she is revealed in her own writings. Analogously,
Roland Murphy advises his students to go directly to the psalms:
"This honest struggling with the word, which comes from writing
one's own commentary, as it were, must precede recourse to commentators or notes by the experts. Only then is a commentary truly
profitable."[4] This advice applies to the reading of Teresa of Avila
once one has had a solid brief introduction to the text at hand.

The Interior Castle, in Spanish *Las Moradas* (*The Mansions*), is
the acknowledged masterpiece of Teresa of Avila. She was directed
to write these, her most mature reflections upon mystical prayer,
by Jerome Gracián toward the end of her life when she was sixty-
two. Her autobiography was at the time unavailable as it was still
in the hands of the Inquisition. Teresa began composition of

The Interior Castle on the feast of the Holy Trinity in 1577. She
completed her work on November 29 of the same year. It was a trou-
blesome year for Teresa and her fledgling Carmelite reform. Difficulties left her little time for writing; in fact, the actual
time within which she was free to write is estimated to have
been two months.[5] *The Interior Castle* is a brief book, especially
in comparison with her lengthy autobiography. It has a prologue,
seven sections called Mansions, numbered First through Seventh,
and an epilogue. The sections are divided into chapters, twenty-
seven in all. Ever a reluctant author, Teresa, nevertheless, at
the completion of her task felt good about her achievement which
she credited to the Lord. She expressed this satisfaction with
her characteristic good humor.

> Although when I began writing this book I am sending
> you I did so with the aversion I mentioned in the
> beginning, now I am finished I admit the work has
> brought me much happiness, and I consider the labor,
> though I confess it was small, well spent. Con-
> sidering the strict enclosure and the few things
> you have for your entertainment, my Sisters, and
> that your buildings are not always as large as
> would be fitting for your monasteries, I think it
> will be a consolation for you to delight in this
> interior castle since without permission from the
> prioress you can enter and take a walk through
> it at any time.[6]

One needs to keep in mind that translations unavoidably dull
Teresa's lively humor. Native Spanish speakers are said to chuckle
often as they read her writings. Her humor and her common sense
abound. One is well advised to sample liberally from among her
some four-hundred-and-forty letters[7] before reading her more formal
texts in order to be conscious of the lively personality who despite
her mystical gifts always kept in touch with the daily events of
her family and friends, with the practical issues of the reform,
and with responsibilities of her own.

The final version of her *Life* was finished in 1565, twelve
years before the composition of *The Interior Castle*. Since the
completion of the former, Teresa had grown both in the mystical
life and in her understanding of mystical prayer. She speaks of
these advances: "And although in other things I've written the
Lord has given me some understanding, I know there were certain
things I had not understood as I have come to understand them now,
especially certain more difficult things."[8] She confirms her
new understanding once more.

> These are something most difficult to explain, if
> His Majesty doesn't do so, as was said in another
> book I wrote fourteen years ago, more or less, in
> which I dealt with these experiences to the extent
> of my knowledge of them at that time. Although
> I think that I now have a little more light about
> these favors the Lord grants to some souls, know-
> ing how to explain them is a different matter.[9]

She returns to the same theme.

> It's possible that in dealing with these interior
> matters I might contradict something of what I
> said elsewhere. That's no surprise, because in
> the almost fifteen years since I wrote it the
> Lord may perhaps have given me clearer understand-
> ing in these matters than I had before. Now, as
> then, I could be completely mistaken--but I would
> not lie, because by God's mercy I'd rather suffer
> a thousand deaths. I speak of what I understand.[10]

With her growth in mystical prayer and in her understanding
of that prayer--and with orders from Gracián--Teresa had ample
reason to compose *The Interior Castle*. To the wisdom of her earlier
writings on mystical prayer, she added the wisdom of her intervening
years of experience. She had become an improved guide for her Carmelite sisters for whom she wrote her books. It is important to
realize that Teresa in *The Interior Castle* was sharing with her
sisters her experience and her understanding of mystical prayer.
The Interior Castle is not a treatise on the nature of ordinary
Christian prayer and certainly not a handbook on how to pray.
Teresa writes about mystical prayer, what she calls supernatural
prayer, what later generations have referred to as infused prayer.
Teresa of Avila describes the special activity of God within the
soul of the mystic. She wants to help her sisters discern the
presence of that gifted prayer which is completely beyond the
achievement of any human effort. With verve, Teresa writes about
the distinction between what can be achieved in prayer through
grace by the human person and what God accomplishes within the
human person through the gift of mystical prayer, using in her famous Fourth Mansions the word *contentos* (consolations) to describe
the former and *gustos* (spiritual delights) to speak of the latter.[11] These Fourth Mansions mark the transition from graced human effort to mystical prayer. The very structure of the interior
castle highlights this all-important distinction. The first three
Mansions describe the ordinary Christian life of dedicated prayer
and virtue especially with emphasis on self-knowledge, humility,
and detachment. The Fourth Mansions inaugurate the beginning of

supernatural experiences. It is crucial to the understanding of
The Interior Castle to keep in mind that Teresa means by the word
supernatural mystical or infused. As Saint Augustine is the doctor
of the western theology of grace, I would propose that Teresa of
Avila is the doctor of the experience of mystical grace. Her
constant preoccupation is with a description of this supernatural
prayer.

To specify Teresa's central concern as mystical prayer is not
to imply that she considered mystical prayer as constitutive of
holiness. Much less does she ever imply that mystical phenomena
such as visions and locutions are the signs of holiness. For Teresa
of Avila, holiness (perfection) consists in the conformity of the
human will with the will of God.

> The whole aim of any person who is beginning prayer--
> and don't forget this, because it's very important--
> should be that he work and prepare himself with de-
> termination and every possible effort to bring his
> will into conformity with God's will.[12]

She is precise on the point that mystical prayer is not the exclusive way to union with God.

> It will be good to avoid giving the impression that
> those to whom the Lord doesn't give things that are
> so supernatural are left without hope. True union
> can very well be reached, with God's help, if we
> make the effort to obtain it by keeping our wills
> fixed only on that which is God's will.[13]

To become one with the will of God has been Teresa's lifelong
desire. "This union with God's will is the union I have desired
all of my life; it is the union I ask the Lord for always and
the one that is clearest and safest."[14] For Teresa of Avila, the
will of God is not some vague ideal.

> What do you think His will is, daughters? . . . Here
> in our religious life the Lord asks of us only two
> things: love of His Majesty and love of our
> neighbor. These are what we must work for. By
> keeping them with perfection, we do His will and
> so will be united with Him.[15]

Teresa combined insights into the meaning of lofty mystical
experiences with an ability to give her readers quite practical
advice. Thus she offers down-to-earth guidance for those who
wonder whether or not they love God.

> The most certain sign, in my opinion, . . . is
> whether we observe well the love of neighbor. We
> cannot know whether or not we love God, although
> there are strong indications for recognizing that

> we do love Him; but we can know whether we love
> our neighbor. And be certain that the more advanced
> you see you are in love for your neighbor the more
> advanced you will be in the love of God . . . .[16]

Teresa does not make love of neighbor identical with love of
God; in fact, she sees that love of neighbor is rooted in the experience of the love of God.[17]

Why turn to *The Interior Castle* with its almost exclusive
emphasis on mystical prayer if one is not experiencing these
mystical gifts? Teresa is not lost for a reply to this question.
Her book has been written "for the glory of God, who lives and
reigns forever and ever,"[18] and she beckons us to praise God for
the spiritual graces experienced by herself and others. Teresa of
Avila makes it possible for us to stand in awe of gifts we may not
experience. These are, however, gifts that open up vast new horizons not only for the recipients but also for the rest of us who
know them only in accounts like Teresa's. She does much if her
story produces awe in even a few modern minds where wonder enters
all too infrequently. In speaking of mystical favors, she says:

> Sometimes He does so [grant spiritual favors] merely
> to show forth His glory. . . . Hence, He doesn't
> grant them because the sanctity of the recipients
> is greater than that of those who don't receive
> them but so that His glory may be known, as we
> see in Saint Paul and the Magdalene and that we
> might praise Him for his work in creatures.[19]

Indeed, we have in *The Interior Castle* a rare document that
offers an entrée into reports of divine activity in human life.
Although written in the third person unlike the *Life* which is written in the first person, the descriptions are quite clearly of her
own experiences. Teresa weaves into her descriptions of her growth
in mystical prayer her understanding of these experiences and the
precisions made by others whom she consulted. Her writings, along
with those of her younger contemporary John of the Cross (1542-
1591), have dominated Roman Catholic mystical theology since their
time. Teresa's unique combination of experience and understanding
is a contribution both to the contemporary renewal of mystical
theology and to inquiries into the meaning of transcendence and
immanence and into the meaning in general of the elusive issue of
the experience of God in human life. The mysticism of *The Interior
Castle* is a resource for the contemplative, the theologian, the
earnest believer, and an antidote to skepticism about divine activity in human life.

Teresa of Avila's mysticism does not result in a retreat from the human scene. Within the very context of her descriptions of the gift of mystical marriage in the Seventh Mansions, she insists that mystical graces call one to service, not to withdrawal from human life. For her sisters living in small cloistered convents, she insists on this service: "This is what I want us to strive for, my Sisters; and let us desire and be occupied in prayer not for the sake of our enjoyment but so as to have this strength to serve."[20] For Teresa, the contemplative sister is one who loves and cherishes her neighbor, not the distant, unseen neighbor, but her fellow sisters especially those with whom she lives.[21] Prayer, mysticism, and love were not abstract ideals for Teresa who warned her sisters about the potential danger of being unreal. "In sum, my Sisters," she says, "what I conclude with is that we shouldn't build castles in the air."[22]

Teresa of Avila has an understanding of the human person which provides an affirmative foundation for her mysticism. While her attitude about the body is quite in line with the less than positive view common to the western spiritual tradition, it is not uncommonly negative. On the other hand, she calls for an appreciation of the beauty and grandeur of the human soul which gives a positive direction to her mysticism. Her presupposed anthropology is in this respect one of profound respect for the dignity of the human soul. She insists that "the things of the soul must always be considered as plentiful, spacious, and large; to do so," she continues, "is not an exaggeration."[23] This foundational theme she stresses at the beginning of *The Interior Castle*.

> I don't find anything comparable to the magnificent beauty of a soul and its marvelous capacity. Indeed, our intellects, however keen, can hardly comprehend it, just as they cannot comprehend God; but He Himself says that He created us in His own image and likeness. . . . It [is] almost impossible for us to understand the sublime dignity and beauty of the soul.[24]

An acknowledgment of Teresa's appreciation of the human soul runs head-on into her self-deprecatory remarks that appear regularly throughout her writings. It is disconcerting to hear Teresa speak of her stupidity and to find that she ends her discussion of the Seventh Mansions asking her sisters "not to forget this poor wretch."[25] One must constantly remind oneself that Teresa is writing in an era without psychological self-consciousness. She has no awareness of a theory of human emotions. Her negative comments cannot be judged as if she had any notion of the consequences

of a poor emotional self-image. Yet, these comments are annoying
to the modern reader and can be a hindrance to an appreciation of
her message. On her behalf, one recognizes that Teresa writes
so spontaneously, is impatient to get finished with her writing,
and so wants to be on with other matters that she obviously makes
no effort to screen out her negative self-estimates. Moreover,
Teresa's stress on self-knowledge and humility as basic to the life
of contemplative prayer gives her no pause to hold back her true
feelings. With the modern theory of the neutrality of feelings,
perhaps we can accept a woman who shares her feelings just as she
experiences them. Whatever the reasons, Teresa of Avila makes no
attempt to hide her feelings about herself or about anything else
for that matter.

The prospective reader of *The Interior Castle* must be ready
to participate in the personal narrative that characterizes Teresa's
story. It is not a book with much profit for the detached spectator. Hers is a story, in the words of John S. Dunne, to which we
must be willing "to pass over." Teresa is an artful storyteller
who shares her mystical experiences spontaneously and with a flair
for compelling imagery. In her *Life*, the use of water as an image
to communicate the progress in mystical prayer has become classical. She informs us also of her discovery of the imagery which is
central to the telling of the story of *The Interior Castle*.

> Today while beseeching our Lord to speak for me
> because I wasn't able to think of anything to say
> nor did I know how to begin to carry out this obe-
> dience, there came to my mind what I shall now
> speak about, that which will provide us with a
> basis to begin with. It is that we consider our
> soul to be like a castle made entirely out of a
> diamond or of very clear crystal, in which there
> are many rooms, just as in heaven there are many
> dwelling places.[26]

By means of this image of the castle and with a continual
flow of other images such as that of the butterfly, Teresa takes
us on a journey through the many-storied apartments of her soul to
its deepest center where the journey culminates in union with God
celebrated as spiritual marriage. Teresa makes full use of the
imagery of bridal mysticism; in fact, she is one of the chief ex-
ponents of this rich western tradition that has been so influenced
by the Hebrew Song of Songs.

Teresa reminds us in a simple, lively way that the journey
to full union with God is a mystery, one that cannot be reduced
to a one-dimensional perspective nor to logical sequences. She

does so using the *palmetto*, which illustrates the multi-dimensional
character of the journey to God.

> You mustn't think of these dwelling places in such
> a way that each one would follow in file after the
> other; but turn your eyes toward the center, which
> is the room or royal chamber where the King stays,
> and think of how a palmetto has many leaves sur-
> rounding and covering the tasty part that can be
> eaten.[27]

However, it is not only the mystery of the mystical life that
makes Teresa's narrative impossible to plot in logical order. Like
her personality Teresa of Avila's language and style are warm and
colorful, sprinkled with vivid images. This untrained lady writes
with a spontaneity that has no regard for the niceties of logic or
grammar. For the reader, this experience is exhilarating but also
quite frustrating. One cannot expect from Teresa a consistency
either in terminology or in the patterns of her story. Teresa
writes poetry, but it is not as a poet that her gifts are displayed.
It is her prose that is enduring because, despite disconnected
thoughts and rambling sentences, she communicates intensely with
her reader. One truly feels like a companion on her journey even
though one may never have experienced any of the events which she
describes. Teresa takes her reader into unknown terrain without
causing fright because she so manifestly cares for anyone who is
following her text.

   There are pitfalls that await the unwary reader of *The Interior
Castle*, obstacles that can be not only frustrating but also thor-
oughly confusing. If one has no acquaintance with the psychology
of late medieval scholasticism, one will be frequently baffled by
Teresa's terminology which, by the way, she does not always use
with complete accuracy. Her language about the faculties of the
soul such as the imagination, memory, intellect, and will can be
understood properly only in the context of the scholasticism of
the sixteenth century. The best brief guidance for understanding
Teresa's use of the faculties is provided by a book that is unfortunately out of print, E. W. Trueman Dicken's *The Crucible of Love:
A Study of the Mysticism of St. Teresa of Jesus and St. John of
the Cross*.[28] Serious errors in judgment arise without some background in the scholastic understanding of the geography of the soul.
Knowledge of scholastic psychology will aid one in understanding
not only Teresa of Avila and John of the Cross but also many other
texts in medieval and subsequent spiritual traditions.

   For almost every reader, there is also a need for patience in
sorting out the meaning of Teresa's terminology about the

extraordinary phenomena of mystical prayer. She devotes extensive
coverage, especially in the Sixth Mansions, to such matters as
visions, locutions, and so forth, not considered by her as in any
way essential to union with God. Perhaps she does so because these
phenomena were so widely experienced and discussed in the religious
culture of sixteenth-century Spain. In her eagerness to avoid being misunderstood, Teresa tries to be clear about the nature and
meaning of the phenomena of the mystical life. Happily she wrote
a document, "Spiritual Relation V," sometimes known as "#59,"[29]
in which she provides her clearest exposition about the meaning of
the terminology for these phenomena. One can turn here with profit
to Dicken, this time in understanding the way Teresa speaks of the
phenomena of the mystical life.[30] There is not much help anywhere
for our generation in coping with Teresa's frequent references to
the devil. Yet, the exercise of trying to understand the attitudes
of a previous age about the activity of the devil in the spiritual
life can aid one in necessarily reaching beyond the confines of a
contemporary purview.

This essay would do its readers a disservice were it to convey
the notion that one's path through *The Interior Castle* were strewn
only with frustrating obstacles. That is hardly the case. The
obstacles are real and must be dealt with realistically if one is
to profit from this adventuresome journey into the interior of the
soul. But the joy and exhilaration that come from accompanying
so lively a guide on the inner journey to self and God are also
real. Many of the stimulating aspects of this journey have already
been noted. Yet, one quite important theme of *The Interior Castle*
must be mentioned if this text is not to be shortchanged. In
The Interior Castle and elsewhere in Teresa's writings, there is
an affirmation of the explicit place of the humanity of Christ in
mystical prayer. Teresa is adamant in her conviction that the mystic must not abandon conscious contact with the humanity of Jesus
Christ.[31] This emphasis is, in fact, a hallmark of her mysticism.
Her unambiguous affirmation of the place of the humanity of Jesus
in the experience of God is an important moment in the western
mystical tradition.

The Interior Castle is one of the most buoyant texts of western Christian mysticism. No one can predict his response to its
challenges. For a religious culture which so infrequently speaks
of hope and where gloom has often been pervasive, this creative
story of divine activity in human life wherein the human person is
drawn into intimacy with God deserves to be prayed over and

reflected upon. No better conclusion to this particular introduction to *The Interior Castle* comes to mind than Teresa's own introduction to the Seventh Mansions, which appears to be a recapitula-
tion of the entire journey and its story:

> You will think, Sisters, that since so much has
> been said about this spiritual path it will be im-
> possible for anything more to be said. Such a
> thought would be very foolish. Since the greatness
> of God is without limits, His works are too. Who
> will finish telling of His mercies and grandeurs?
> To do so is impossible, and thus do not be surprised
> at what was said, and will be said, because it is
> but a naught in comparison to what there is to tell
> of God. He grants us a great favor in having com-
> municated these things to a person through whom we
> can know about them. Thus the more we know about
> His communications to creatures the more we will
> praise His grandeur and make the effort to have
> esteem for souls in which the Lord delights so much.[32]

This quotation is reminiscent of Augustine of Hippo whose inspiration Teresa acknowledges in both her autobiography and in *The Inte-
rior Castle*.[33] Like Augustine in *The Confessions*, Teresa of Avila
praises the Lord for his mercies, his activity among human persons.
In *The Interior Castle*, Teresa sings the praises of the Lord for
His communications to creatures, the mystical favors received by
herself and others and of which she has so unique an understanding.
She is indeed a doctor of grace. She affirms a central message of
Christianity: God himself is life's great gift. The castle of
Teresa of Avila is a castle for our times, for all times. It
challenges us to seek out the horizon of joy and optimism lest we
be swept away into the gloom and pessimism of a single horizon.

Pablo Picasso is supposed to have said that he painted not
what he was looking for but what he discovered. Another Spaniard,
Teresa of Avila, also imparts the sense that she has described the
inner journey to self and to God, not as she wanted it to be but
as she found it. Picasso's paintings and Teresa's writings will
endure. However, each succeeding age must turn to these paintings
and to these writings in order to discover what is there, not what
it wishes to be there. Teresa of Avila's story of her journey into
the interior castle is an invitation for others to embark with the
help of her experience on the inner journey where one always is
an explorer.

NOTES

[1]Malachi Martin, *The New Castle: Reaching for the Ultimate*
(New York: Dell, 1974), p. 13.

[2]*Ibid.* p. 14.

[3]See Ernest E. Larkin, O. Carm., *Spiritual Awakening: The
Mystical Prayer of Teresa of Avila and John of the Cross* (eight
cassette tapes with study guide published by *National Catholic
Reporter*, Kansas City, Mo.).

[4]Roland E. Murphy, O. Carm., "The Faith of the Psalmist,"
Interpretation, 34 (1980), 230, n. 5.

[5]Teresa of Avila, *The Interior Castle*, The Classics of Western
Spirituality, trans. Kieran Kavanaugh, O.C.D., and Otilio Rodriquez,
O.C.D., Introduction by Kieran Kavanaugh (New York: Paulist Press,
1979), p. 18.   All quotations from *The Interior Castle* in this
essay are taken from this translation.   Henceforth: *The Interior
Castle*, with Mansions, chapter, and section indicated.

[6]*The Interior Castle* (The Epilogue, 1), p. 195.

[7]*The Letters of Saint Teresa of Jesus*, ed. and trans. E.
Allison Peers, 2 vols. (Westminster, MD: The Newman Press,
1950).

[8]*The Interior Castle*, I, 2, 7.

[9]*The Interior Castle*, IV, 1, 1.

[10]*The Interior Castle*, IV, 2, 7.

[11]*The Interior Castle*, p. 203, under "Chapter 1, n. 1." The
translations above for *contentos* and *gustos* are taken from this
note.

[12]*The Interior Castle*, II, 1, 8.

[13]*The Interior Castle*, V, 3, 3.

[14]*The Interior Castle*, V. 3, 5.

[15]*The Interior Castle*, V. 3, 7.

[16]*The Interior Castle*, V. 3, 8.

[17]*The Interior Castle*, V, 3, 9.

[18]*The Interior Castle*, Epilogue, 5.

[19]*The Interior Castle*, I, 1, 3.

[20]*The Interior Castle*, VII, 4, 12.

[21]*The Interior Castle*, VII, 4, 14.

[22]*The Interior Castle*, VII, 4, 15.

[23]*The Interior Castle*, I, 2, 8.

[24] *The Interior Castle*, I, 1, 1.

[25] *The Interior Castle*, VII, 4, 16.

[26] *The Interior Castle*, I, 1, 1.

[27] *The Interior Castle*, I, 2, 8. Peers speaks of this plant as one which Andalusian children strip of its leaves in order to eat its center. E. Allison Peers, "St. Teresa," *Studies in the Spanish Mystics*, I (London: The Sheldon Press, 1927), 213. This essay is still a most helpful and informative introduction to the writings of Teresa of Avila. A useful vade mecum is E. Allison Peers, *Handbook to the Life and Times of St. Teresa and St. John of the Cross* (Westminster, MD: The Newman Press, 1953).

[28] *The Crucible of Love: A Study of the Mysticism of St. Teresa of Jesus and St. John of the Cross* (New York: Sheed and Ward, 1963). See Chapter 12, "The Anatomy of the Soul."

[29] *The Complete Works of St. Teresa of Jesus*, ed. and trans. E. Allison Peers, I (London: Sheed and Ward, 1944), Relation V, 327-33. *The Collected Works of St. Teresa of Avila*, trans. Kieran Kavanaugh, O. C. D.,and Otilio Rodriquez, O. C. D., I(Washington, D.C.: Institute of Carmelite Studies, 1976), Spiritual Testimony 59, 355-61.

[30] *The Crucible of Love*. See Chapter 14, "Visions, Locutions, Trances, Raptures," and *passim*.

[31] *The Interior Castle*, VI, 7, 5. See the indices under Christ, Humanity, *The Interior Castle* and in *The Collected Works of St. Teresa of Avila*, I.

[32] *The Interior Castle*, VII, 1, 1.

[33] *The Book of Her Life* in *The Collected Works of St. Teresa of Avila*, Chapter 9, nos. 7-8; Chapter 13, n. 3; Chapter 40, n. 6. *The Interior Castle*, IV, 3, 3; VI, 7, 9.

HEROIC SANCTITY AND CONTEMPORARY CULTURE:

SOME REFLECTIONS ON HAGIOGRAPHY*

Lawrence S. Cunningham

In a seminar lecture on Max Weber, my colleague Richard
Rubenstein once said that a scholar is one who wrestles with a
fundamental problem so persistently that his vision is enlarged
well beyond the range of his original inquiry. Thus, Weber, who
was preoccupied with understanding how capitalism arose in Europe
at a certain moment in historical time, was led to write books and
articles on subjects as diverse as Mandarin culture in China and
the religions of India. I thought of Rubenstein's comments recently
when I tried to figure out how I ended up, possibly the last person
in contemporary America, spending my afternoons reading lives of
the saints. It is a bit more clear to me now that I have had a
chance to reflect on it. Some years ago I became interested in
those persons in modern western culture who were very close to religious belief but who seemed incapable or unwilling to enter into
any formal allegiance with organized Christianity in general and
Roman Catholicism in particular. What held Simone Weil back from
the church? Why did an Ignazio Silone resolutely refuse Catholicism? Is there more than a joke in Luis Buñuel's quip "I am an
atheist, thank God"? What explains the tensile strength of Irish
Catholicism that kept James Joyce so bound to its aesthetic horizon?
In the course of my studies I began to notice that many such
writers and artists in the modern period concerned themselves a
great deal with saints; in fact, they seemed to be the only persons
in the western world who were talking about saints in a seriously
new way. Silone's hero Pietro Spina, in *Bread and Wine*, after all,
says as a youth that the one thing that he wants to be is a saint if
only he can figure out a way to avoid ending up as a plaster statue
in a dead church. Graham Greene wrote a whole series of novels in
the forties and fifties in which he tried to depict saints not as
canonized heroes but as flesh and blood figures who suffered all
of the inhumanity and weakness of our flesh. I have argued elsewhere, for example, that while the whiskey priest in *The Power and*

*Delivered as a plenary address to the College Theology Society
at its 1979 Annual Meeting.

the Glory is a direct and conscious anti-type of Father Miguel Pro,
a real martyr in Mexico, Greene saw both of them as saints.[1] In
fact, when the whiskey priest is led, shakily, to his execution,
he feels only a great sense of disappointment as if he had missed
an appointment; he knows the one thing that counts is for him to
be a saint. Likewise, Albert Camus, in *The Plague*, has the character Tarrou say to the hero of the novel that the one thing in
life that is important to him is to be a saint. When the hero,
Doctor Rieux, replies that Tarrou does not believe in God, the
latter responds that that is precisely the problem: how does one
get to be a saint, when one does not believe in God?

     It was this theme of the saint among the writers who were
"Outsiders" that led me more and more to think about saints. But,
what is a saint? How does one go about recognizing one? At first
blush, every Catholic should be able to answer that question but,
on closer examination, the idea of the "saint" is imperfectly ar-
ticulated in the Christian tradition and what little is understood
at the popular level is encrusted over with fabulation, supersti-
tion, neglect, lack of theological reflection, or, for many, massive indifference. In fact, there are a number of reasons why it
is very difficult to think about saints in the Catholic tradition
in a reasoned and critical way. I would like to outline some of
those difficulties in the first part of this paper while the second
part suggests why the whole area of hagiography is a neglected
source for critical, spiritual, and theological reflection.

                                   I

     The first problem in any serious consideration of the saints
comes, I suspect, from a certain way of remembering the saints
which we have inherited from our own upbringing and education.
While not even the best efforts of well meaning but overly pious
biographers and hagiographers can destroy the luminously singular
personalities of a Saint Joan of Arc or a Saint Francis of Assisi,
there are other saints who have a deservedly bad reputation. My
own memories of being presented with images and lives for emulation
when I was young has left me with a certain remembered complex of
characteristics which I find, in this stage of my life, either
faintly ridiculous or compellingly repulsive. Representative saints
of youth (at least male youth) tended to be priggish young Europeans
with three characteristics: they were all religious novices; they
were all afflicted with consumption or what was once called "a weak
chest"; they all seemed to be excessively preoccupied with the

possibility that they might look directly at a woman. Aloysius
Gonzaga, it was reported, spoke to maids in his home only through
a closed door and never felt comfortable being alone in a room with
his own mother. Modern youth does not value tuberculosis (Susan
Sontag's *Illness as Metaphor* has amply demonstrated how declassé
a disease it is today) and any healthy young male who did not look
at women would be sent to the school counsellor.

But beyond the mere impressions of insufficiency that one has
inherited from one's youth there is the further--and more real--
problem of the saints as a category in Catholicism. The category
of saints, as everyone knows, came into the Christian church as a
result of the Roman persecutions.[2] We have ample evidence to show
that by the third century there was a well developed cultus of
martyrs in the Roman church.[3] This cultus was having an evident
impact both on the liturgy and spirituality of the church. By the
middle of the fourth century, again at Rome, we had a developed
calendar for saints' days, together with an increasing fascination
with the martyrs as miracle workers.[4] It is well to remember that
the first person who began to compile treatises on the miracles of
the saints in the west was not some credulous medieval monk, but
the great Saint Augustine who, in fact, founded the genre. He
showed evidence of his fascination with the saints and the miraculous in Book XXII of the *City of God*.

With the waning of the persecutions there were no more addi-
tions to the rolls of the martyrs, but an interesting shift in the
understanding of martyrdom was taking place--a shift that would
insure that the Kalendarium of the saints would continue to swell.
Martyrdom was now taken to mean any heroic effort in the life of
virtue. A comment of Saint Athanasius in his influential *Life of
Saint Anthony* was typical: in his fastings, prayer, watches, vig-
ils, and mortifications, Anthony was daily a martyr.

The extension of the notion of martyrdom in the post-Constan-
tinian church did raise a problem: how does one certify a martyr
(in the extended sense of the term) as a saint? Death was the older
criterion, but now violent death was not the way that these new
"martyrs" ended their days. The answer was that the new heroes
would have to prove their heroic sanctity by their capacity to per-
form an egregious number of miracles in their lifetime with more
to be produced through their intercession after death. By the sixth
century, as Agostino Amore has recently shown, saint and miracle
worker became synonymous terms.[5] Lives of saints really became
lives of miracle workers. This was as true in the days of Saint

Martin of Tours as it was in the Middle Ages. It is, to a certain
extent, true today in that the official *relationes* of a canonized
saint must include evidence of the miraculous before one is called
to the altars in the beatification and canonization process.

Canonization as a process brought its own problems to bear on
this definition of the saint. In the early church the martyr's
cultus arose rather spontaneously. After the sixth century the
saints were usually proclaimed and their cultus established by the
local bishop. It was only in the twelfth, and especially in the
thirteenth, century that Rome began, first, to concur and, then, to
monopolize the process of canonization. In the post-Tridentine
period the whole dynamic of canonization was rigorously legislated,
the mainlines of that legislation finally entering into the Code
of Canon Law.[6]

The development of a jurisprudential canonization process was
a much needed reform in the church, but it brought with it its
own problems, problems that we are much more aware of today than we
were in the past. The formal canonization is very expensive, time
consuming (as a rule the process does not start until after the
candidate is dead fifty years), and loaded with historical and
cultural biases that narrowly restrict its scope: the element of
the miraculous is strongly present, and there is a very strict inquiry into doctrinal orthodoxy which begins at the diocesan level
before there is any process at the Roman level.

Beyond that, since the canonization process is so bureaucratic,
one must have access to the bureaucracy in order to take advantage
of its dynamics.[7] While it has often been alleged that the pre-
dominance of clerics and vowed religious in the calendar of saints
is the result of an elitist conception of the perfection of life
coming from a vowed existence, there is also a sociological explanation for such a phenomenon. Religious Orders have the talent (historians, writers, etc.), the access, and the money to push the canonization process. The post-Tridentine calendar of saints results
from the structures of the institution as much as from certain ideas
about spiritual perfection.

In order to summarize the above argument, let me offer some
test cases. If I were to pick out a "perfect" candidate for canonization under this official dispensation, I would choose someone
like the late Padre Pio, the Italian stigmatic. First, he was a
Capuchin friar and the generalate of the Capuchins is in Rome with,
conveniently enough, an historical research center for the Capuchins
also located in Rome. Secondly, Padre Pio was a man of eximious

piety who had a reputation in his lifetime as a miracle worker.
Thirdly, he never uttered an original theological word in his life.
Fourthly, he was ecclesiastically obedient to a fault. Fifthly,
there is a lot of residual sentiment in Italy in his favor as his
image on practically every cab dashboard in Rome and Naples readily
will testify. I would not, contrariwise, put many dollars on
Teilhard de Chardin's cause. While the cause of John Henry Newman
has been initiated, he will not beat Padre Pio. One finds it hard
to think of the fastidious Englishman as a very willing miracle
worker despite his defense of the thaumaturgical in the appendices
of the *Apologia Pro Vita Sua* and in other works.

To this point we have discussed the shaping of the image of
saints as it has *de facto* occurred in the long history of the Catholic tradition. When we ask about the insights of theologians on
the subject of the saints, we have practically nothing to offer.
Unlike the Christian Orthodox tradition where the development of
theology is closely tied to liturgical and spiritual sources,
Western theology has tended to separate itself from such contacts.
In fact, were one to look at the comprehensive manuals of theology
for some sense of what theologians had to say about saints, there
would be precious little to find. What one did find would be scat-
tered hither and yon, with the material on the saints ordinarily
taking the form of an *obiter dictum*. In the manuals there is a
discussion of saints when the distinction between adoration and
veneration is treated. There is an equally short discussion about
whether or not papal proclamations of canonizations come within the
purview of the charism of papal infallibility, and some mention of
the saints under the treatment of the communion of the saints and
the eschatological nature of the church. That is about all. As
far as I can determine there is no theological manual in modern
times that has anything further to say on the subject.

Because of this *parvitas materiae*, I began to look into theological and religious writers in the twentieth century to see if
there was anyone who had addressed this topic *in extenso*. Curiously
enough, the only three serious writers who came to my attention
were the Protestants William James in *The Varieties of Religious
Experience* and Paul Tillich in his *Systematic Theology*, and an extended essay of Karl Rahner in *Theological Investigations* IV as
well as the entry under "Saints," derived largely from that essay,
found in *Sacramentum Mundi*.[8] There are a few basic ideas that seem
to be common to them all that need to be enumerated.

First, all of these authors deny that saints should be equated
with miracle workers. In this they stand apart from such phenome-
nologists of religions as G. van der Leeuw who think that function-
ally saints are, by definition, thaumaturges.[9]

Secondly, both Tillich and Rahner are careful to point out
that when we talk about saints we need to remember that *hagios*--
the saint--is a term used in the New Testament of every person who
is a member of the believing and professing Christian community.
So the question becomes how one distinguishes the saint in the
Pauline sense from those that the Christian tradition has designated
as saints in a more specific and specialized way.

Thirdly, all of the authors--while using quite diverse termi-
nology--see the role of the saint as being one in which his life
and his perception of the religious tradition as it is manifested
in his life bears witness either to the intense possibility of
religious living or shows forth a new way of understanding what it
means to be a religious person. In that sense, the saint is seen
less as a wonder worker and more as a paradigmatic figure. Rahner
insists that the witness of the saint is such that others can say
that even in *this* way someone may be a Christian.

Fourthly, James and Rahner note that the life of the saint is
often at odds with the prevailing religious *zeitgeist*. Precisely
because this or that person sees a new need or a new way of living
out the implications of the Gospel message, he often assumes roles
that are either consciously or implicitly prophetic. Now that we
have safely enshrined them it is easy to forget that John of the
Cross was put in prison because of his style of life; that Robert
Bellarmine was in trouble with the Roman authorities for, God save
us, not being sufficiently maximalist in his theological approach
to the papacy; that Joan of Arc was thought to be a witch; that
the Curia was very nervous about Francis of Assisi given its past
experience with such evangelical reformers; and so on.

None of the authors mentioned above has worked out a thorough
theology of saints, but what they have done is made some extremely
perceptive comments about the role of the saint as a carrier or
messenger of new insights into the living of the Gospel while, at
the same time, distancing that notion from a concept of the saint
which is too narrowly restrictive. Furthermore, their understanding
of the saint as a paradigmatic figure allows us a certain flexibil-
ity about how we use the term saint and to whom it may be applied.
It would seem to me that the acid test for sanctity would be a
judgment about the applicability of the saint's life for the life

of others. This need not be understood in terms of *imitatio* as
much as a *fons potentiae* (a source of inspiration). It would be
difficult, for example, to get the "cause" of Thomas Merton through
the bureaucratic process; indeed, I believe that a good number of
people would be chagrined at the idea of Merton as a saint, as we
usually understand the term. But, in the sense that Merton has
touched the lives of innumerable persons, that he carried on a
vast spiritual correspondence with a wide range of personalities,
that he could reach, even after his death, those who looked for
some vision of transcendence--in that sense, at least, he was a
saint. Merton was something of an anomoly; he was hard to define
(was he a conservative? liberal? a theologian? a poet? an ascetic?),
yet it is clear that he made a unique contribution in showing
others new and different ways of leading the contemplative life in
the monastery and extending that kind of life, *mutatis mutandis*,
outside the cloister.

II

According to the *Oxford English Dictionary*, the word "hagiography" was first used by Robert Southey in 1821 to refer to lives
of the saints and its first usage was already a pejorative one.
Southey referred, in an article in the *Quarterly Review*, to "Romish
hagiography." The word has not shaken off its pejorative sense
in the course of time. For my purposes here I am going to concede--
and it is not much of a concession--that hagiography is uncritical,
given to fantastic embroidery, moralistic, and generally inac-
curate.[10] It should be pointed out that there are, as the re-
searches of the Bollandists have demonstrated, historical kernels
in much of the tradition of hagiography, but the kernel yields itself to us only after mighty labors and imaginative guesses.[11]
With that concession in mind, there are still a compelling number
of reasons why the hagiography of the past deserves more reflection
and attention than it receives and, furthermore, why we can, with
a bit of sympathy, understand that hagiography has persisted, in
new and different forms, into our own period. This section of the
paper then proposes to offer some hints in defense of, and proposals
for, a more sympathetic approach to the hagiographical tradition.

First of all, hagiography tells the story of Christianity
"from below" as opposed to systematic theology that reflects on
Christianity "from above." In that sense there is far less control on the imagination of the hagiographer than on the ratiocina-
tions of the theologian. At times (as Johann Huizinga demonstrated

years ago in *The Waning of the Middle Ages*) this free associating
imagination got out of hand. Nonetheless, there is in hagiography
a view of the development of spiritual styles quite diverse from
the official view that comes down from the top.

The position of women in the church is a case in point. We
are all familiar with the "stars" of female sanctity--Saint Teresa
of Avila (cf. Egan's essay) and Saint Catherine of Siena--but
what is often overlooked is that a close reading of hagiography
shows an importance of women that one would never guess if one
were to read only the historical chronicles or the writings of
theologians. Today, for example, we are slowly recovering some
sense of the role of women in the early church, but there is much
more to do.[12] What, we must inquire, was the position of the women
who were the confidants of Saint Jerome? How was Paula, an aristo-
crat and founder of monasteries both in Rome and Bethlehem, perceived in the early church? What was her relationship to Jerome?
Likewise, more attention needs to be given to the abbesses in the
Anglo-Saxon church who were often more powerful and influential
than later commentators would be willing to credit. Hilda of
Whitby is a case in point: she not only founded and ruled over a
monastery with both male and female inmates, but also trained the
clergy and many of the most important bishops of the seventh-
century church. She was, as the chronicles of the Venerable Bede
make plain, the hostess for the Synod of Whitby which settled the
Easter date in favor of the Roman usage and, parenthetically, reinforced Roman as opposed to Celtic customs in the English church.
The great medieval mystics of Germany are yet another area which
should be of increasing interest to us. Much has been made of the
influence that the Rhineland mystics have made on the subsequent
character of both popular religion (their impact on artistic iconography has been significant) and spirituality. However, accounts
about some of these valiant twelfth-century women have not been
adequately explored. We know that Hildegard of Bingen, to cite one
example, was a prolific writer on topics as diverse as botany and
theology. She produced commentaries on the Scriptures and wrote
a play. What does that say about the conditions for learning among
women in that period? How much of it has been overlooked in our
haste to talk about the male bastions of the schools of Paris or
the monastic centers of learning? The "Lives" of these women (are
they just the tip of the iceberg?) are yet to be restudied in the
light of contemporary feminist concerns.

Next, we must admit, and then reflect on, the fact that a good deal of hagiography is pure fiction. A figure like Saint Veronica (cf. *veron icon*--a true image) is a product of an unknown hagiographer's imagination. Yet, that symbolic person, given life from the bare mention of the holy women who followed Christ to Calvary, has played a significant part in the popular devotion of Western Catholicism since the Middle Ages. She is not an unworthy creation, nor is her literary existence without edification and deep symbolic significance. We could multiply examples of such "fictionalized" persons--Saints George, Christopher, and Barbara come immediately to mind--but the point I want to advance here is that the fictional elaboration of the lives of the saints should not be an occasion for making a too obvious inference, i.e., since these stories about the saints are not "true," we have an added reason for relegating saints to the dustbin of history. On the contrary. The proper question should be: what characters, written larger than life, have the power to serve as models and paradigms for the religious pilgrim of this age? What stories, whether fictional or true, give us some sense of what it means to be religious in our age?

It should be noted in this regard that the fiction of Albert Camus served the fifties and sixties as a sourcebook of what it meant to be an authentic person engaged (engagé) with the humanization of the world. The fact did not engage the attention of many of the mainline theologians, but it did not escape the notice of sensitive commentators like Michael Novak or Thomas Merton, both of whom found authentic value and "saintliness," for example, in the character of Doctor Rieux in *The Plague*. Nor is it tangential to my argument that beyond the more obvious sources of biblical and ascetic spirituality, the most powerful influences on the *Catholic Worker's* Dorothy Day has been from the world of the fictional: one need only remember her constant references to the characters of Alyosha and Father Zossima from the *Brothers Karamazov* and her repeated references to such works as George Bernanos' *The Diary of a Country Priest*.

There is an obvious lesson here that goes well beyond the plea for a sustained dialogue on the part of the theologian and the artist. It is, in brief, to recall that one source for the continued reflection on what it means to be a Christian derives from the deep spring of the charged imagination. In fact, were I able to press my argument further I would do more than recall the suggestive formulations of Karl Rahner and Bernard Lonergan, both of whom set

out in their work the intense religious horizon of the aesthetic
imagination. Rahner defines the artist as the person who is "capable of speaking the primordial words (*Urworte*) in powerful con-
centration," i.e., the artist gives currency to those words in our
human culture which reflect the deep meaning and deep significance
of the experience of being, against the deep meaning and mystery of
Being itself.[13] Lonergan, for his part, echoes that insight in
his typically economical and laconic manner: "Prior to the neatly
formulated questions of systematizing intelligence, there is the
deep-set wonder in which all questions have their source and
ground. As an expression of the subject, art would show forth that
wonder in its elemental sweep."[14] Obviously, I cannot apply here
the insights of these theologians to the creative act of fiction;
suffice it to say that these two theologians reflect that which
has been worked out in any number of other ways: creativity has
roots far beyond the mere fact of "imagining" and "making up."
What the hagiographer did at one time for a largely illiterate population, the fiction writer can do for our age: give us real models
and goals for living in the fullness of being.

A third reason why we need to reapproach the hagiographical
tradition with more seriousness is this: As we read through some
of the materials dealing with the lives of the saints it is easy
to note that, in a seemingly disparate amount of material, there
are certain threads that run through the tradition. We may see a
certain style of life emerging in a certain period of the church's
history, that style may produce certain extremely able representa-
tives, and then it will seem to submerge itself, only to appear
again in a new and different guise. My feeling is that, if such
threads may be disentangled from the tradition of hagiography, we
may learn a good deal about our own time.

What I am seeking to articulate may be clarified by using the
example of the desert tradition of spirituality which emerged very
early in the history of Christianity; indeed, it emerged before
the period of the persecutions were over. The period of the desert
ascetics saw large numbers of people in North Africa and the
Holy Land leave the cities and towns of the Empire for a life of
penance and seclusion in the desert wastes. It was from this movement that the whole tradition of monasticism was eventually to
evolve. One characteristic of this flight from the world was the
conceptualization of the desert itself as a place which held a
dual significance: it was the fearsome and generally uninhabitable
land which was the home of the demonic and it was the place that

one went to meet God. This idea of the desert has its roots in
the similar experience of the children of Israel and of Jesus,
both of whom went to the desert to wrestle with temptation and to
seek communion with the absolute. The idea of Saint Anthony
wrestling with the demons in order to be purified for the contemplation of God is an old symbol in Christian iconography which
still kept its fascination for Gustave Flaubert in the last century
and Salvador Dali in the present one.

The eremitical movements of the Middle Ages continued this
idea of the desert traditions but with a somewhat new twist. Religious orders such as the Carthusians and the Camaldolese did not
go out into the deserts; they created them. Though their hermit-
ages were in isolated places, their spirituality was still filled
with the imagery of the desert and its underlying dialectic of
struggle against the demonic and its search for the pure vision of
contemplation. That eremitical tradition never died out in the
west, and in our own time we see a renewed interest in the desert
experience. Largely under the influence of Thomas Merton, there
has been a place for the eremitical in the otherwise communal style
of life of the Trappists. Beyond that it is easy to see evidences
that this ideal of the desert is getting serious consideration within many of the religious orders. Examples abound: the "deserts"
of the Carmelites; the contemplative retreats of the Franciscans;
the founding of new religious communities or the restoration of
old ideals within more established groups.

But beyond these more obvious continuations of the desert
tradition there are other, more subtle, manifestations of the desert spirit in this century. The one truly new and creative attempt
to reinterpret traditional religious life in our time has been that
of the "Little Brothers and Sisters of Charles de Foucauld"--a
religious order that was conceived in the desert wastes of North
Africa but which developed in the industrial world of the west.
The unique insight of the Little Brothers and Sisters is that the
deserts of today are not to be found in the natural wastelands of
nature but in the humanly created deserts of the industrialized
world. Thus, the Little Brothers and Sisters find no need to re-
convert Arizona dude ranches into centers for meditation and contemplation. They have sensed that the urban slums of the world are
every bit as sterile and every bit as filled with the demonic as
the ancient Thebaid of the Desert Fathers. The small communities
of these dedicated men and women are a living laboratory of the
desert ideal. They live poorly and in contemplation amidst the

silences and terrors of the new deserts of our time.

If the followers of Charles de Foucauld indicate the latent
strength of the desert tradition, Teilhard de Chardin shows forth
the power of the desert as a source for a new way of conceptual-
izing the mysteries of the faith. It is easy to forget that Teilhard, a mystic by temperament, found the proper *milieu* for his
religious speculations in the lonely trips that he made to the
desert wastes of Northern China and Inner Mongolia in the twenties,
Anyone who has read carefully *The Letters from a Traveller* should
reread those letters while mentally comparing them to the tradition
of the *Verba Seniorum*. Just as the ancient sages of the Egyptian
desert formulated a peculiar vision of perfection based on their
experience in a particular environment so Teilhard, touched by the
vast reaches and awe-ful silences of the desert, began to recon-
ceptualize the whole notion of Christ, seen, not as a person for
a person, but as the Cosmic Christ who engages the world in its
totality. In that regard, Teilhard's justly celebrated *Mass on
the World* can be seen as a perfect expression of the desert spirituality for a person of this time.

All of the desert witnesses that we have mentioned to now--
Saint Anthony, the medieval Carthusians, and the moderns like
Teilhard de Chardin, Charles de Foucauld, and Thomas Merton--shared
one thing in common: they went to the desert willingly. What
seems to be new in our time is the creation of vast deserts in which
people are sent against their will. (Richard L. Rubenstein explores
this phenomenon from another perspective in the opening essay to
this volume as well as in his masterful work *The Cunning of History*.)
These deserts have names: Treblinka, Belsen, Auschwitz, and the
Gulag Archipelago. From these deserts we are getting an entirely
new kind of hagiography: letters, poems, memoirs, novels, diaries,
and oral memories of the attempts of the new ascetics to wrestle
with the pure face of the demonic, a demonic not created by the
imaginative and the phantasmagorical, but the demonic of the cold
calculation of the human will.

I have argued elsewhere that Elie Wiesel tells the story of
his own experiences in Auschwitz with a reversed language of the
Exodus story where terms like "going out" and "election" take on a
new, and perverse, signification.[15] Just as the early desert ascetics had to make some sense out of God in the terrifying absences
of the Egyptian wastelands, now the new desert dwellers ponder the
sense of transcendence, truth, and God in a new way. Just as
The Life of Anthony profoundly touched the lives of searchers in

late Roman times (cf. the testimony of Augustine in the *Confessions*
about the power of that book), so now humanity must raise new questions about ultimate destiny as it begins to assimilate the language
of the camps and the death factories, the new deserts of our time.

These reflections on hagiography have been wide ranging and
allusive. I make not one argument, but several. Part of the
allusiveness is intentional; for I had a purpose in mind when I
wrote, a purpose that was larger than the mere conveying of information. At the bottom is an implicit plea to look again at some
of the eddies of the Catholic tradition to see if, in our desire
for the modern and the socially acceptable, we may not have neglected hidden resources and abandoned treasures that we might
search for once again. I have chosen to explore one of them: the
long tradition of the saints.

If we are a people with a history, then we need to recover a
sense of that history and refuse to trivialize and sentimentalize
it. We need to look for saints today--the ones who will show us
how to live--as we had to look for them in the past. They are the
persons who revivify and set forth symbols of hope. They are the
epiphanies of truth that make the Gospel credible. They appear
often in the most unexpected of places, even as unlikely as the
artist's imagination. It was put this way by Garry Wills:

> Rome is always dying (partially) from the head
> down while being (in part) resurrected from the feet
> up. New forms of life have come from unexpected
> places-- from Athansius at local councils, Benedict
> in the monasteries, Thomas and Albert in the univer-
> sities, Francis of Assisi in the lanes and roads,
> Ignatius alone with a penitent making the *Spiritual
> Exercises*, Xavier and Ricci out at the rim of the
> world, Acton and Newman with pamphlets and
> journals.[16]

Wills ends his catalogue with the nineteenth century. What interests me is those who will have a place in that catalogue for
our century; since they will be the ones who will teach us of the
worthy character of listening in a time which has been described
as the time of God's silence. After all, "To apprehend/The point of
intersection of the timeless/With time, is an occupation for the
saint" (T. S. Eliot, "The Four Quartets").

NOTES

[1]Lawrence S. Cunningham, "The Alter-Ego of Greene's Whiskey Priest," *Modern Language Notes* (September, 1970), pp. 50-52.

[2]The literature on this question is vast. A useful survey is W. H. C. Frend, *Martyrdom and Persecution in the Early Church* (Garden City: Doubleday, 1967). On the legal question about the persecutions, see the essays on the subject by Saint Croix and Sherwin White in *Studies in Ancient Society*, edited by M. I. Finley (London: Routledge and Kegan Paul, 1974), pp. 210-62.

[3]Josef A. Jungmann, *The Early Liturgy* (Notre Dame: Notre Dame University Press, 1959).

[4]Hermanus A. P. Schmidt, *Introductio in Liturgiam Occidentalem* (Roma: Herder, 1959), pp. 528-635; Kevin Donovan, "The Sanctoral," in *The Study of the Liturgy* (New York: Oxford University Press, 1978), pp. 419-31.

[5]Agostino Amore, "Culto e canonizzazione dei santi nell' antichità cristiana," *Antonianum* (January-March, 1977), pp. 38-80.

[6]For a brief overview, see Paolo Molinari, "Canonization," in *New Catholic Encyclopedia*, III, pp. 55-59, and the same author's "Canonization of Saints" in *Sacramentum Mundi*, V (New York: Herder and Herder, 1970), pp. 401-02. The pertinent canons are CIC 1999-2141.

[7]For an analysis of the canonization process as a bureaucratic one, see Amitai Etzioni, *A Comparative Analysis of Complex Organizations* (New York: Free Press, 1961), p. 243 et passim.

[8]William James, "Saintliness," in *The Varieties of Religious Experience* (New York: Mentor Books, 1958), pp. 207-91; Paul Tillich, *Systematic Theology* (Chicago: University of Chicago Press, 1967), *ST* I, 120ff. and *ST* III, 270ff.; Karl Rahner, "The Church of the Saints," *Theological Investigations*, III (Baltimore: Helicon, 1967), pp. 91-105.

[9]Gerardus van der Leeuw, *Religion in Essence and Manifestation*, I (New York: Harper Torchbook, 1960), p. 185.

[10]The best work on hagiography is still Hippolyte Delehaye, *The Legends of the Saints*, trans. Donald Attwater (New York: Fordham University Press, 1962).

[11]On the work of the Bollandists, see David Knowles, *Great Historical Enterprises: Problems in Monastic History* (New York: Nelson, 1962).

[12]One sees, for example, many more papers at national meetings of the American Academy of Religion studying such topics; this is a hopeful sign.

[13]Karl Rahner, "Priest and Poet," in *Theological Investigations*, III (Baltimore: Helicon, 1967), pp. 294-321.

[14]Bernard J. F. Lonergan, *Insight: A Study of Human Under-standing* (London: Longmans Green, 1958), p. 185. I am using these theologians as a kind of synecdoche for the whole area of theology and the imagination--a topic so relentlessly investigated today.

[15]Lawrence S. Cunningham, "The Anti-Exodus of Elie Wiesel," in *Responses to Elie Wiesel*, ed. Harry Cargas (New York: Persea Books, 1978), pp. 23-29.

[16]Garry Wills, *Bare Ruined Choirs: Doubt, Prophecy, and Radical Religion* (Garden City: Doubleday, 1972), pp. 262-3.

PART THREE

Art,

Worship,

and

Imagination

CRITICAL RITUAL STUDIES:

EXAMINING AN INTERSECTION OF THEOLOGY AND CULTURE*

Mary Collins

Near the end of Flannery O'Connor's novel *Wise Blood*, the
protagonist, Haze Motes, who earlier had blinded himself, has begun
to wear three strands of barbed wire wrapped around his chest. His
landlady, when she becomes aware of this development, chides him,
"Mr. Motes, what do you do these things for? It's not natural."

He simply contradicts her. "It's natural."

She persists. "Well, it's not normal. It's like one of them
gory stories, it's something that people have quit doing--like
boiling in oil, or being a saint, or walling up cats. There's no
reason for it. People have quit doing it."

"They ain't quit doing it as long as I'm doing it," he says.[1]

When we approach the subject of the significance of ritual
studies for theology and culture, we are forced to say that, despite all the rational arguments that have been marshalled to explain the impotence, the impertinence, or the insignificance of
traditional religious ritual, "they ain't quit doing it." People
regularly worship their God corporately and publicly, ritually, in
cities, towns, and villages everywhere on this continent and on
this planet.

T. S. Eliot had looked at the western world early in the
twentieth century and grieved that traditional worship of God was
fading. He wrote:

> But it seems that something has happened that has never
>   happened before:
>   though we know not just when, or why, or how, or where.
> Men have left GOD not for other gods, they say, but for
>   no god; and this has never happened before
> That men both deny gods and worship gods, professing
>   first Reason,
> And then Money, and Power, and what they call Life, or
>   Race, or Dialectic.
> The Church disowned, the tower overthrown, the bells
>   upturned, what have we to do
> But stand with empty hands and palms turned upwards
> In an age which advances progressively backwards?[2]

Whether students of religion and culture are preoccupied with
those myriads who have quit or those who keep on with the public

*Delivered as a plenary address to the College Theology Society at
 its 1979 Annual Meeting.

worship of God according to traditional or reformed rites, they
have reason to ask what the phenomenon of ritual action is about
and to wonder what inner dynamic of religious rituals gives them
their power both to engage and to estrange contemporary women and
men. Nor should it be overlooked that some apparently secular
phenomena are either cryptically or residually religious events.
The modern Olympic games, for example, had their origins in the explicit intent of their nineteenth century founder to provide a
ritual celebration of the new religion of humanity.

I

    Despite the ubiquity of human ritualization generally and re-
ligious ritual specifically, ritual studies have had a modest academic existence up to the present. In the study of primitive
society and primitive religion, cultic behavior has been an important datum because textual materials were scarce or non-existent.
But in the study of the so-called higher religions, academic interest has focused on the study of religious texts. The liturgical
churches--Eastern Orthodox, Roman Catholic, Anglican, Lutheran,
for example--have regularly taught their own ritual traditions.
However, study of these traditional Christian rites was often limited to the study of proper performance according to the discipline
of the tradition.
    Since the nineteenth century, historical studies of Christian
liturgy have sought to recover long-buried layers of that received
tradition. But it was commonly said in the churches that the
glory of liturgical rites was their objectivity. And that claim of
objectivity in form and content, so assumed, went unexamined.
Meanwhile, throughout the past century, advances in textual criticism and exegetical technique and methods of theological reflection
on religious writings overran the world of religious studies. Critical study of ritual activity and religious rituals specifically,
to the extent that it advanced at all, has developed in the newly
emerged field of social and cultural anthropology. Sociologists
examining modern societies have, for their part, bypassed ritual
action as insignificant data until quite recently.
    Some years ago the Orthodox liturgical scholar Alexander
Schmemann had noted that liturgical theology--the theological reflection on the public worship of the believing community--was
peculiarly in danger of being arbitrary in its interpretations of
ritual data. But Schmemann himself had offered no methodological

solution to the problem.[3] It was possible to document liturgical
history on the basis of extant texts. It was possible to investigate what had been said by earlier believers about the meaning of
the texts and rites. It was possible to provide a phenomenology
of a rite. But there was no orderly critical way to uncover the
comprehensive meaning of an actual ritual event.

The phenomenon of ritual flux in the western churches in the
latter part of the twentieth century--involving both adaptation
and invention--compounded the problem. What has been lost? what
discovered? what retained? The historical and phenomenological
approaches to ritual studies have been strained by these developments. A new approach to critical analysis and theological interpretation has not yet been clearly refined. But some significant
developments are occurring. This essay will identify some of the
issues at stake and note what is evolving methodologically, sim-
plifying--though I hope not unnecessarily--what is in reality
complex.

At issue are fresh approaches to the exegesis of liturgical
rites[4] and new methods of critical reflection on the meanings present in ritual acts. These developments should be of interest to
and have a bearing on work currently being done in the interplay
of theology and culture. For religious ritual, like religious
literature, is a cultural artifact, expressing transcendent meaning
through non-verbal limit language--a language of acts which press
participants beyond the world of ordinary human existence.[5]

With the use of methodological resources adapted from the
human science of anthropology, it is possible to explore critically
what the rites of church, synagogue, mosque, temple, and sacred
circle express about the faith of the believers. Such investigation shows that ritual faith is not simply static and objective.
Effective ritual acts celebrate faith selectively, choosing themes
and emphases for celebration from questions of ultimacy put to the
tradition in particular cultural and historical situations, and
using symbolic forms that are available within the culture posing
the question.[6]

It is common enough to assume that the meanings available and
operating within ritual assemblies are reducible to those meanings
consciously available within the doctrinal and theological traditions of a faith community. It is common enough to assume that
old or archaic ritual symbols convey constant traditional meanings.
Anthropological approaches to the study of religious ritual suggest
that these assumptions must be examined. In times of cultural flux,

when a living faith tradition is tested and strained, ritual assemblies are likely to anticipate the new themes and to attempt
the new syntheses which are only subsequently thematized and systematized verbally. They do so non-consciously. The new themes are
often experienced as dissonant and even disruptive or incongruous.
But it is the work of the ritual action to join into a whole again
and again what is in fragile relationship and always in danger of
disintegration, namely, the future, the present, and the past of
a people. It is the work of researchers to observe, to analyze,
to interpret, and to evaluate what is set out ritually. If the researchers are Christian theologians, they will examine what they
uncover in the light of the gospel.

Ritual assemblies have been and continue to be the point of
sustained contact with mystery for most people within most religious
traditions. Because of this they constitute a fertile ground for
religious studies and ought to evoke uncommon interest. They are
a prime, if neglected, theological source.

A single case study illustrates the point that ritual activity
warrants more careful scrutiny from persons interested in the interplay of theology and culture. A short time ago I began a study of
Roman Catholic rites for the profession of vows by women religious.
First, I considered the received tradition of the profession ritual
in the group under investigation, considering texts as well as
available historical interpretations of them. Next I studied texts
of seventy-two recent performances of the rite of profession in
twenty-four communities that share that common ritual tradition.
In doing this I focused on the period from 1969 to 1975, a period
when such rites were in flux due to persistent pressures from the
larger society, from the larger church, and from the communities
themselves. I assumed the role of participant observer in one
such ritual assembly and did an in-depth analysis of it, incorpo-
rating interviews with a dozen other participants in the ritual
event.

Independent of actual ritual development in such assemblies,
the officially revised Roman rites of religious profession were
promulgated in 1970. These included the rite of religious profession and the pontifical rite of the consecration of virgins. Both
continued to set out as a central theme the received tradition of
the theology of religious life for women, a theology focused on the
symbol of virginal espousal to Christ.[7] However, my investigation
of indigenous local celebrations among Benedictine women from 1969
to 1975 shows that the received tradition of meaning and the symbols

that expressed that meaning were giving way. The symbols bearing
those meanings had been consistently transformed, at times even
eradicated. Veiling disappeared, as did the crowning; so did the
prayers accompanying these, with their references to prudent virgins and nuptials with Christ the true spouse. Less consistently,
a new cluster of symbolic themes and actions began to emerge,
reflecting a search for new meaning for the vowed life of women in
religious communities.

These developments had occurred in ritual assemblies under
circumstances in which authoritative ecclesiastical interpretation
was suspended. In such circumstances, the ritual action constituted
"serious play" related to real life within the Roman Catholic
church.[8] Ecclesiology, Christology, pneumatology, and Christian
anthropology as it speaks to the identity of women were all undergoing exploration.

It was evident in this case that ritual reinterpretation of
received meanings was preceding systematic theological reflection
on that form of Catholic Christian life, and was in fact offering
operative new themes to any researcher prepared to gather and to
interpret the data and to reflect upon it theologically. Every
ritual assembly is self-expressive to some degree in the ritual
choices it makes. Because of this, the ritual assembly is a public
forum in which professionals can consult the faithful on matters
of faith. In this forum, however, one must be trained to gather
not only self-conscious meanings but also the unthematized, ambiguous efforts at new syntheses.

To state the basic position of this paper succinctly, ritual
studies are worth pursuing by researchers interested in the interplay between theology and culture precisely because ritual acts
constitute a distinctive kind of religious and cultural expression,
one which is corporate in its manifestations and bodily and non-
discursive in its presentation of content. These very characteristics make ritual inaccessible to ordinary theological methods,
which work with texts.

Ritual acts are fundamentally traditional. But they are always the actions of some particular people gathered in a particular
place and time who use the available ritual forms for their own
purposes. So a "universal" ritual is always local and contemporary
in performance. Participants are touched and shaped by the rituals
they celebrate, but they also interpret and elaborate the received
tradition as they participate in it. This phenomenon of ritual
action deserves more attention than it normally receives in the

study of theology and culture.

How can ritual activity be better attended to in the church?
What biases must be overcome in the attending?   What are the im-
plications for the theological tradition of new attention to rites?
These matters must be addressed.

II

In the recent past religious studies and theological method
have been influenced significantly by researchers attending to
questions put to them by the human and social sciences.   The impact
of sociology, both the sociology of knowledge and the sociology
of institutions, comes immediately to mind.   A similar influence
has come from the field of psychology--from depth psychology,
social psychology, and communication theory.   In contrast with the
established importance of these fields for the work of religious
studies, one must characterize as inchoate the dialogue between
social and cultural anthropologists on the one hand and theologians
of western religions on the other.   Urban T. Holmes captured the
spirit of the current exchange when he entitled a review article
in the *Anglican Theological Review* "What Has Manchester to Do with
Jerusalem?"[9]

Manchester is the home of the Anglo-American school of social
and cultural anthropology, a school of thought characterized by its
concern for developing empirical methods for the study of cultural
systems.   In its earliest procedures, social and cultural anthropology operated with a presumption of cultural stability and studied
ritual action as a function of that cultural stasis.   So much was
this heuristic premise of stability in control that social and
cultural anthropology looked exclusively at primitive, and presumably stable, societies.[10]   Accordingly ritual study was originally identified with and determined by the study of primitive religious
cultures, not with the religious traditions of the west.

Presently, cultural and social anthropologists are coming to
terms with the role of ritual activity as a function of change.
They are increasingly interested in it as a manifestation of the
social drama.   They come to ritual action to investigate aspects
of the symbol formations of a cultural system--whether Roman Catholicism in Mexico or Yemenite Judaism in modern Israel[11]--and to
analyze the dialectical interaction between the patterns of symbols
and the power relationships operating in that system.   According
to Abner Cohen, one of the operating premises of social anthropology
is the following: patterns of symbolic action persist from the past

into the present not because of inertia or conservation but because
they play important roles within the contemporary social setting.
As a result, says Cohen, the history of a cultural trait or a
ritual unit will of itself tell only a little about its significance within its present setting. Symbolic forms of earlier eras
may persist in the midst of changes in meaning and power relationships. On the other hand, meanings and relationships from an
earlier era may persist despite a change in symbolic forms.[12] New
and old meanings and symbolic forms can coexist even when they seem
incompatible from an historical or logical perspective.

Accordingly, a Roman Catholic theologian can and should wonder
what doctrine of church and church order is intended in the 1968
rite of Roman Catholic presbyteral ordination. The rite offers
worshippers a sixth century ordination prayer for priests, which re-
calls the world of the ecclesiastical hierarchy of Pseudo-Dionysius
in which spiritual gifts descend from highest to lowest ranks. Yet
this ordination prayer comes after a ritual unit which provides
for the community's public endorsement of suitable candidates for
ordination to that hierarchy--suggesting either that lower ranks
can judge the higher or that the local ecclesial community is the
locus and source of all ordering. Ambiguity in the rite provides
for interpretation in the performance. And it is in local performance that operative meanings will be evidenced. Moreover, it is
most likely that actual interpretations will reflect existing power
relationships in the local church.

Because social and cultural anthropology have begun to develop
methods of inquiry into the ritual process and into the dialectic
between symbols and power in a system, these fields are a resource
for religious studies generally and for theological reflection on
a living faith tradition itself in process of development.

Reference to the symbol formations and power relations of a
cultural system calls for some clarification. Clifford Geertz's
1966 essay on "Religion as a Cultural System" has gained the authority of a classic position statement in the relatively young
discipline of cultural anthropology.[13] Geertz's definition of a
religion has been cited so faithfully in some academic circles that
the words have taken on a creedal quality. Moreover, Geertz's
definition has had its authority confirmed by being rendered in
short form for the convenience of students, field workers, and
lecture audiences. Briefly, according to Geertz, a religion is
(1) a system of symbols (2) that refer to problems of ultimate
meaning and (3) thereby formulate an existential order.[14]

In his seminal essay, Geertz notes that ritual plays the central role in religion. He writes, "It is in ritual . . . that this
conviction that religious conceptions are veridical and that religious directives are sound is somehow generated. . . . Whatever
role divine intervention may or may not play in the creation of
faith--and it is not the business of the scientist to pronounce
upon such matters one way or the other--it is primarily, at least,
out of the context of concrete acts of religious observance that
religious conviction emerges on the human plane."[15]

Geertz's criticism of anthropologists in 1966 was that they
were not sufficiently disciplined in their analysis of the system
of meanings embodied in the symbols which make up a religion.
Too often they were taking for granted the meanings that most needed
to be elucidated through careful ritual exegesis.[16] The field of
anthropology has developed some disciplined methods of inquiry in
the ensuing decade which would support the study of ritual as a
theological source. For even in 1980, it is easy for interpreters
of religion and culture to work with *a priori* meanings for ritual
symbols which have been disembodied from actual ritual events.
What, for example, do rings in rites mean?

Once ritual activity is recognized and acknowledged for the
distinctive source of meaning that it is, careful study of ritual
data is a necessity, with research techniques appropriate to the
data. Because some of that data is ritual texts in particular
religious traditions--Roman Catholic, Protestant, Orthodox, and
Jewish liturgical texts are all cases in point--appropriate methods
of textual criticism, exegesis, and interpretation are in order.
But much of the ritual data of world religions, including those
just mentioned, is not textual. Other methods of investigation
must be found, therefore, to deal with the complexity of the content ritual action embodies--texts, but also gestures, movements,
objects, exchanges, rhythms, sounds, which produce a single coordinated impact.[17] The single effect is like that created by disparate pieces of clothing, many of them redundant, which are worn
simultaneously to produce the layered look, as contrasted with those
same pieces of clothing on hangers in a closet.

Cultural anthropologists would read the data of ritual events
by attempting to uncover the inner coherence and intelligibility
of a ritual symbol formation within a total symbol system, whether
that system is Catholic Christianity or the culture of the televised
professional football game. They will aim to identify the root
metaphor and the dominant ritual symbols of a cultural system and

then to interpret the complex and subtle elaborations of these
which operate in the various ritual acts of the performing group.

Social anthropologists would look at the same ritual data,
but look at it somewhat differently, namely as a manifestation of
political or social process. Geertz's observation that a religion
is a cultural system with ritual at its heart will help to con-
cretize this point. Geertz specifies that the investigator should
focus on whatever action constitutes a system's fullest public
manifestation in order to see its symbolic formation fully elaborated ritually.[18] The point is true for any cultural system; its
most elaborate public ritual will set out its dominant symbols.[19]
Any number of people have proposed, for example, that the interplay
of symbols of youth, sex, money, physical force, male dominance,
and consumer goods in the ritual of televised professional football
constitutes the central cultural performance of the United States
at the end of the twentieth century.[20] This ritual event is perceived as programmatic. It presents in condensed symbolic form
the beliefs and aspirations of a cultural system. When the social
anthropologist takes up the examination of the system of symbols,
interest lies in the dialectic between the symbolic patterns and
the power operating in the cultural system. This will be reflected
in ritual events.

In the Christian ritual tradition as presently restored in
all the so-called liturgical churches of the west, the full rite
of Christian initiation culminating in the eucharistic meal on the
night of the resurrection of Christ is judged to be the fullest
elaboration of Christian ritual performance. In that sense, the
rite can be expected to be programmatic; that is, it should contain
within it the dominant ritual symbols which have borne the beliefs
and the hopes of the community from the beginning to the end of the
twentieth century. Moreover, the actual use of the symbols may be
expected to--and do--say something about power relationships.
For example, control of dominant Christian symbols, e.g., water,
oils, wine, bread, the Word, normally lies with the ordained. Rules
for extending use also originate with power wielders.

It is possible, by considering all known versions of the rites
of Christian initiation, to uncover those elements which are basic
structure and those which are "structural zeroes." In the case of
the rite of Christian initiation, covering the movement from entering
the catechumenate to participating in the Easter rites, the dominant
symbols emerge: signing with the cross, laying on hands, giving
salt, anointing with oil, transmitting new light, pouring or

plunging into water, attending to a living Word, sharing bread and wine, and ordering the assembly.

The ritual components which are "structural zeroes" are not thereby meaningless. They are instrumental and are regularly used to establish, maintain, or clarify power relationships. Postures, for example, can and often do serve such a purpose. So does the conferring of insignia designating role or status—rings, croziers, the pallium, or the veil. Controlling access to certain ritual spaces is another way of ritualizing power relationships.

The dominant ritual symbols and the instrumental ones recur in various combinations and recombinations throughout the total Christian ritual system, expressing beliefs and hopes and also establishing and maintaining historical relationships. An exegete investigating rites can gather the conscious meanings easily enough, by consulting the participants and the authoritative sources of the living tradition. But the non-conscious meanings are harder to establish. Disciplined observation of the performance of a rite can provide a starting point. What are the external forms and the visible characteristics of ritual objects or ritual transactions? Pursuing this line, the researcher may find iconic significance in the choice of substantial or insubstantial bread, the marking of a "dry" cross on the head of a catechumen and one with chrism on the initiate, the range of physical response or emotion permitted or controlled.

Further, what are the significant contexts in which the ritual events occur? Pursuing the second line, an investigator should learn what are suitable times and who are suitable subjects and agents for the various ritual actions, what spontaneous elements have been introduced into a performance, what predictable elements omitted, and for what purposes. As with any exegetical task, the intelligence and creative imagination of the investigator shapes and guides the work of gathering significant data.

What will result from critical exposition of the contents of a single ritual performance, which is only part of the larger symbolic formation of the religious tradition, is a plethora of meanings. Investigation will yield a list of ambiguous, redundant, and often apparently disconnected meanings. But there are ways for interpreting the disparate data. Victor Turner's research has led him to hypothesize that the meanings for any ritual unit tend to cluster around two poles, as in a single magnetic field, one attracting affective meanings, the other normative ones.[21] Ritual participants will be drawn affectively to meanings that have to do

with personal identity and destiny, with living within the mystery
of a loving God. So, for example, Christian ritual anointings
speak of personal transformation by the Holy Spirit of the Risen
Christ.

From a theological point of view, one could inquire into the
distinctive content of each of the several forms of ritual anoint-
ing--during initiation, at the time of illness, and for the consecration of a bishop. Anointings intend to affirm personal existence in relation to Christ, to his Spirit, and to the Creator.
Yet, anyone who attends to the ritual anointings carefully, past
and present, learns without words of an ambiguously different relationship with Creator and Redeemer for women and for men. That
anointing which asserts fullness of authority in the Spirit through
Christ is proscribed for women. Rites intend to make statements
about identity which affirm but also constrain.

Accordingly, rites make normative ethical and institutional
statements. They set limits and define. The ritual participant
will be caught up in and engaged with all of these simultaneously.
Ritual anointings establish relationships and roles within the community as well as with the triune God. The normative meanings are
fundamentally socio-political, having to do with authority and
power, roles and duties, privileges and obligations.

Turner further hypothesizes that the two poles in the magnetic
field of a dominant ritual symbol exert power over those who enter
openly into ritual action. The identity and destiny in God promised
in the anointings makes acceptable and even attractive the roles
and obligations of life in the community of believers. Effective
rituals can transform lives.[22] Esther Ticktin shows an intuitive
sense of this in an essay she calls "A Modest Beginning," in a collection entitled *The Jewish Woman*.[23]

Ticktin had come to feel a need, as a Jewish woman, for traditional Judaism to confront the diminished status of women in that
covenant community. She proposed ritual confrontation with the
dilemma rather than further rabbinic argument. Ticktin suggests:
let the men who study Torah zealously and say they can find no
resolution to modern women's needs in the face of Torah's obligations themselves participate ritually in the experience of exclusion from the covenant community. Let them do it in three ways,
straining and testing their own identity.

First, let them separate themselves from any assembly of God's
people which separates and secludes women, even if the women claim
to agree with the separation. Second, let them deny themselves

their right to read the Torah portion in a synagogue which denies
this to women. Finally, let them exclude themselves from participating in any circle of male dancers who rejoice in God's gifts
and presence if the circle has no place for the dance of women.
And as they strain their own religious identity, let them meditate
on their experience in the light of the text, "For you were strangers in the house of Egypt, and I brought you out."

Ticktin's sense of the power of ritual tells her that, should
the men of Israel ever confront this impasse ritually so that they
can feel the issue as well as discourse about it, the community of
Israel would move beyond what it now understands of the power and
demands of Torah. Rituals are distinctive social and religious
actions precisely because they use the human body in disciplined
ways to express, explore, and even transcend available human and
religious meanings.

But if Esther Ticktin is optimistic about the power of creative religious ritual to press a people beyond the limits of the
possible, many more have noted the loss of power of the traditional
religious rituals in the past decades. British sociologist Robert
Bocock observed that even in the 1970's most Britons still looked
to Christian rituals, especially life-stages rituals, for significance, but he contends that they confronted in these rituals elements which contradicted their own basic feelings about themselves.
They were not caught up in the identity the ritual offered, but
came away further confused. Bocock asserted that the dissonance
arose at the level of identity because of the overt and hidden
ritual denials of the goodness of bodily existence.[24] He further
argued that the ascendancy of rock music and the decline of participation in church rites were correlative developments in Britain,
and that rock rituals arose through pre-conscious resistance to
operative religious anthropology in church rituals.

Before passing too quickly over Bocock's judgment, we should
consider it in relation to some frequently cited research by Andrew
Greeley. Both researchers address the question of contemporary
women and men rejecting Christian rituals. They do so by looking
at different poles in the magnetic field of identity and obligation
that Turner hypothesizes. Bocock finds Britons turning away from
a God whose worship requires them to reject their own bodies while
Greeley sees American Catholics disdaining a church which burdens
them with guilt about their sexuality when they assemble for
worship.[25] In the first case, personal identity is the issue;
in the second, institutional norms and obligations.

In 1973 Mary Daly wrote in *Beyond God the Father* that women
specially had to say "no" to the false identities, obligations,
and roles set out for them in religious rites. In 1978 she published an extensive critique of the religious and social rites that
have diminished women physically and psychologically.[26] Inevitably,
the whole religious community has some faith-inspired nay-saying
yet to do in the face of conventional religious anthropology.
Basic to such a conversion is critical theological inquiry into
the cognitive content of the liturgical tradition of the churches.
The resources of cultural anthropology will aid that task.

III

Bocock and Geertz offer correlative reasons for stressing
ritual studies among the human sciences: to understand western
culture generally, and to understand also the distinct cultural
system which a religious tradition constitutes. But, currently,
ritual studies have only a modest place in the theological investigation of religion and modern culture. Some of this, Bocock
indicates, can be attributed to the western world's preconceptions
with the primacy of reason and rational discourse as the privileged
vehicles of meaning.

Since the enlightenment certainly, modern culture has been
driven by a pursuit of rationality and correspondingly uncritical
of its real limits. As participants in modern culture, the Christian theological community has been caught up in this preoccupation
even while it talked of mystery.

More recently, mere rationality is coming to be recognized as
an inadequate foundation for human meaning, whether social or
religious. We do not live now and never have lived by head alone.
Ritual says this insistently because it requires the human body to
articulate human and transcendent meaning. Bocock notes that the
very act of bodily presence is the basic ritual action: one must
participate "in person." He adds, "The use of the body . . . places
ritual at the center of our attention if our concern is with the
split in our culture between the body and the mind."[27]

Nevertheless, despite the general cultural bias that persists,
there has been a remarkable indifference to ritual study in the
Roman Catholic theological tradition, given the functional centrality
of liturgical rites for the celebration, transmission, and appropriation of religious beliefs within the tradition. Something more
than the general bias seems to be operating. Obviously, anthropologists look more readily than theologians at the ways in which

rituals employ bodies in limit-testing behavior. Rituals engage
humans in movements, exchanges, and transactions which strain to
effect an integration of paradoxical transcendent meanings.[28]
They do this in ways fully as immediate and imaginative as the
limit-shattering language of a religious tradition in its primary
expression. Why, then, have ritual studies been relatively insignificant in the study of western religion and culture?

It seems plausible that the human body's very centrality to
ritual action may be the prime reason that rites are judged by
academics to be insignificant sources of transcendent meaning.
At least two implications of such a judgment warrant investigation.
The first is more immediately accessible to view, a cultural truism;
the other, more remote.

Because of the cultural dualism that has pervaded the western
theological tradition, ordinary people--even the baptized and especially women--have been viewed primarily as manifestations of
unredeemed humanity in need of salvation, not as icons of the divine. While being bodily present in the worshipping assembly is
indeed the basic ritual act, no one is bodily present in the abstract. Specific postures and gestures required, permitted, or
prohibited themselves communicate the participant's attitude toward
self. The ritual use of the body makes it a vehicle for integrating positive and negative religious feelings. A ritual assembly embodies whatever self-understandings are active, whether official or unofficial. When there are tanks of holiness to be affirmed, or distinctions between groups, the ritual use of the body
communicates the appropriate religious feeling.

Some theologians have argued that the basic western attitude
toward the human person which surfaces in rites is anti-incarna-
tional. Nevertheless, the western Christian theological tradition
has effectively rationalized the diminishment and distrust of the
body--thus, of historical persons. Reevaluation of ritual studies
as a font capable of yielding data for critical reflection on the
Christian faith presupposes a certain readiness to discover religious significance in what people do in and through their bodies.

It is doubtful that the attitudinal change required to bring
about a new valuation of ritual studies as a theological source
can be effected simply by rational discourse while negative Christian feeling about the body is in control. Such feeling has been
learned by participation in the very rites that invite analysis.
Clerics have imposed their values not by talking about them but by
participating in ritual actions that reinforce feelings of clerical

separation and superiority. Women have appropriated womanly piety
by participating in rites that reinforce feelings of inferiority
and religious dependency. Because there is a characteristic concealment of emotion operating in ritual activity, it is difficult
for participants to recognize the depth of ritual communication
and to analyze it intelligently.

Discussing the problems inherent in the anthropological interpretations of rites, Victor Turner notes among the main characteristics of rites the tendency to stress the harmonious aspects
of relationships and to suppress latent conflicts within the
rites.[29] This suppression might take the obvious form of elimination from ritual speech of matters about which participants are
fully aware; but more complex concealment of what is consciously
known is also possible, as Turner indicates:

> It may be said that any major ritual that stresses
> the importance of a single principle of social
> organization only does so by blocking the expres-
> sion of other important principles. Sometimes
> the submerged principles, and the norms and customs
> through which they become effective, are given
> veiled and disguised representation in the symbolic
> pattern of the ritual; sometimes . . . they break
> through to expression in the spatial and temporal
> intersection of the procedure.[30]

The point Turner makes is illustrated by a familiar element within
the Jewish Passover ritual.

The shank bone of a lamb is included on the plate of ritual
foods used during the Passover Haggadah. Although the narrative
tells the story of Yahweh's choice of a people, it omits the dark
side of that relationship, manifested in the destruction of the
Jerusalem temple. The bone, not mentioned in the ritual narrative,
nonetheless calls attention to the end of the temple and temple
sacrifice. The matter is frequently more complex and the disguise
more effective, though, than selective inattention to one item
among ritual foods.

Gregory Bateson, an interpreter of iconic communication, of
which ritual is one form, carries the matter of concealment further. He notes that iconic communication regularly expresses much
that has sunk to the level of the unconscious, for whatever reasons.
Further, what is expressed iconically and metaphorically has its
own distinctive "grammar." Among other things, iconic communication about relationships lacks the grammatical capacity for simple
negation. So, says Bateson, the actors find it necessary to
"say the opposite of what they mean in order to get across the

proposition that they mean the opposite of what they say" (emphasis his).[31]

Redundancy, the patterning of a message in several codes simultaneously, sustains and reinforces the unconscious data. Through ritual redundancy humans participating "in person" both appropriate and reinforce non-conscious messages through their bodies. Quite literally without thinking, participants situate themselves in this space and not that, or move in and out of designated spaces; they wear these garments and not those, or exchange garments, assume these postures and not those, or vary postures and gestures according to sexual and social classifications. Nonreflective participation does not negate the presence of complex symbolic meaning. Moreover, it is possible that what is expressed and represented may be a sustained ritual inversion of the actual state of affairs known by what Bateson calls "primary process," that level of unconscious mental activity concerned with comprehending relationships.

The fact that religious ritual deals simultaneously with religious feelings about the self and about ultimate relationships--some of which are consciously suppressed and some of which are nonconscious perceptions known only at the level of primary process--makes the critical study of rites a potentially challenging enterprise within the western theological community. Western theology has been historically wary of the images that have expressed the religious feelings of mystics, visionaries, and devotees, regularly eradicating this content from the corpus of significant theological data. Nevertheless, it is unexamined ritual activity which sustains uncritical "religious" feeling about the self and about ambiguous distinctions between the "saint" and the reprobate, between the ordained and the unordained, or between male and female. That power of feeling and the feeling of power reinforced culturally and religiously through ritual acts may be the crucial factor inhibiting serious engagement with ritual studies in both the academic and the theological communities.

Still, persons who study theology and culture critically have reason to inquire into the dynamics that control what meanings are expressed and which remains concealed. Similarly, they have reason to question the theological mode of operation which disregards ritual study as a fertile source of human and religious meaning. The renewal of theological anthropology or the emergence of the practical political theology of the human subject cannot be accomplished in abstraction from the understanding of human persons, male and

female, set out in liturgical assemblies.[32]   It is here that the
investigator can consult the church of any era about its perception
of ultimate realities.

For example, the Roman Catholic church's official promotion
of motherhood in contemporary society is belied by its ritual
attitude toward the saving power of wombs that bear and breasts
that nurse. It is true that there is new-found academic fascination with the mystical vision of Julian of Norwich that Jesus is
indeed mother as well as brother. But there is no sign of institutional readiness to introduce into public liturgy biblical
imagery that points to the pregnant woman and the nursing mother
as a human icon of the One who gives both body and blood for the
life of the world. In fact, post-Vatican II reformers suppressed
the rite of the blessing of women after childbrith. Having arrived at a judgment that the traditional rite carried a genuine
denigration of women's experience in giving birth, they wittingly
or unwittingly continued to assume that there is in childbearing
nothing positive to celebrate which is revelatory of the paschal
mystery. Ritual attention and inattention alike communicate.[33]

Profound transformation of religious feeling and consciousness
will be required before the Christian assembly can proclaim the
praise of the Creator who has given the world in a mother as well
as a father an icon of God and the mystery of salvation available
in Jesus Christ.[34] The religious imagination is clearly capable
of such iconic recognition and symbolic transformation. Yet the
sole institutionally sanctioned image of the divine savior remains
the celibate male, paradoxically set out as the perfect icon of
the divine lifegiver and guardian of creation.

But a caution must be sounded against a too facile interpretation of available but disconnected ritual data, whether one is
looking at overtly religious or professedly secular ritual events.
Meanings are found through a study of the total system of symbols.
At the level of theory the social anthropologist hypothesizes that
in the dialectic between power relationships and symbol systems
minor or temporary shifts in power are seldom immediately accommodated by corresponding changes in symbolic forms.[35] The papacy is
a case in point. Only with John Paul II--more than a century after
the real change in power had occurred--was there an explicit public
eradication of the tiara, as a ritual symbol of the papacy, and a
substitution of the cross.[36] The ambiguity of symbols readily
allows for long-term discrepancy. Moreover, even when changed
power relations begin to take a firm hold, symbolic changes are

generally seen as idiosyncratic in their first manifestations, as
part of the personal biographies of those who are struggling to
reorder power relationships.   John XXIII, Paul VI, and John Paul I
lived with the ambiguity of papal power and the tiara.   John
Paul II has suppressed the medieval symbol.   He has nevertheless
revealed his intention to wield the power it symbolized.

Critical students of traditional ritual can learn to observe
the idiosyncratic.   Because ritual symbols are characteristically
redundant, ritual manifestations of the effort to create new syntheses of meaning and power will be diffuse and can be expected to
show varying degrees of creative imagination.   They will also embody ambiguity and concealment.   Therefore, investigators of the
religious meanings operating in liturgical rites must learn to observe, to collect the data, to analyze it within the context of the
whole system, and to interpret it in the light of the actual use of
power.   But they must also learn to ask the critical questions:
are these rites congruent with human experience and helpful to
human existence?   is their expression of relationships the gospel
truth?

The first set of tasks is foundational and their performance
can be aided notably by drawing upon the post-structuralist methods
of cultural and social anthropology.   The second matter is more
properly theological; it invites systematic reflection on the
Christology, pneumatology, ecclesiology, theological anthropology,
and eschatology manifest within the ritual transactions that make
up the liturgical event.

Because cultural systems, religious and secular, continuously
impinge on one another and so create mutual instability, the theories and methods of cultural and social anthropology constitute a
potentially important resource for the dialogue of theology and
culture.   Ritual studies may have languished to date because of the
cultural-religious bias which split mind and body.   It may also be
the case, however, that theologians have lacked the proper tools
for opening up the many languages of rites.   Yet theologians past
and present have mastered ancient languages and ancient philosophical systems in their efforts to expose the historical dialogue
between religion and culture and reflect upon it theologically.
Ritual studies might well be undertaken now with the tools of social
and cultural anthropology in the hopes of understanding the contemporary expressions and developments of living religious traditions.
Rites are after all as abundant as texts.   To date, most students
of religion and most theologians have been blind to rites.   And

the rites, themselves, in turn are mute. What has Manchester to
do with Jerusalem? It can facilitate the dialogue between theology
and culture!

NOTES

[1]Flannery O'Connor, *Wise Blood* (New York: Signet Books,
1962), p. 122.

[2]T. S. Eliot, "Choruses from 'The Rock,'" in *Selected Poems*
(New York: Harcourt, Brace, and World, 1964), p. 120.

[3]Alexander Schmemann, *An Introduction to Liturgical Theology*
(London: Faith Press, 1966), pp. 11-23.

[4]Exegesis is used here in its fundamental sense of critical
exposition of meaning. Textual exegesis has established methods;
such is not yet the case with ritual exegesis.

[5]David Tracy, *Blessed Rage for Order* (New York: Seabury,
1975). Tracy explores the concept of "limit language" in some detail in chapter six, "Religious Language in the New Testament,"
pp. 119-145. He notes that a full development of theological
method has to attend also to the study of ritual; see p. 15, n. 5.
This essay proceeds from a comparable premise.

[6]Mary Collins, "Critical Questions for Liturgical Theology,"
Worship 53 (July, 1979), pp. 302-317.

[7]René Metz, *La Consecration des Vierges* (Paris: Presses
Universitaires de France, 1954). "Le symbole de la *sponsa Christi*
constitue . . . le fil d'Adriane de cette liturgie," p. 118.

[8]That "serious play" about life within the Roman Catholic
Church today risked some challenge to patriarchal institutional
structures, but in the nature of the case religious profession of
women within the church involves some acquiesence to patriarchy,
whether as a sinful situation to be overcome from within or as a
sign of divine providence.

[9]Urban T. Holmes, "What Has Manchester to Do with Jerusalem?"
Anglican Theological Review, 59 (January, 1977), pp. 79-97.

[10]Abner Cohen, *Two-Dimensional Man* (Berkeley: University of
California Press, 1974), p. 18 f.

[11]See, for example, an investigation of the power of religious
symbol in public events in Victor Turner's study of Mexico, "Hidal-
go: History as Social Drama" and his study of medieval England,
"Religious Paradigms and Political Action: Thomas Becket at the
Council of Northampton" in *Dramas, Fields, Metaphors* (Ithaca: Cornell University Press, 1974), pp. 60-97 and 98-155. For a comparable investigation of religious symbolism in the Middle East, see
Schlomo Deshen and Moshe Shokeid, *The Predicament of Homecoming*
(Ithaca: Cornell University Press, 1974).

¹²Cohen, *Two-Dimensional Man*, p. 3. Feminist criticism points
to the persistence of the patriarchal structuring of society
throughout successive political shifts within patriarchy. See
Elizabeth Clark and Herbert Richardson, eds., *Women and Religion*
(New York: Harper and Row, 1977), pp. 1-14.

¹³Clifford Geertz, *The Interpretation of Culture* (New York:
Basic Books, 1973), p. 90.

¹⁴Deshen and Shokeid, p. 156.

¹⁵Geertz, p. 112.

¹⁶*Ibid.*, p. 125.

¹⁷See Gregory Bateson, *Steps to an Ecology of Mind* (New York:
Ballantine Books, 1972); "Redundancy and Coding" discusses patterned
and coded behavior, pp. 411-425. For a judgment on the implications of Bateson's theory for liturgical studies, see Gerald Lard-
ner, "Communication Theory and Liturgical Research," in *Worship* 51
(July, 1977), p. 306.

¹⁸Geertz, p. 113.

¹⁹Victor W. Turner, *The Forest of Symbols* (Ithaca: Cornell
University Press, 1967), p. 20.

²⁰See, for example, Eugene Bianchi, "The Super-Bowl Culture
of Male Violence," in Eugene Bianchi and Rosemary Ruether, *From
Machismo to Mutuality* (New York: Paulist Press, 1976), pp. 54-
69.

²¹Turner, *The Forest of Symbols*, p. 28.

²²*Ibid.*, p. 30.

²³Esther Ticktin, "A Modest Beginning," in *The Jewish Woman*,
ed. Elizabeth Koltun (New York: Schocken Books, 1976), pp. 129-
135.

²⁴Robert Bocock, *Ritual in Industrial Society* (London: George
Allen and Unwin, Ltd., 1974), p. 38.

²⁵Andrew Greeley, *The American Catholic: A Social Portrait*
(New York: Basic Books, 1977), pp. 126-151.

²⁶Mary Daly, *Beyond God the Father* (Boston: Beacon Press,
1973), pp. 140-146; also, *Gyn/Ecology: The Metaethics of Radical
Feminism* (Boston: Beacon Press, 1978) on Indian suttee, Chinese
footbinding, African genital mutilation, and European witchburning,
chapters three to six.

²⁷Bocock, p. 34.

²⁸Roger Grainger, *The Language of the Rite* (London: Darton,
Longman, and Todd, 1974), p. xi.

²⁹Turner, *The Forest of Symbols*, pp. 32-41.

³⁰*Ibid.*, pp. 40-41.

³¹Bateson, pp. 140-141.

[32]Johannes Metz, for example, speaks naively of "the human
subject" when he proposes a theological criticism of middle-class
religion without adverting to the clear structural distinction
maintained within both middle-class religion and society concerning
suitable roles for male and female subjects, and in proposing memory as a basic category of practical critical reason without adverting to the implications of distinct sexual roles for that basic
"human" memory. See *Faith in History and Society* (New York: Seabury, 1980).

[33]Walter von Arx, "The Churching of Women After Childbirth,"
in *Liturgy and Human Passage: Concilium 112*, ed. David Power and
Luis Maldonado (New York: Seabury, 1979), pp. 62-72. The article,
which narrates the history of the rite and the reasons for its
suppression, does not take into account the general liturgical
status of women. This matter will not be "forgotten" simply by
suppressing the churching rite.

[34]See Bernard Lonergan, *Method in Theology* (New York: Herder
and Herder, 1972), pp. 238-244, for a discussion of religious conversion as the basis for both intellectual and moral conversion.
For a related discussion of conditions which block insight, see
Insight (San Francisco: Harper and Row, 1978), pp. 191-203.

[35]Cohen, pp. 36-37. Complexity, ambiguity, density, redundancy, and concealment are all characteristic of ritual behavior.
The correlative absence of any transparency of meaning should pre-
clude all hasty judgments about the significance of isolated epi-
sodes or manifestations of corporate meaning.

[36]John Paul II made prominent use of the cross at the close
of his rite of installation in October, 1978. Earlier, he had
drawn attention to the suppression of the triple tiara in his installation homily. In his address to Polish workers at Nowa Huta,
delivered from the nearby Shrine of the Cross in Mogila on June 9,
1979, he spoke of the power of the cross as a symbol for himself
and for Polish workers. *Origins*, 9 (June 21, 1979), pp. 76-77.

THE LIMINAL SPACE OF RITUAL AND ART

Marchita B. Mauck

Liminality (from the Latin *limen*, threshold) is a term belonging to the study of psychological anthropology. Victor Turner
describes the attribute of liminality or liminal people as

> necessarily ambiguous, since this condition and these
> persons elude or slip through the network of classifi-
> cations that normally locate states and positions in
> cultural space. Liminal entities are neither here nor
> there; they are betwixt and between the positions as
> signed and arrayed by law, custom, convention, and cere-
> monial. As such, their ambiguous and indeterminate at-
> tributes are expressed by a rich variety of symbols in
> the many societies that ritualize social and cultural
> transitions. Thus liminality is frequently likened to
> death, to being in the womb, to invisibility, to dark-
> ness, to bisexuality, to the wilderness, and to an
> eclipse of the sun or moon.[1]

Liminality is the middle of three stages in all rites of passage,
as described by the anthropologist Arnold van Gennep.[2] It is
characteristically brief and intense, and anti-structural in that
it suspends the regular rules and expectations of society. Liminality precedes the reintroduction back into the community.
Liminality can be described as a space/time in which we allow mystery to unfold, and in which we are willing to surrender to the
power of symbol to penetrate our being and lead us deeper into
mystery. Liturgy and art function most effectively in such a space/
time.

Contemporary visual exemplars abound in which the spectator is
led into realities beyond the surface of the image. For example,
purity and luminosity of color become an expression of a vitality
that often has spiritual content. The works of Mark Rothko immediately come to mind. His late works consisted mainly of huge rec-
tangular areas of color which seem to float, suggesting an expansion of space to even cosmic dimensions. The spectator experiences
the total sensuality of color in a most provocative as well as
evocative way. In the paintings for the Rothko Chapel in Houston,
Rothko achieves with immense subtlety the illusion of an open,
sacred, celestial infinity, dark and brooding and inscrutable, in-
viting contemplation.

That sensation of floating, hovering color which induces in-
trospective reveries appears also in works of the so-called color

field painters such as Helen Frankenthaler or the stain paintings
of Morris Louis or Paul Jenkins. Color ebbs and flows, sometimes
obscured by a mysterious vein effect, with a primal life force
that silently but continually washes over the surface of the
painting.

Such perceptions represent what Urban Holmes refers to as the
"land east of the river" in the landscape of consciousness, the land
of receptivity. Holmes describes a fascinating map of human consciousness in his book *The Priest in Community*. He supposes a
"land bordering on a fathomless ocean, which crashes against the
shore with infinite energy."[3] The shore line is varied from beaches
to steep cliffs. It slopes upward, toward a plateau. Moving away
from the ocean, in a westerly direction, the land is a wilderness
with its own fauna and flora, with its friendly and treacherous
plants and animals. "There are water holes shaded by tall trees,
and there are also geysers of boiling sulfurous liquid."[4] As you
travel, you have ambiguous feelings about this strange, eerie, but
tantalizing world. Eventually you discover a path leading toward
the west, and you suddenly discover others travelling with you,
just others with no distinctive dress or titles. You talk to others, sharing whatever it was that brought you to this wilderness.
You talk about the ocean depths from which you have come, and where
you hope to go. You share intimate details of your life. The
path becomes clearer, and you finally come to a great river. On
the other side of the river the wilderness seems to end. There are
fields, houses, planned villages. The great river divides the
liminal anti-structure, which Holmes calls the receptive mode, from
the structures or the action mode. The raw energy, the Word of
God, emerges from the abyss from whence we came. We discover the
primal symbol of Christ, "the primordial representation of the self
and the embodiment of God's love enabling our wholeness."[5] As we
move west we become conscious of the root metaphor for Christians,
the process of death and resurrection. Our Christian myth is what
Holmes describes as a primordial myth, "the true story about the
relationship between us and our God who lies beyond the fathomless
ocean, from whence we have come and to which one day we must return."[6] The primordial myth of Christians, the life and death and
resurrection of Jesus, is enacted in our rituals, sung about, and
retold, one to another. And we live it. While we are operating in
the receptive mode of consciousness, we are open to all possibilities and all risks. Faith occurs first in the land east of the
river, the land of no control, the land in which we must surrender

control.

Across the river things are different. The power of our
stories carries us across and we want to do something with our
stories. But here our fears are gone and things are comfortable
and predictable. There is security. We analyze what has happened
to us and objectively attempt to grasp our world and be in control
of it. Ambiguity vanishes and the risk of the unpredictable is
gone. The villages give way to the suburbs of a great city where
people work smoothly together. In Holmes' allegory, everyone knows
what to do and how it will be done. This land of structures is the
land we know well, that of our western culture, and certainly that
of our institutional church. We have moved from a world of story
to one of systems. Sign rather than symbol dominates. In a society of laws, signs are important. Their clarity is indisputable.
But, Holmes points out, "the only problem is they lack passion.
They are boring. They cannot inspire a great love, the building of
a cathedral, or a journey around the world on a raft. Nobody dies
for a sign."[7] The only real comfort, in a strange sort of way, is
that the more we know about how those computer analyzed systems and
structures function, if we penetrate them deeply enough, we will
discover the chaos of their structures and, as Holmes says, find
ourselves on the shores once again of the fathomless ocean.[8]

We obviously have to live on both sides of the river. But as
a people who have spent time in the "wilderness" and have discovered
some of the truths which transcend the verities of structures, we
have difficulty with the balancing act of one foot on each side of
a treacherous abyss. We are afraid that if we cross the river to
the western side, we will soon forget our experiences in the east.
What is the solution? Surrender, I suggest, to the power of liturgy
and art to direct us. The intention of both is to help people live
comfortably with the world of myth, story, ritual, and at the same
time the secular, technological world. Both have the dynamic of
parable to catapult us back into the receptive mode where we find
God and rehearse again our sources, our roots, our journey, our
goals.

Roger Grainger observes in his book *The Language of the Rite*
that "the artistic or theatrical nature of ritual serves to produce
a special 'atmosphere for encounter,' in which we are enabled to
meet one another and so discover ourselves as we really are. The
rite provides what Antonin Artaud has called 'the structure in time
for that meeting for which the being of man ceaselessly cries out

but which in life it can so rarely achieve.'"[9] This quotation in-
corporates Grainger's main premises; namely, that ritual is a means
of encounter which proclaims the reality of relation, that ritual
wrests timelessness from temporality, and that ritual provides a
place/space for meeting.

Ritual is primarily a corporate activity. One of the important
things which happens is that ritual encounter reveals one's awareness of belonging to his particular environment and thus helps secure his identity and sense of himself. But other things also happen in this context. One's sense of himself is often that of alienation, the inability to attain the *being* he seeks, the awareness
of a distance between what is and what should be. Within this abyss
of discontinuity and lack of relation one yearns for unity and
wholeness. Ritual experience, in its corporate sharing, provides
the option of bridging the existential chasm between self and being by moving from the self to the other--giving of oneself both
to others and to the Other who affirms us in being. We ceaselessly
cry out for the resolution of this tension between self and the
Other. Recognition of the gulf separating the soul from God paradoxically makes him less distant, and ritual makes immediate our
simultaneous comprehension of God's summoning us across the gulf
of alienation. Ritual provides a vehicle for satisfying the rest-
lessness of the human soul which urges it to attempt continually
to merge with the Other in unity and harmony.

The implication of ritual's function as a means of encounter
with others and the Other is awesome. The encounter is simultaneously so down-to-earth human and divine. It is a matter of val-
idating the divinity in which the individual shares, as he or she
moves toward the Other, toward being. The context of the ritual
must be hospitality, and there must be an invitation to mystery.
The language of ritual will be a foreign language babbled to the
wind if the atmosphere does not proclaim that this time and this
place are special because of what is happening here. Everything
must be planned and arranged so that in this time and in this space
one feels an overwhelming desire and necessity to surrender to the
mysterious reality of the past and future made present and immediate. The power of the rite must be allowed to function! Grainger
says that "in ritual, a person comes home, he returns to a primal
richness and satisfaction; and because home is *really* home, when
he emerges again to continue his wanderings he does so refreshed
and renewed, in mind, body, and spirit."[10] In ritual we cross
back to the land east of the river for the strength and inspiration

to survive on the western bank. Ritual is the bridge across the
river, the bridge Holmes calls the power of our stories.

The turn toward Otherness which is the basis for encounter
and relation occurs in time. Grainger says that the shape of the
rite creates an atmosphere of timelessness--time stands still to
the extent that the truth perceived transcends time and delivers
one "from the temporal ambiguity of things and events and gives
life stability and permanence."[11] It is important that time be
interrupted so that eternity can be confronted and understood as
distinct from the flux and commotion of ordinary time. We surprisingly create a ritual context of "spiritual space" for the
penetration of the world of faith. The rite becomes an event which
distracts from the demands and pressures of the moment, leading
the participant into another time/space within which encounter with
the divine can occur. In fact, Grainger points out, the present
moment becomes all time and the place of revelation is a type of
everywhere.[12] His thesis is that only by means of the perception
of eternity can real life in time be attained. In that "spiritual
space" of timelessness--the land east of the river--the ritual requires that one participate, and even more surrender to the experience. The experience to which one surrenders is first of all
the ritual recalling of the past in order to make it present now.
To transcend the past requires "killing" it in order to progress
toward the future. In a Christian context this means dying to sin,
and in personally experiencing this event, we destroy temporality.
Recalling the events of salvation history allows them to transcend
time and become immediate for the participants, and simultaneously
redemptive by association. These ritual events carry great intensity, and it is their intensity which helps suspend time. Dying
in order to begin again is a negative/positive experience, traumatic
at the beginning and life-giving and renewing at the end. The
corporate nature of ritual enables the sharing of the concomitant
anxiety and the possibility of drawing on a pooled fund of courage
to face the future.

Ritual makes us free from time so we can be free for time,
time to contemplate the new beginnings. It is the "dreaming time
of van Gennep's liminal stage, and the dream time to which A. Artaud refers which is at the same time a dreaming place."[13] Reaching
the moment of stasis--that timelessness in which new creation and
revelation can unfold--is a fragile equilibrium. The individual
immediately recognizes that he belongs, and that something is occurring here which concerns his relatedness and his freedom to

respond. If he feels enticed to respond, then ritual has been
successful in encouraging him to affirm his relatedness, to assemble with others, to reach out to God, and in so doing to bridge
the gap between the self and the Being for which he is yearning.
Then the power of ritual is free to transform lives by proclaiming
and sanctifying the authenticity of human reality. It enables us
to define and recognize the goodness of our humanity because we
feel our incarnate Lord drawing us to himself.

In the receptive mode, that liminal territory of timelessness,
of ritual, of encounter, it is clear that the work of art, as a
thing of beauty, reflects some artist's journey in the land east of
the river. Even the most mundane subject matter can introduce the
viewer of a work of art to a reality which transcends the apparent
theme. In the fifteenth century Jan van Eyck celebrated the sheer
glorious materiality of substances. Such an appreciation of the
density and substance of objects in creation reflected in medieval
times a response to Thomas Aquinas' conviction that physical objects are corporeal metaphors of things spiritual. Photographical-
ly realistic paintings of gleaming Airstream trailers by Ralph
Goings, the intricate detail of shiny reflective carburetors in Tom
Blackwell's paintings, or David Parrish's famous motorcycle paintings, all ultimately refer to the value system of the American culture of the 1970's. The contemporary artist Richard Estes recon-
structs cityscapes of store façades mirroring traffic and other
buildings in pristine, sunny transcriptions of incredible complexity which mesmerize spectators. In the work of both Estes and
van Eyck there is an emphasis on *being* rather than *doing* within
the context of carefully orchestrated glittering labyrinths. The
metallic shine of a precision-tooled engine can visually express
the same exuberance as the jewelled crown in a fifteenth-century
painting. Both represent an appreciation of the density and complexity of matter in the universe. The high compression engine is
no less spiritual because it is a representation of a machine, or
the embroidery on the Virgin's gown any more secular because its
rich, expensive reflective surfaces are acknowledged. Both refer
to realities other than the immediate object.

In the first quarter of the twelfth century, in the French
city of Autun, the artist Gislebertus sculpted the entrance portal
and all the column capitals of the interior nave and the outside
cloister of the church of St. Lazarus.[14] Gislebertus had the
courage to claim his humanity! An inscription across the portal
sculpture reads "Gislebertus of Autun made this." If we take a

look at the incarnation through his eyes, it begins with Eve--
a rather shocking figure for the period, for Eve here assumes
flesh. She is not a type of the female, but a real woman. Only
a man who knew a woman is soft and seductive could have created
this image. She is real, with no apologies, and she deliberately
reaches for that apple. That gesture sets in motion a series of
events which will eventually require the coming of God as man to
set things right again. An angel arrives to awaken the kings and
send them on their journey. The simple gesture of the touch which
awakened the first king who opens his eyes is the same gesture by
which God the Father quickens Adam into being in Michelangelo's
evocation of creation in the Sistine Chapel. There is something
so human about the details. One of the kings attentively listens
to Herod. Joseph awaits the birth as do all fathers in all times,
with a weary, helpless endurance as he rests his chin in his hands.
He perks up considerably after the worries are over and a perfect
baby has been born. He peers off into the distance at the approaching magi. As they offer their gifts, the child, all so humanly,
grasps the nob to remove the lid and look inside the jar. As in
John Shea's "Prayer to the God beyond God," this is the baby who
is the "Architect, Body-Moulder, Breath-Giver, Mountain-Thunderer,
Goatherd, Sky-Dweller, Dream-Stalker, Freedom-Fighter, Desert Sheik,
Bridegroom, Wine-Grower, Potter, Law-Giver, King-Breaker, Jealous
Husband Judge, Ruler, Priest Father Flame, Wind, Gentle Voice,
Grave-Robber, Spirit-Giver"[15] for all time. The scenario plods on
its inevitable course as the Holy Family begins the journey that
will lead to death and life. The journey is not a mystical abstraction. Joseph and the donkey in scumbled line stumble over what
looks like Oreo cookies as they proceed to their destiny--and ours
--in such a painfully human way. It is in walking with one another
along that same dusty road in the wilderness east of the river,
represented literally and symbolically by Gislebertus, that we will
get to know who God is.

    What Gislebertus accomplishes in his images, guiding us into
the ambivalence of the land east of the river, is the function of
symbol. Symbols mediate for us when we get too close to the holy.
They give us access to the event itself. Artists seem to know what
Paul Tillich speaks of when he says that when you participate in
symbol you participate in being itself. For Tillich, symbols send
a root into the power of being and let us participate.[16] Authentic
existence means letting the self surrender to the power that can
help us participate in being. That Being, in Karl Rahner's terms,

is manifold, multi-valent, and it always seeks expression in an-
other. A symbol is the expression of one thing in another.[17]
Abbot Suger understood this in describing the beauty of his new
Abbey Church at St. Denis, at its dedication in 1144. He said:

> When--out of my delight in the beauty of the
> house of God--the loveliness of the many-colored
> stones has called me away from external cares, and
> worthy meditation has induced me to reflect, trans-
> ferring that which is material to that which is im-
> material, on the diversity of the sacred virtues:
> then it seems to me that I see myself dwelling, as
> it were, in some strange region of the universe
> which neither exists entirely in the slime of the
> earth nor entirely in the purity of Heaven; and
> that, by the grace of God, I can be transported
> from this inferior to that higher world in an ana-
> gogical manner.[18]

Here we see that the strategy of symbol is metaphor which makes
the transaction of symbol possible. Gislebertus' donkey plodding
along, or the details of a stained glass window, or paintings of
glittering metallic machines can be grasped at a literal level; but
we are seduced into, plunged into a deeper significance where meaning emerges if we surrender to the power of the symbol. When we
surrender, new disclosures occur; we are ripped open to the possibility of new perceptions. We are set on a new journey of discovery. Art and liturgy both function in the land east of the
river, along with literature and music and dance and the poetry of
space and the space of time. They seduce us into a surrender to
being, into a contemplation of and participation in ultimate
Being. There is no hope of survival on the western side without
them. Both art and ritual shape an extraordinary space/time conducive to an encounter with transcendent reality. The presence of
the Other can penetrate our awareness when we surrender to the
liminal experience of *being* rather than *doing*, when we let ourselves
celebrate mystery.

NOTES

[1]Victor W. Turner, *The Ritual Process: Structure and Anti-Structure* (Chicago: Aldine, 1969), p. 95.

[2]Arnold van Gennep, *The Rites of Passage* (Chicago: University of Chicago Press, 1960), p. 11.

[3]Urban T. Holmes, *The Priest in Community* (New York: Seabury Press, 1978), p. 20.

[4]*Ibid.*

[5] *Ibid.*, p. 24.

[6] *Ibid.*, p. 25.

[7] *Ibid.*, p. 28.

[8] *Ibid.*, p. 30.

[9] Roger Grainger, *The Language of the Rite* (London: Darton, 1974), p. 162.

[10] *Ibid.*, p. 167.

[11] *Ibid.*, p. 131.

[12] *Ibid.*, p. 166.

[13] *Ibid.*, p. 162.

[14] For illustrations of the Autun sculptures, see Denis Grivot and George Zarnecki, *Gislebertus, Sculptor of Autun* (New York: Orion Press, 1961).

[15] John Shea, *The Hour of the Unexpected* (Niles, IL: Argus Communications, 1977), p. 88.

[16] Paul Tillich, *What is Religion?* (New York: Harper and Row, 1969), pp. 76-77, ff.

[17] "The Theology of the Symbol," in *A Rahner Reader*, ed. Gerald A. McCool (New York: Seabury Press, 1975), pp. 120-130.

[18] Erwin Panofsky, ed., *Abbot Suger on the Abbey Church of St.-Denis and Its Art Treasures* (Princeton: Princeton University Press, 1979), p. 21.

THE ARTIST AND IMAGES OF INCARNATION

Eugene M. Geinzer

To the conscientious Christian analyst of culture, it would
seem that the Incarnation has not taken effect. Why, for example,
do images of our integration so repeatedly suffer setbacks. We
feel alienated from God, stranger to or enemy to our neighbor,
divided within the very house of our own being. Not only do we
fight our way through a suspicious spirituality (the Old Man/New
Man dichotomy), but also what could be a supportive community to
us is a tangle of incommensurate expectations. Moreover, even in
our prayerful moments we seem to be assured over and over again
that there is no power, no person who resonates with our needs.
How then can the letter to the Ephesians shamelessly exclaim:
"This means that you are strangers and aliens no longer. No, you
are fellow citizens of the saints and members of the household of
God" (Eph. 3:19)?

We can locate tentative answers to these problems, I propose,
by asking what images we expect of the Incarnation. If we discover
that we have been assigning univalent characteristics to the images
which constellate around the Incarnation, we may note that what we
have actually done is anesthetize those very load-bearing images.
We may actually have made the Logos monosyllabic, fixed, and non-
nutritive of a new creation, of a genuinely new image: a new face
of the earth. Yet if we use the word *image* in the way in which
Genesis seems to use it, namely, to body forth, we have a rich new
perspective. An artist sees images as multivalent, unfixed, necessarily ambiguous. This is also, I suggest, a fact of the Incarnation; its physiognomy is ambiguous. It can be described only in
its multivalences. We can then understand the image of God making
his home with mankind as a bodying forth of all the complexities of
personal encounter.

The marks of all images allow us to reread that "body" language
of the Incarnation. First, images are *self-discursive*. Prior to
our introspection of personal imagery, we are unconsciously revealing ourselves. Secondly, images are *ecstatic*. Were it possible
for us to be conscious masters of ourselves, still our self-image
would leap beyond every original personal project. Finally, images
are *dialogic*. No matter how idiosyncratic we--like God--pride

ourselves in being, our image is derivative and yet a progenitor
of other images. It is of the essence of images to be bartered.
Images disclose one another.

In looking for the imagistic patterns of the Incarnation, it
is essential then not to resort to superficial identifications.
It is my hypothesis that if we interrogate the images of our culture, we will unearth, at any one of these three phases, a trajec-
tory that corroborates the fact of the Incarnation. My reasoning
is analogous to John Dewey's in his book *Art as Experience*. It is
the task of the artist-theologian to reveal the *continuum* between
the "art" of God and that of our everyday life.

Rather than choosing either extreme of idolatry of iconoclasm
as we investigate the images of this world, we should choose a
middle ground in which heaven and earth meet. This nexus, I believe, is the location of the central images of the Incarnation.
An idolator finds the most seductive image of the Incarnation con-
clusive. An iconoclast repudiates any image. Mircea Eliade prof-
fers a middle ground: "Rightly to understand the structure and
function of such an image, one must remember the dialectic of the
sacred: any object whatever may paradoxically become a hierophany,
a receptacle of the sacred, while still participating in its own
cosmic environment."[1] Thus when I accept my own image and the
contextual images of this world, then, I believe, I am beginning
to accept the image of the Incarnation.

Why, one may ask, add any more images to an already congested
landscape! The truth of the matter is that we are ourselves images
and we cannot help but replicate ourselves. Even the first jerky
movements of a child are images of excitement or pain at the very
felt experience of deprivation or presence of food. Piaget has
well documented in *The Construction of Reality in the Child* the
way a child begins to situate himself in space, locating who and
what can be ingested.[2] As his fine motor eye-hand coordination
develops, it becomes obvious that his gesticulation patterns who
he is, what he wants, and where he thinks that desired object might
be. Compare the early developmental gesture of a child of six
months to that of an amateur golfer:

> He lets go of a toy as he raises his right arm. (He
> is lying down.) The toy falls to the level of his
> waist; he searches for it at once with his hand,
> lowering his forearm without displacing his upper arm.
> (He knocks against the object as it happens to be
> located in the trajectory of his hand.) Throughout the
> whole search his glance is aimed in the right
> direction.[3]

A primitive consciousness directs the configuration of this child.
The very way he constructs the image of his body allows him to
achieve his purpose. So it is with a golfer or swimmer. His
body image expresses his purpose and achieves his goal.

In his elaborate treatise on the coincidence of the revelatory
process and the imaginative process, Ray L. Hart isolates some of
the dynamics which account for the evolution of an image.[4] He
speaks of imaginative language (and by language he includes all
aural, visual, and tactile images) as "event-inverbalizing." That
is, with as little prejudice to the whole experience, an image
gathers up the whole import of the event.[5] Unlike discursive and
self-conscious languages that would subject the event to inspection
and systematization, images allow the event to remain free. For
example, how much more comprehensive is the image of body as
swimming than an explanation of how a body moves through water.

Yet images, for all their compression, for their ability to
communicate immediately, are a source of much puzzlement. Somehow
they can never be "unpacked" adequately. Images instantly body
forth and simultaneously resist analysis. Chagall's inverted
angels and floating animal heads are immediately accessible--but
then again they are elusive. His images invite us back for repeated
inspections. Archetypal forms are re-invented. They become imbed-
ded in private imagery. They reappear again. What past event has
been caught fast? Where can one begin to unpack the event that has
been "inverbalized"? We shall not begin to interrogate the image
as long as we treat the image as univalent, as forever bound up
with one meaning, as a transcription of "my" personal history. It
is only when we notice the "shock" of where we are in our temporary
dislocation with reference to any image, what Hart calls "ontological instability," that our self-image will begin to re-construct
itself in response to the newly felt image.[6] Only a meeting with
a new alternative or the resurgence of some older suppressed image
will "shock" the imagination into forming new images. This is what
we must allow to happen to ourselves vis-a-vis the images of the
Incarnation: we must allow the divine image to have repercussions
in our own image.

There are at least three moments of "shock" or "ontological
instability" that cause a crisis for our body-images--and here we
may also apply our analysis to the discussion of disappointment in
images of the Incarnation. William Lynch has suggested two image
constellations that have promoted this creative havoc. The first
he calls "Prometheanism-in-reverse," a kind of puritanism. It

is an image of contempt for the breathtaking self-assertions of
technological man; it holds our progress as folly. It wants to
halt advancement and return to some primeval image.[7] We may detect
this naive primitivism in the "White Flight" to suburbia in the
fifties and sixties. We lost heart midstream and fled our polluted cities.[8]

The second type of image "shock" is described by Lynch as
"Pirandellism." It is the ritualistic drama of demasking and de-
nuding everything. Lynch writes, "Everybody wishes to get below
the surface."[9] The most recent variations of this theme are demyth-
ologizing political heroes, psychoanalyzing our conversation, and,
as Edward Albee expressed it in *Who's Afraid of Virginia Woolf?*,
"peeling the label." Especially when a culture fictionalizes
images, it is likely that the same culture will suspect every
image.

A third instance of "shock" to the body-image, I submit, is
akin to the image crisis that the First Letter of James writes
about: "A man who listens to God's word but does not put it into
practice is like a man who looks into a mirror at the face he was
born with; he looks at himself, then goes off and promptly forgets
what he looked like" (Jas. 1: 23-24). It is an epistemological
problem, at least. It is frequently also a memory problem. Our
memories are not Xerox duplicators, nor are our images static. So,
it is impossible to freeze how we once looked in a mirror. Rather
we are many "posturings" before a mirror: it is how we *willed* to
stand before that mirror of our imaginations that is important.
It is all important how we exposed ourselves to ourselves--how we
caught ourselves looking into the mirror to question all that was
synopsized of our immediate past.[10] Since we cannot reify that
self-image, we are in crisis: we seem to lose touch with ourselves.
Let us call this kind of image crisis that of "split images."

The man who walked away from the mirror and forgot the image
of the face he was born with is a metaphor for the disillusionment
we experience with the Incarnation. The problem involves three
issues. First, the split image that originates in the encounter
of Creator and creature. Was I ever really in touch with God?
Did I ever have the freedom not to be in touch with God? Was I not
born with His face? Is my image, therefore, distinct from God?
Secondly, if I once saw myself--however momentarily--in touch with
his word, how am I now related to that former being-in-touch? If,
on the other hand, I did integrate God's Word, who is this new
amalgam? This is a question of self-identification: does

congruency with Christ obliterate my person? Thirdly, the very
process of recognizing myself in the mirror requires the imaging
capacity of other creatures. I cannot know myself without my
fellows' images. How does my self-knowledge through others distinguish me from those others? Each of these split-image tensions
requires analysis in turn.

    Creating Image / Created Image: Genesis, in its first ac-
count of creation, affirms the Creator's relationship to his
creature in this way: "God created man in his image; in the divine image he created; male and female he created them" (Gen. 1:
27). *The Jerome Biblical Commentary* remarks: "The Semites knew
of no dichotomy in man in *our* terms; the whole man, as a complete
personality, had God's image."[11] There is a terrible intimacy between creator and creature. The relationship is never so easy as
in Hart's description of human creativity: "But for [artists] the
act of delivery is also the act of clean discovery; the after
birth is quickly sloughed; and the work of art lives its own flesh,
gurgles its own joys and weeps its own sorrow."[12] Even though an
artist can become dispassionate about some of his works, there is
no way he can deny responsibility for them. If it is difficult
for the artist to make little of his progeny, how much more so the
parent! How hard it is to separate from one's children. What then
must be the trauma for one who creates images in his own divine
likeness and allows them autonomy! Reciprocally, how difficult it
is to be allowed "on one's own." How desperate is our prayer if,
like Cal in Steinbeck's *East of Eden,* we make loving gestures to
an impassive and withdrawn father. When, on the other hand, we
tire of our tedious prayer and conclude that our interlocutor is
dead, "living without God" becomes a scary freedom. Such is the
freedom of modern man haunted by his radical search for non-condi-
tionality.[13] We are desperate to know that we are legitimate
heirs of this universe. We wish to know our ancestry; we fear to
acknowledge this paternity and so compromise our unconditionality
as person and responsible agent for this world. Even in setting
out to achieve this world mastery, we have intimations of our
failure and resort to petitionary prayer, such as "God, make this
thing work out!" Despite the salutary quality of such appeal, we
must not deceive ourselves into thinking that God will intervene
and usurp our creative freedom--even momentarily. We are still
free in failure.

    Whitehead, I think, proposes an excellent way of understanding
human freedom vis-a-vis God's intentionality. He understands God's

creative urge through the category of "primordial nature." For
Whitehead, it is God's sifting of possibilities into this world.
Secondly, it is marked by "the lure for feeling, the eternal urge
of desire."[14] In this understanding, God lures the world on, but
he does not manipulate its freedom. Whitehead sees another pole
to God's personality; it is his "consequent nature," the "weaving
of God's physical feelings upon his primordial concepts."[15]
Whitehead's own resume in *Process and Reality* best articulates
this receptive nature of a God who encounters his creation:

> The revolts of destructive evil . . . are dismissed
> into their triviality of merely individual facts;
> and yet the good they did achieve . . . in the intro-
> duction of needed contrast, is yet saved by its re-
> lation to the completed whole. The image--and it is
> but an image--the image under which this operative
> growth of God's nature is best conceived, is that of
> a tender care that nothing be lost.[16]

The Old Man / New Man: There is much ambiguity in the Pauline
letters with regard to the nature of our resurrection in Christ.
It seems to be a "now you see it, now you don't" game of identity.
Even though we know we have been newly incorporated, the transition
is slow. Paul exhorts us to "act as though" it has all been accomplished: "This we know; our old self was crucified with him
so that the sinful body *might be destroyed* and we *might* be slaves
to sin no longer. In the same way, you *must consider* yourselves
dead to sin but alive for God in Christ Jesus. Do not, therefore,
let sin rule your mortal body and make you obey its lusts" (Rom. 6:
6, 11, 12, my emphases). It is difficult to regard our identity
as partial, even tentative. In Hart's language, the image of
ourselves in baptism and adult confirmation is one of "dominant
intention." The principal option has been taken, yet every inter-
mediate act is not necessarily well integrated. Thus our day by
day choices *attempt* to extirpate ego-centrism in behalf of a future
and thorough self-transformation. Still, we are rightfully incred-
ulous. We make a donation of ourselves in love, yet find ourselves
still in possession of that very self.

There are two dangerous tendencies in western culture that
attempt precipitously to hasten the integration of the identity.
The first is a kind of false mysticism. It yearns for ecstatic
union with the New Man in Christ by sublimating everything else.
Full realization of the new man is not achieved by releasing oneself of this body. We cannot negotiate our body-images for
mystical union. Neo-Platonism partakes of this illusion. Taking

its cue from Plato, that the soul, "after its fall, has been captured," Neo-Platonism expounds something dangerously close to a
split identity: "[The soul] is said to be in a tomb, and in a
cave, yet, by turning again towards ideas, it frees itself from
its bonds."[17] We must be scrupulously alert to all sinister attempts to inhibit the coalescence of body and soul by choosing a
pseudo-spirituality that abhors the body. For there is no way the
spirit can speak except through the body.

A second set of forces impedes the integration of self. It
is a fear not unlike that of the Sanhedrin which resented the
implication of Jesus that he, a human, was also divine. It is the
pervasive suspicion of iconoclasm; it is forever discriminating:
"We are extensions of Christ's incarnation, but we are not Christ."
"We are in Christ, but only metaphorically." "Christ empathized
with our humanity, but he never became our humanity." All these
cautious discriminations leave Christ on the other side of the im-
passable chasm that divides our person. He is always divine, we
are relentlessly human. In fact, such a spirit construes created
autonomy a defiance of God, not a gift. It resents collaboration
with Christ as a cheap concession to conditionality. Lynch
characterizes this image of man as that of a "creature who must
live and die unbowed and unsubmissive to the world."[18] The marvel
of this form of self-image is that it supposes that it can profess
the Incarnation of Christ and yet exclude his palpable ingredience
in the affairs of man. Thus, in the long run, this attitude rejects the very image of man which could put man together. That is
surely self-spite.

Self-Image / Fraternal Images: The dependence of self-images
on fraternal images is the source of the third tension that is consequent to the Incarnation. In the First Letter of John we read:

> We, for our part, love because he first loved us.
> If anyone says, "My love is fixed on God," yet
> hates his brother, he is a liar. One who has no
> love for the brother he has seen cannot love the
> God he has not seen. The commandment we have from
> him is this: Whoever loves God must also love
> his brother (1 John 4: 19-21).

Just as our motivation to love is dependent on God, so the actualization of our loving is dependent on the existence of someone to
love. Here is the ambiguity of the Incarnation at its greatest:
how to begin to move towards that which is anonymous, amorphous,
even perhaps antagonistic. And should we find the object of love,
then we begin to fear the possibility of dissolution of self in

the act of loving. Images can only be brought to light by one
another; images fear being distorted by that very self-evolution.
    Mutuality is the hallmark of a creature in an environment.
To be human is to entail the rest of creation: we feed on one
another. "All societies," Whitehead writes, "require interplay
with their environment; and in the case of living societies the
interplay takes the form of robbery."[19] Thus we must be acutely
moral in our bilateral relations with the world. Image-making is
a two-edged sword. No matter when or how I gesticulate, my self-
image is projected onto the universe. Even the solipsist is an
audience to himself. The very gesture I make, besides limiting
the number of gestures I will make, configures by attraction, and
contrasts with the images that others will make. My image shapes
other images which, in turn, will rebound to me. To clarify the
interpenetration of images, I cite Maurice Merleau-Ponty. His is
an epistemology of objects. To suggest an epistemology of image,
I have presumed to substitute the word *image* every time he uses
object.

> To look at an [image] is to inhabit it, and from
> this habitation to grasp all things in terms of the
> aspect which they present to it. But in so far as I
> see those things too, they remain abodes open to my
> gaze, and, being potentially lodged in them, I al-
> ready perceived from various angles the central [image]
> of my present vision. Thus every [image] is the mir-
> ror of all others when I look at the lamp on my
> table. I attribute to it not only the qualities
> visible from where I am, but also those which the
> chimney, the walls, the table can "see"; the back
> of my lamp is nothing but the face which it "shows"
> to the chimney. I can see therefore an [image] in
> so far as [images] form a system or a world, and
> in so far as each one treats the [images] around it
> as spectators of its hidden aspects which guarantee
> the permanence of those aspects by their presence.[20]

    The mutuality of image-making, then, actually becomes multi-
valent. And each pulse of my own image in this world catalyzes,
feeds, and defines other images which in turn are variously deployed.
At the same time, an unexpected moral factor comes into play; my
very imagining could endanger other images. Lynch is fully cognizant
of this dilemma when he writes: "I would hope that this secular
man could come near to saying, 'Your image is not mine; but it
leaves mine intact and has not destroyed me. I can live and breathe
and work with it.'"[21] Only through my fellows' images can I come
to know myself--and as other than them. Thus, great humility is
required of this mutuality if I am to come to heal the tension of
the split-image.

No matter how obvious the impact of the images of the Incarnation ought to be, that impact does not always register for reasons just enumerated. Usually we would simply prefer to pigeonhole images just as we do ideas so as to conserve energy. A contemporary analogue is the viewer at a modern art gallery. The casual visitor relegates the image to "smeary streaks and scratches." He wants the painting to tell a story he knows. He wants a "visual cocktail." All of our images will rush by in this manner if we are so cavalier; we will thus miss many of the signs of the Incarnation. To provide a paradigm for investing more energy in living with an image, I have proposed that we consider three characteristic marks of images. That images are self-discursive, ecstatic, and dialogic needs now further amplification.

Images are Self-Discursive. The most obvious, and most over-looked, fact of images is that they are intensive expressions of the person who made them. So, when God creates his own image, it is Christ, a man. That tells us a great deal about God. Christ is obviously not an image God hunted around for. Images are simultaneous to the imaginer. For example, when I am elated, I do not pause to consider which image might best capture my elation. Ray Hart writes: "We do not first get hold of a subject, then shop around for just the right language in which to package it. Language and apprehension (at least that apprehension susceptible of articulation) arise together in the mind's act."[22] So, the Father's self-expression is immediate from all eternity. Rahner describes the self-expressive quality of the Father's image, Christ:

> The Word is 'generated' by the Father as the image
> and expression of the Father. The process is neces-
> sarily given with the divine act of self-knowledge,
> and without it the absolute act of divine self-
> possession in knowledge cannot exist. The Father
> is himself by the very fact that he opposes to him-
> self the image which is of the same essence as him-
> self, as the person who is other than himself; and
> so he possesses himself. But this means that the
> Logos is the 'symbol' of the Father: the inward
> symbol which remains distinct from what is symbol-
> ized, which is constituted by what is itself.[23]

We might also note with Rahner, inasmuch as we often suspect images as mere contrivances, that Christ is the same image to us that he is to his Father:

> The humanity of Christ is not to be considered as
> something in which God dresses up and masquerades--
> a mere signal of which he makes us, so that some-
> thing audible can be uttered about the Logos by
> means of this signal. When God, expressing himself,

exteriorizes himself, that very thing appears
which we call the humanity of the Logos.[24]

Consequently, if God is imaged as Christ, who is man, something
wonderful is happening to our humanity. Our image is of the
greatest value because it is also the Father's self-image. Our
fear of being jettisoned from God at the moment of creation is a
fiction then. His identity is ours. We are not making vain protestations of love. They are his protestations also, crying "Abba,
Father!" within us. Neither are our temporal images lost in the
flux of the world: "The consequent nature of God is the fulfillment of his experience by his reception of the multiple freedom of
actuality (our actuality) into the harmony of his own actualization. It is God as really actual, completing the deficiency of his
mere conceptual actuality."[25]

   Finally, we need make no apology to the iconoclast who decries
our anthropomorphisms:

> If God himself is man and remains so for ever, if
> all theology is therefore eternally an anthropology;
> if man is forbidden to belittle himself, because to
> do so would be to belittle God; and if this God
> remains the insoluble mystery, man is for ever the
> articulate mystery of God. We do not think that
> we could see what is behind man except by seeing
> through him into the blessed darkness of God himself
> and then really understanding that this finite being
> is the finitude of the infinite Word of God himself.
> Christology is the end and beginning of anthro-
> pology.[26]

If Christ, the Father's self-image, reveals something about himself,
so too must we, whose anthropology is actually a Christology, be
revealing contemporary palpable images of the Incarnation. Thus
we are working out God's image in time. And if in time, then, the
image also changes. Mircea Eliade writes: "Every new valorization
has always been conditioned by the actual structure of the image,
so much so that we can say of an image that it is awaiting the fulfillment of its meaning."[27] And if an image's ramifications flower
as it moves through time, is it not appropriate to say that an image
in the future has leapt beyond its original import? This we call
its *ecstatic* quality.

   Images are Ecstatic. One of the distinctive modalities of the
image of Christ is that it is always transfigured. In fact, subsequent to the Resurrection we need to speak of his image as not
only transfigured but also transfiguring. The nearness of this
transfigured person allows dumb men to speak, the blind to see, and
the poor to rejoice. Our own image is transfigured, moved beyond

the selfish and temporal bounds that once contained us. History
itself is changed:

> Judaeo-Christianity presents us with the supreme
> hierophany: *the transfiguration of the historical
> event into hierophany*. God not only intervenes in
> history, as in the case of Judaism: he is incar-
> nated in a historic being. What his incarnation
> presents is like an audacious effort to save the
> historical event itself, by endowing it with the
> maximum of being.[28]

What accounts for the transfiguration of the image that the
letter to the Philippians speaks about? "Though he was in the form
of God, he did not deem equality with God something to be grasped
at. Rather, he emptied himself and took the form of a slave, being born in the likeness of men" (Phil. 2: 6-7). Paul imagines
the transfiguration as an emptying experience. The ecstasy of God's
image is usually accounted for as pure love. Whatever the analysis,
that ecstasy beckons us to reciprocate that burst of energy.
Rahner writes:

> God takes on a human nature as his own. The inde-
> finable nature, whose limits--'definition'--are the
> unlimited reference to the infinite fulness of the
> mystery, has, when assumed by God as *his* reality,
> simply arrived at the point to which it always
> strives by virtue of its essence. It is its *meaning*
> to be that which is delivered up and abandoned.
> This is done in the strictest sense and reaches
> an unsurpassable pitch of achievement, when the
> nature which surrenders itself to the mystery of the
> fulness belongs so little to itself that it becomes
> the nature of God himself.[29]

Thus, our own nature is invited to burst out of its own skin and
become the nature of God. We are invited at the precise point at
which we feel most frail, the image of our own humanity (the
"ontological instability" of Ray Hart), and lured on to "be finished."[30]

The solution to the problematic of my identity vis-a-vis
Christ's is resolved in a startling way--by way of an ecstasy. Our
personal history of images so interpenetrates his that we share
the same time frame, the same spaces, the same words. And he, for
his part, goes to the extent of even imagining with our images,
"according to all the things that have parallelism and resonance
for the body and the spirit of man: its density to touch, its
light and colors."[31] The ecstatic word of God does not return emp-
ty-handed. It returns as the Son of Man who draws all things
up to heaven in himself.

In the same fashion our image-making is ecstatic. Our images
reach deeper than our own experience and make contact with the
archetypal images, the timeless questions and answers that form
the backdrop of every novel image.[32] Our images even exceed the
archetypal images, providing a "new valorization of an archetypal
image which crowns and consummates the earlier ones."[33] Our
images in their making catalyze words, gestures, shapes, physical
materials to leap far beyond every connotation, every limit they
had ever known before. Finally, we ourselves, the instigators of
these images, are superseded, surpassed by our own created images.
Our "superject," as Whitehead would name it, projects our very
being beyond our original image limits; we are transfigured.[34]
Here we are, more than we ever could have imagined!

    Images are Dialogic. The problem with being an accretion of
images--which we are!--is that by isolating the various component
images, we risk damaging the cohesiveness of the resultant images.
Paul writes well of this:

> If the body were all eye, what would happen to the
> hearing? If it were all ear, what would happen to
> our smelling? As it is, God has set each member of
> the body in the place he wanted it to be. If all
> the members were alike, where would the body be?
> There are, indeed, many different members, but one
> body (1 Cor. 12: 17-20).

Our images must be mirrored back, imaged back in order for them
to perdure, in the manner of Parker's Byzantine Christ in Flannery
O'Connor's story "Parker's Back." First we have to be loved: we
have to be known before we can know and love ourselves. The very
rubbing together of the myriad images of the Incarnation is of the
very essence of the Incarnation. Without such interaction an image
dies. In a sense, this third dimension of image, its dialogic
nature, is a re-capitulation of "the image as self-discursive" and
"the image as ecstatic." Because if there is dialogue, an image is
invited out of itself (ecstasy) and shows itself to be what it is
(self-discursive). Once an image engages other images it shares in
the histories and futures of other images, in the concatenation
with archetypal and prophetic images, in the mutations that dialogue
always precipitates. For example, the image of a church is consequent to its dependency on the archetypal expectations of its con-
gregation: it reveals itself in the acting out of its liturgy, in
its services to the poor, the blind, the stranger. It exceeds
itself in those rare ecstatic moments when it is one people, united,
empathizing with all people. In this dialogic process it is

significant that an image prospers not only through what it har-
moniously amalgamates but also by what it eschews [Whitehead's
"negative prehensions"]. Thus, the image of a church also suffers
or is enhanced by what it is not, by what it has not admitted into
itself.

It is probably due to this modality of images, the dialogic,
that images most frequently put us in a growing place, that moment
of "ontological instability," because most often images of the Incarnation startle us by their apparent buoyancy in the midst of
disaster; or they shame us because the tax-collectors and prosti-
tutes are entering heaven ahead of us. Or, ultimately, we are
shocked to find that God looks like nothing more than our very own
humanity. We are forced by this startle, shame, and shock to
imagine how radioactive pollution and fresh yellow jonquils, bartered peace and self-emptying love, an unlimited life possibility
and sudden death fit together to reveal that God is in this
world.

Images, because they are the co-incidence of all three levels
of experience--of self, of God, and of other--compel us to manifest
ourselves, to leap beyond our own perimeters to speak to others.
To ask the question "What are you?" about any one layer of an image
is to provoke reverberations among the other two. For this reason, he who does not love the Incarnation he can see cannot love
the God whom he cannot see; nor can he ever love himself. Thus,
the art of God's hand is only whole when "the collaborating, co-
operating, answering imagination of its perceiver is thrown into
act."[35]

The assumption at the basis of the preceding exposition is
this: until man appreciates the collusion of images that comprise
his own image, he will never be able to appreciate any image of
the Incarnation. That is why it is essential to grapple with the
apparent internal dichotomies we experience with ourselves, with
God, with our neighbor. Until we realize that we can and should
be of one fabric with the world, the images of the world and
Christ will always seem antagonistic or simply foreign. In that
case, our image would always be "over-against" every other image.

But we cannot allow that because our images of self are micro-
cosms of the world. And the images of the world are macrocosms of
us. Are our private chambers cluttered with selfish thoughts and
debris? So are New York's gutters. Is there anonymity in a
suburban shopping center? So is there coolness in rote greetings
to our neighbors. Can we really find rest in our mountain resorts

as long as our cities are restless? There is no circuitous route
back to a wholly integrated image of self through some fantasy
condominium complex. There is no innocence in escapist America
because our escapes will be taxed to underwrite the renovations of
our deteriorating urban centers. Every image finally evokes every
other image--and those latter are frequently the images we tried
to forget.

To read an image accurately is to read it within the "rules
of the game" each image has in mind. We may neither under-read nor
over-read an image if we are to glean its subtle nuances. As in
a good work of art, there can be no component that is not accounted
for without the work breaking into pieces. Every aspect of an
image is integral to its understanding. If you under-read a work
of art such as Faulkner's *Absalom, Absalom!* or Picasso's "Guernica,"
you will find yourself wondering why the "imaginer" invested so
much energy in such an inchoate scramble of images and ideas. And
if you over-read the face of some current fad, such as disco or
pornographic shock, you will have to infer heroic motives to account for the grossness of gesture. But if you listen to the register in which an image is set--e.g., a Jazz composition--it will
tell you its thematic device, its rhythms, the ground rules of its
improvisation. It will disclose itself to you, stir your feelings,
and cause you to respond with your very own images of joy or
sadness.

As we have seen, the emergence of an image, whether conscious
or unconscious, makes ripples on the face of this universe. What
is more, because of the threefold valence of images, they interlace
the primordial regions of our Incarnational experience: self,
Christ, and world. To touch one level of imagery is to open insight
on all three. So, water, great heights, an old man on a bench,
gnarled fingers, lithe steps, a dead policeman, a new bud--every-
thing can open us to an understanding of the Incarnation. These
images reveal themselves, exceed themselves, speak to one another
of birth, of life, of death. Inevitably they spring out of the
imagination of the Incarnation. For, as we have seen, Christ did
not merely identify with us as person, but through the creation
of the world every scent, color, device, sound, everything, even
God, was accommodated to the imagination of man. But not merely
accommodated, rather Christ became an ingredient "in the collective
unconsciousness that it may be saved and fulfilled. The Christ
descended into hell. How, then, can this salvation reach into our
unconsciousness without speaking its language and making use of

its categories?"[36] Belief in the image of Christ provides apertures
through which we understand still more images: how washing,
feeding, healing can mean the tenderness of a God. With these images we can return to our stifled cities to do what our univalent
understanding of these gestures was insufficient to actualize.
At the very same time we will not spurn the technological project
as contemporary towers of Babel, but as man trying to be regenerated
by the witty, buoyant, clever, decorated images of his life.

So the task of believing that God made the world good is the
task of re-imagining our community image, of retrieving our city's
image, of rebuilding our psychic image: of refacing the earth
with our images. If we do not imagine what the world can look like,
the more violent will surely make images that will try to obliterate
the face of Christ. If the Incarnation were instantaneous and
complete, there would be no more imagining: all the images would
be perfect. Since this is not so, we must daily attend to the
gestures others make, for these new images catalyze the power to
constellate still greater images of this world. In the assimila-
tion and absorption of these tentative images, we experience our
little deaths, though "in daily death, Christ's life becomes manifest in our bodies" (2 Cor. 4: 10).

NOTES

[1]Mircea Eliade, *Images and Symbols*, trans. Philip Mairet
(London: Harvill Press, 1961), p. 82.

[2]Jean Piaget, *The Construction of Reality in the Child*, trans.
Margaret Cook (New York: Basic Books, Inc., 1954), pp. 97-218.

[3]*Ibid.*, pp. 115-116.

[4]Ray L. Hart, *Unfinished Man and the Imagination* (New York:
Herder and Herder, 1968), pp. 109-311, passim.

[5]*Ibid.*, pp. 48-49, 252, 282.

[6]*Ibid.*, p. 216.

[7]William F. Lynch, S. J., *Christ and Prometheus* (Notre Dame:
University of Notre Dame Press, 1970), pp. 19-20.

[8]Wolf Von Eckardt, "Cities, The Age of Recovery," in *Mainliner
Magazine*, Vol. 23, No. 2 (Los Angeles: East/West Network, Inc.,
March, 1979), pp. 93-95.

[9]Lynch, pp. 21, 48.

[10]Hart, pp. 194-196.

[11]Eugene H. Maly, *Genesis*, Vol. I of *The Jerome Bible Commentary*, ed. Raymond E. Brown, S.S., Joseph A. Fitzmeyer, S.J., Roland E. Murphy, O. Carm., 2 vols. (Englewood Cliffs: Prentice-Hall, Inc., 1968), p. 11.

[12]Hart, p. 12.

[13]Lynch, p. 39-53.

[14]Alfred North Whitehead, *Process and Reality* (Toronto: Collier-Macmillan, 1929), p. 406.

[15]*Ibid.*, p. 407.

[16]*Ibid.*, p. 408-409.

[17]Plato, *The Republic*, VII, 514ff., quoted in Eliade, p. 117.

[18]Lynch, p. 18.

[19]Whitehead, pp. 124-125.

[20]Maurice Merleau-Ponty, *Phenomenology of Perception*, trans. Colin Smith (New York: Routledge & Kegan Paul, 1962) p. 68.

[21]Lynch, p. 9.

[22]Hart, p. 27.

[23]Karl Rahner, "On a Theology of the Symbol," in *More Recent Writings*, Vol. IV of *Theological Investigations*, trans. Kevin Smyth (Baltimore: Helicon Press, 1966), p. 236.

[24]*Ibid.*, p. 239.

[25]Whitehead, p. 411.

[26]Rahner, "Theology of the Incarnation," in *More Recent Writings*, p. 116.

[27]Eliade, p. 159.

[28]*Ibid.*, p. 169.

[29]Rahner, "Theology of the Incarnation," p. 109.

[30]Hart, pp. 122-123, 171-176.

[31]Lynch, p. 71.

[32]Hart, pp. 297-299; Lynch, pp. 89-90.

[33]Eliade, pp. 163-164.

[34]Whitehead, pp. 58-59, 259-260.

[35]Hart, p. 259.

[36]Fr. Beirnaert, "La Dimension Mythique dans le Sacramentalisme Chrétien," in *Eranos Jahrbuch*, 1949, Vol. XVII (Zurich, 1950), pp. 255-286, quoted in Eliade, p. 161.

PART FOUR

Religious Pilgrimage

and

Cultural Horizons

QUEST FOR SELF/QUEST FOR GOD

Mary Jo Weaver

In these days of eager self-discovery and confessional autobiography, it is not unusual for people to share their individual
"stories" with one another. I have noticed, however, that some
people cannot contain themselves in simple narrative, but require
more mythic forms and prefer to think of their lives as odysseys
or sagas. What interests me specifically is the tendency to describe one's personal story as myth, as *pilgrimage*, a term which
is traditionally and properly religious. A pilgrimage is a journey
to a holy place undertaken for motives of devotion and for purposes
related to a divine/human interaction of some kind (thanksgiving,
supplication, reparation); yet people use the word pilgrimage to
describe a personal journey that has nothing to do with religion.
The propensity of people to define their own lives as pilgrimage
is partly explained by a desire to endow self-discovery with the
status of divine revelation; as such it is a brand of narcissism.
A more intriguing reason for the confusion, however, is the similarity of experience between the quest for self and the quest for
God, between self-understanding and pilgrimage.

Contemporary literature has, in some sense, secularized
religious terms and processes and has seemed, as a result, to have
effectively separated the quest for self from the quest for God.
Whether the two can, in fact, be separated is an interesting theological question[1]: Karl Rahner suggests that there is a fundamental, dialectical unity between the experience of God and the experience of the self, that one could draw up a table of correspondences between the history of one's self-experience and one's God-
experience.[2] Such a table of correspondences has emerged for me
as I worked through an understanding of pilgrimage from a religion
and literature perspective.

There are at least four points where I think the experience
of the self seeker and the God seeker are similar if not identical:
the loss of identity, dark nights, urgency, and a community of
intimacy. Before I exploit these areas, I must say a word about
my method of exploitation and make a case for a paradigmatic text
which suits both my method (religion and literature) and my problem
(pilgrimage). I will use *The Divine Comedy* as a central (religious

177

and literary) text on pilgrimage, draw out the points of correspondence, and then relate those points of correspondence to similar
ones in contemporary literature.

What shapes the journey we call pilgrimage? Surely part of
the answer lies in beliefs--what a person believes about the self
and/or about God is essential to whether and how the journey will
be conceptualized and pursued. That begs the question, however,
for what we really want to know is how beliefs are understood and
felt by people, how they function to motivate one's decisions.
One way a person can understand and in some way "experience" a belief is to read a story about it, to have the imagination awakened
and sustained by a particular perception of reality. Literature as
the embodiment of perceptions about the world has the power to
shape people's understanding. A person who fancies himself or herself a pilgrim needs to be supported by beliefs and a community,
but also by *stories* about saints and pilgrims. Whether those stories are about spectacular people or more ordinary folk, they are
helpful because they provide clear images of the results of a pilgrimage and what one may expect along the way. In that way, stories
provide stimulation and support for the imagination.

Stories that sustain a pilgrim need not be religious ones.
Since art mirrors life, we can learn something from the artistic
conception that may not be as sharply focused or as nuanced in
overtly religious literature. It is appropriate to look to "secular" literature for religious understanding precisely because "religion" is not an encapsulated matter. At the same time, because
pilgrimage is a religious term, one needs a normative text which
is both literary and religious and which is bound up intimately with
pilgrimage.

Dante's *Comedy* is not only the great pilgrimage text of religious literature, it is a major literary work which has been ex-
ploited and understood outside of any religious dimension. It is
not only a superlative text for a literary and religious understanding of pilgrimage, it combines a quest for self with a quest
for God so as to point to the similarities and differences.

The *Comedy* is first of all a *story*.[3] An old Hasidic tale has
this punch line: "God made people because he loves stories." If
the Bible is a good indicator, it must be true. Stories get our
attention and sometimes have an uncanny power to draw us into and
beyond themselves. Chesterton said that the most profound theological lessons of his life were given to him in the nursery by way
of fairy tales,[4] and C. S. Lewis argues that stories draw us into

another world where we are fortified and nourished for the tiresome
ordinariness of life.[5] Other authors suggest that there are stories
a plenty in this "ordinary world," but that it is difficult for us
to pay attention to the profound implications of what goes on around
us all the time. There is a tendency sometimes to think that the
power of everyday concerns to distract or overwhelm us is a modern
one, that in the "good old (medieval) days" life was simpler and
anxious introspection unnecessary. The enduring attractiveness of
The Divine Comedy lies in its power as a *story* and in its perceptive
descriptions of human feelings of loss, cowardice, despair, exhilaration, progress, and regression. There is a two-steps-forward-
one-step-back kind of progress in the *Comedy* that draws one to its
author, and there is such a range of failure and triumph in the
individual stories that most of us can find ourselves somewhere.

If pilgrimage is a religious quest, then it must have some
relation to God. On this level, it is clear and unarguable that
Dante's work is an important piece of pilgrimage literature--it is
the soul's search for God stretched cosmically over heaven and
hell. What may not be so obvious is that Dante's story is also
very much bound up with the quest for *self*--it is not just about
the soul and not just about God. A pilgrimage may be a "journey
to a holy place" (in the *Comedy*, a journey to heaven itself), but
how does one begin a journey until one knows where one is starting
from? Part of the understanding of the starting point lies in a
clear understanding of the self--we need to know who we are before
we can know where we are going.

It is not unusual to find great religious writers interested
in themselves as well as in God. Augustine, for example, is remembered for knowing the *end* point of the pilgrim: "Our hearts
are restless until they rest in Thee." What is sometimes forgotten
is that he clearly knew the *beginning* of the quest as well: "Let
me know myself that I may know thee, O Lord."[6] People are attracted
to Theresa of Avila because she clearly knew who she was, a feat
that appears more compelling these days than mystical awareness of
the deity. Dante, in the *Comedy*, is no exception to the need to
know the self before one knows God--the quest for self may or may
not lead to pilgrimage (quest for God), but no pilgrimage can occur
without it.

In contemporary literature the quest for self has taken on
such dimensions that it sometimes eclipses the quest for God. The
medieval mystics were united in believing the journey to the boundless depths of God to be unceasing. It appears to be true that

the exploration of the self is also endless, that people find themselves infinitely fascinating, that the private islands of one's
own soul form an endless chain of new places. Who are we, after
all? In *Ulysses*, James Joyce says, "Every life is many days,
day after day. We walk through ourselves meeting robbers, ghosts,
giants, old men, young men, wives, widows, brothers in love. But
always meeting ourselves."[7] Our fascination lies not only in self-
discovery, but in the ability to change our minds about ourselves,
to re-interpret our experience of ourselves. Rahner says that our
freedom lies in that ability, as well as in our ability to change
our minds about our experience of God; his main point, of course,
is that these things are so intertwined by nature that they form
a unity.[8] Dante perceives this unity, albeit not in such overtly
theological terms.

The most beautiful and least read book of the *Comedy* is
Purgatory. Here Dante does what many of us want to do--he comes to
terms with the self as it is and, where possible, moves beyond its
foibles. Before he could choose the penitential and adventurous
journey through Purgatory and into Heaven, however, he had first
to come to terms with his worst possibilities--the journey to Hell
was a necessary first step in his self-understanding. When Dante
finally arrived in highest heaven, he fancied he understood God.
More than that, however, he understood *himself* in relation to God
and interpreted his whole journey in relation to God's light:

> That light doth so transform a man's whole bent
> That never to another sight or thought
> Would he surrender, with his own consent
>
> For everything the will has ever sought
> Is gathered there, and there is every quest
> Made perfect, which apart from it falls short.[9]

The confluence of quests in the *Comedy* makes it an appropriate text
for an exploration of the quest for self and the quest for God.
An archaic translation of *Matthew* 9:39 reads, "He who seeks only
himself, brings himself to ruin." One of the central paradoxes in
Christianity is how one finds the self by losing it. In the *Comedy*,
Dante seeks for more than himself, but never at the expense of himself; the quest for God requires a vigorous and parallel quest for
self.

The four points at which I think the quest for self and quest
for God are similar in experience have been suggested to me partly
by Dante and partly by reading some historical literature of pilgrimage. On the whole, however, I think they come from a random

reading of novels and a preoccupation with what is called "the
spiritual life." Those people who doggedly search for God in their
lives appear to me to have certain common experiences: they often
begin a spiritual journey in the throes of a great personal crisis
or in some experience of loss or frustration; with the possible
exception of Julian of Norwich, they experience a "dark night," a
period of abandonment or the feeling of being stranded in a dark
valley somewhere, with the power only to wait and the need to
participate in the darkness; there is a sense of urgency, that the
journey to God cannot wait once one is ready for the venture; and,
finally, those who seek after God have a profound sense of community,
a need to participate prayerfully with others either here (on earth)
or beyond (the communion of saints in heaven). Spiritual experience
has other aspects, but these are the ones I find relentlessly present in what used to be called "spiritual reading" or the lives of
the saints.

What interests me is that these same experiences occur in
novels. Modern literature, concerned with the quest for self and
the ability to perceive the enormous implications of the world
around us, is full of descriptions of characters that are similar
to the ones found in the lives of the saints at least in terms of
some of their *experiences*. The experience of not knowing who one
is or where one is going, as embodied in a wide range of modern
novels, is a common one. Moments of personal crisis may set modern
protagonists on a quest for self or a search for a home as surely
as they inspired medieval mystics to search for God. The search
appears to be endless, with moments of profound angst, a sharing
of the experience of the dark night. Many novels embody a sense
of urgency, of finding out *now*, of beginning *today* to solve the
mystery of the self. Finally, in the personal journey, one finds
the need for community, companionship, some sense of being with
others.

In order to relate the quest for self to the quest for God
and to measure both against the *Comedy*, I will describe each of
these kinds of experience as it relates to the search for God and
the search for self in Dante's work. In order to draw the whole
conception more directly into other literature, I shall then make
some suggestive parallels between what can be found in the *Comedy*
and how that might be illuminated by stories from other quarters.

I. The Loss of Identity as a Starting Point

The *Comedy* begins with a frightening scene of Dante "lost in
a dark woods." He is trapped by hardness of heart that has crept
in on him as imperceptibly and as surely as middle age. The scene
itself contains several of the themes: he is lost, does not know
who he is, has a great sense of despair (darkness) and an accompanying sense of urgency, made unbearable by the hopelessness of
the situation. It is instructive to think for a moment about the
real Dante as opposed to the Dante in the poem. We know that he
wrote the poem at the nadir of his personal life, that his inspiration came to him at a time when he had lost his youth, possessions,
household peace, and citizenship. Dorothy Sayers says,

> He was stripped bare. He looked outwards upon
> the corruption of the Church and Empire, and
> he looked inwards into the corruption of the
> human heart; and what he saw was the vision of
> Hell. And, having seen it, he set himself down
> to write the great comedy of Redemption, and of
> the return of all things by the way of self
> knowledge and purification to the beatitude
> and presence of God.[10]

From the poem we know that Dante had lost his sense of spiritual
direction, that he had turned his back on grace (Beatrice) and
looked for all the wrong things in all the wrong places. Accordingly, at the beginning of his journey, he was *lost*, he knew neither
who he was nor what he might become, he forgot (if he ever knew)
how he came into the forest and had no idea about how to get out.
His thoughts had nothing to do with God at all; his experience was
simply one of being lost and trapped--the way out of the woods was
up a mountain, but that mountain was blocked by a lion, a leopard,
and a lean and hungry wolf, representing the sins of youth, man-
hood, and old age.

The loss of identity is often experienced as paralysis and
sometimes as confusion--the person either cannot move or cannot
fathom where s/he might move. In the *Comedy* Dante is rescued by
his hero, the poet Virgil. It is interesting that it is *not*
Beatrice (or God) who comes to lead Dante out of the darkness, but
the pagan poet. Under the circumstances it is possible to conjec-
ture that Virgil is the only person Dante could have seen at the
time, that the spiritual blindness or hardness of heart represented
by the forest prevented him from seeing anything much beyond himself. Virgil is a double, a self-reflection of Dante's epic ambi-
tion. As a poet, Virgil gives Dante a sounding board for himself,

reminds Dante of Dante's own poetic context and identity. Dante
can begin his journey when his memory is stimulated and his imagination engaged.

As one looks through spiritual literature there are many people
who sought an enlightened self-understanding and, later, a search
for God, from a point of confusion or loss of identity. Few of the
saints and (with the exception of the enthusiastic Isaiah) none
of the prophets followed a self-chosen path--they were touched, in
moments of crisis or confusion, by an experience outside themselves and often beyond the range of their imaginations. The
wounded Ignatius of Loyola moving from soldier to spiritual leader,
and the frustrated Augustine being led to the gospels he once re-
pudiated as crude are examples of saints who, from all we can determine, experienced a profound sense of loss and confusion about
their identity.

A modern experience of this loss of identity can be found in
an enormous range of novels and short stories--it is the preoccupation of the age and extends itself to all sorts of people: intel-
lectuals and self-deceivers (in the novels of Iris Murdoch), the
bedraggled middle-class (in those of Margaret Drabble), dreamers
and lunatics (in Walker Percy), and reluctant heroes (in the stories
of Graham Greene). It is also found in a kind of literature that
is born of the search for roots. One book of this genre which combines the sense of loss with the stimulation of the imagination and
the need to find oneself in an identifying context is N. Scott
Momaday's *The Way to Rainy Mountain*.[11]

Momaday, a Kiowa Indian and professor of Comparative Literature
at a major university, experienced a strong cultural disjunction
which, stimulated by the death of his grandmother (his last link
to his past and himself in that past), led him back to the stories
of his tribe. He undertook to retrace the journey of the Kiowas
to Rainy Mountain and, in so doing, to intertwine his own reflections and memories with tribal myths, stories from his grandmother
and observations about the land itself in order to draw the reader
into the experience of a lost people and a rediscovered imagination.
His book is divided into three parts: the "Setting Out" which makes
clear that one must know where one is coming from, that the loss
of identity often requires a person to retrace steps rather than
to look for a new path; the "Going On" which implies the importance
of being sustained in one's vision with all the difficulties of
that task; and the "Closing In" which draws the reader into the
experience of being part of a whole people who are lost. The last

part, the "Closing In" (*not* "Arriving"), contains in a poetic way
the whole story of the Kiowas as disclosed through their relationship with horses. Horses transformed the Kiowas from a Plains
people into daring buffalo hunters, into invincible men who knew
who they were and had some power in determining their lives. It
is clear that a man ought to risk his life for his horse and that
enemies will recognize the power that horses give to these people:
when the soldiers took Kiowa lands and imprisoned the Indians on a
reservation, they killed all their horses and so robbed them of
their power--and their vision. When one is astride a horse, one
can see clearly and as never before; being on foot means being
without vision. Because of their power, horses are perfect sacrificial victims and appropriate loci for the sacred: one man kept
the *bones* of his last horse as one would keep relics.

At the end of the book, Momaday observes that no one knows
the Kiowas anymore; but they can imagine them, they can remember--
one is not totally lost so long as memory and imagination remain.
As Momaday begins to understand himself in relation to his roots,
he can or cannot move on to another kind of search. Clearly, however, he could have moved nowhere at all until he began to understand who he was. Dante, too, once he begins to understand himself
in relation to Virgil, can begin to move along in his search for
himself and in his search for God, both of which tasks appear to
be infinite.

II. *The Dark Nights*

Mystics tell us that there are "dark nights of the soul,"
times of great loneliness or a sense of abandonment by God in which
one experiences anguish and darkness. The experience is not unlike
the deep sense of aloneness people have when, for whatever reasons,
communication with their lovers ceases--and, presumably, that is
the nub of the mystical experience, namely, that the beloved has
disappeared. In the quest for self there are moments when we escape ourselves, when we wonder if there has ever been any growth
in us, where we experience ourselves as hopeless and regressive and
lost in a kind of darkness, trapped by guilt or anxiety.

Other kinds of dark nights relate more directly to the quest
for self and to the self as pilgrim--moments of confrontation between the intended/good side of ourselves and the dark/sinful facts
of our lives. One confronts sin when one is forced to recognize
the polarities of intention and action in one's own life. In the

Comedy Dante presents this experience in two ways: *potentially*
(in terms of what he might become--his experience in hell) and
actually (in terms of what he is at the moment--his experience in
purgatory).

Dante's experience of hell is meant to bring him to judgment;
his experience in purgatory is the personal confrontation of himself as he stands under judgment. The journey to hell is not a
privilege for Dante so much as it is the drastic action undertaken
to show him how much danger he is in. In the meeting between Dante
and Beatrice at the top of Mount Purgatory, she tells us why Dante
had to be taken to the potential dark depths of himself, i.e., to
hell. When Beatrice (Dante's singular and overpowering experience
of grace) died, Dante did not turn his eyes to heaven where she
existed in an even more grace-ful state, but forsook her and made
friends elsewhere:

> His mind was turned from me, his heart estranged;
>
> And by wild ways he wandered seeking for
> False phantoms of the good, which promise make
> Of joy, but never fully pay the score.
>
> With inspirations prayer-wrung for his sake,
> Vainly in dreams and other ways as well
> I called him home; so little did he reck
>
> And in the end, to such a depth he fell
> That every means to save his soul came short
> Except to let him see the lost in hell.[12]

If pilgrimage and the quest for self both begin with a sense of
loss of identity, a need to know the self as it is, then it is also
important that one finds out the truth about himself, seeks to
know all sides of the matter.

Saints have often thought of themselves as great sinners, sometimes with such emphasis that many of the rest of us found them
slightly neurotic. In secular literature, too, there is a preoccupation with the dark side of the self and the implications im-
bedded in the preoccupation with that dark side. The clear fascination with the impecunious experience of sin in Wilde's *The Picture
of Dorian Gray*, and the tortured madness of Raskolnikov in *Crime
and Punishment* are classical accounts of the lure and result of
the dark side of the self. Oftentimes the discovery of the dark
side of the self is the principal action of a story.

A very clear Jungian novel about the dark side of the self
is Ursula LeGuin's *A Wizard of Earthsea*.[13] The hero in this story
is a young magician, Sparrowhawk, a boy with great powers. In a

contest with an older boy, a contest fueled mostly by jealousy and
a desire for revenge on Sparrowhawk's part, he conjures up a dark
spirit from the realm of the dead, a spirit so powerful that the
chief magician must wrestle it back to the nether world and lose
his life in the process. Still, a small bit of it, a dark shadow,
escapes into the world where it disrupts the equilibrium and waits
for Sparrowhawk, to take up residence in him and to do evil. No
one knows the shadow's name, and in this world as in ours, names
are power; if something can be named, it can be controlled. Sparrowhawk's secret name is Ged, a fact he shares with only a few
people since sharing it makes one vulnerable. The story line of
the book entails Ged's search for the name of the shadow and his
determination to do mortal combat with it. He tracks it to the
ends of the earth, beyond the boundaries of reason and control. In
a climactic scene, locked in battle with the predatory shadow, Ged
discerns its name--the name of the shadow of Ged, it is himself.

> Ged had neither lost nor won, but, naming the
> shadow of his death with his own name, had
> made himself whole; a man, who, knowing his
> whole true self, cannot be used or possessed
> by any power other than himself and whose
> life is therefore lived for life's sake.[14]

An interesting feature of LeGuin's book is that there is no
divine power at all, no god. There are creatures superior in intelligence to people (dragons) but there is no order beyond the
order of the universe. Still, one must confront the shadow side
of oneself. In the *Comedy* and in overtly religious literature, the
confrontation of the sinful side of the self is bound up with the
religious quest--one confronts sin in order to accept judgment and
thus to proceed along the path to God.

III. *Urgency*

Dante's experience of being lost in the dark woods was a moment
of urgency for him--something had to be done quickly lest he be
past *all* help. The old hymn which begins with "I was sinking deep
in sin" ends with the experience of grace--"love lifted me."[15] Love
lifted Dante, too, but not before it provided him with a drastic
experience of what it meant to sink deep in sin. Because of death,
there is, finally, a moment when an ultimate decision must be made.
The sense of that final moment is what I mean by urgency. One of
the consoling features of the concept of purgatory is that it holds
a place for the late-repentant, those whose decisions were, indeed,
made only in the moment of death. The possibility of salvation

extends right down to the last minute, but not beyond that.

In the search for the self there are also moments of urgency, a sense that one must make decisions *right now* if one is to find the self and be able to live with it. A sense that the presence of the whole self, past and future, is contained in the pulse of one moment in the present gives one an awareness of the need for some drastic action.

There are two ways to perceive this sense of urgency, whether it applies to the quest for self or to the quest for God. In one way of looking at things, the person has *no* sense of urgency--the moment might be cosmic, but the person is relatively unconscious about it. The novels and short stories of Flannery O'Connor deal primarily with people who are beset by an urgency they do not perceive. Her method of bringing the urgency to the consciousness of her protagonists is violence which, she believes, is the only way to break through their thick-headedness. In "A Good Man is Hard to Find," the grandmother is precisely at such a moment of urgency: she is facing her death. She does everything she can think of to ignore or avoid that fact, and it is only in repeated acts of violence to her family and the clear threat of her own violent death that she sees clearly--for a moment--where she is. In that instant of clarity she makes what is apparently the only right decision of her otherwise self-deluded life. The escaped convict who kills her sees this and says, "She would of been a good woman . . . if it had been somebody there to shoot her every minute of her life."[16]

Another way to portray a sense of urgency is to describe a protagonist who experiences the urgency as a desperate need to act. Peter Matthiessen's *At Play in the Fields of the Lord*[17] is a good example. It is the story of two partners, Wolfie, a self-styled "wandering Jew," and Moon, a half-breed American Indian, thrown together in a Latin American jungle with a Spanish Catholic priest and four fundamentalist American missionaries. They all have different ideas about what to do with/to a tribe of wild, jungle Indians: Wolfie wants to bomb them, win the commandant's favor, get his passport back, and get out of there; the priest, being a realist of sorts, wants to leave them alone; the missionaries want to convert them and win them for Jesus. The hero, however, is the half-breed American Indian, Lewis Meriweather Moon. He understands the Indians as his last chance to find himself--they give him a sense of urgency about his life that he has never had before. In a pre-dawn trip (hallucinogenic and actual, i.e., in the airplane he and Wolfie own), he flies into the jungle and parachutes naked into the

midst of the tribe in an effort to be reborn as an Indian, to capture the sense of himself that has been denied in the American
culture. His need to envision himself as an Indian is urgent.
Much like Dante he must act now or never.

IV. *Community of Intimacy*

Ultimately the quest for God is defined in relation to community; one finally knows oneself before God as an individual, but
also as part of a communion of saints, part of a group. The quest
for self, too, requires that one understand the self in relation
to others. In the *Comedy* Dante offers three different descriptions
of community. In the anti-community of hell there is no mutuality,
no cooperation, no regard for one another; there individual souls
exist in illusion and mutual hostility. The experimental community
of purgatory is similar to hell in its social stratification--sin-
ners are divided from one another according to their sin--but similar to heaven in its courtesy, mutual regard, and joy; there individual souls, in a process of purgation, are learning to be a
community of intimacy where one locates the self in relation to
others and to God. The perfected community of heaven is presented
as the apex of religious experience and self-awareness; there the
saints relate perfectly to God and to one another and the total
understanding of the self in relation to others and to God is given
a full range of community contexts.

A novel which reflects the variations on community presented
in the *Comedy* is Charles Williams' *Descent into Hell*.[18] The plot
and Williams' theological assumptions hinge on his understanding of
the atonement as initiating a "web of exchange" which presents
people with the choice of individuality or intersubjectivity (which
he calls "substitution and exchange"). Individual existence, apart
from a community, is a hellish choice according to Williams whereas
willing and joyful participation in the web of exchange is a fore-
taste of the heavenly community. According to Williams, Christ
bore the burden of human sinfulness and set the example for the human race; people, therefore, are to bear the burdens of others.
In the web of exchange, no one bears his own burden; everyone must
bear someone else's. It is a community of interdependence. The
three main characters in the novel reflect three possible choices
and, in doing so, mirror the three descriptive community options
presented by Dante. Wentworth, by his own choice and refusal to
become involved in the life of the community, is damned; he continually and consciously isolates himself from others, prefers

himself over everyone else, and thrives in isolation. His descent
into hell is not surprising. Pauline Anstruther is in the process
of learning or purgation. She has always been alone, terrified of
others, but begins to recognize the community of interdependence
in which people live. Following the laws of exchange and substitution, she takes cn a substantial burden, meets her best and worst
selves, and becomes part of a community that transcends time and
space. Margaret Anstruther, Pauline's grandmother, is so accustomed
to participation in the web of exchange, so discerning about the
needs of others and her role among them that she constitutes a model
of perfection within the novel, an embodiment of a heavenly character. She is so in tune with the community (past and present, here
and elsewhere) that she can see people no one else can see and feel
the power and presence of God through them. As one of the "saints"
she understands herself very well as an individual, and in relation
to a community of intimacy and love.

The quest for self and quest for God have an intimate connection, as the literary/religious parallelism of pilgrimage indicates.
Pilgrimage as a literary form has profound religious implications.
Dante describes pilgrimage as the movement of the soul towards God
and toward the fulfillment of its capacities within the hierarchy
of creation. For all the presence of God in *The Divine Comedy*,
however, it is clear that the pilgrimage would have been impossible
without self-knowledge. By drawing some correspondences between
the quest for self and the quest for God, I have suggested that
the connection is more intimate than one might ordinarily suppose.
It is not unusual to find caricatures of these quests divided one
from another: Some people fancy that medieval religion was designed
primarily to keep people's focus away from themselves and totally
upon God; others interpret contemporary secular literature as being
so devoid of any interest in God that it is totally preoccupied
with the self. A closer look at pilgrimage shows enough correspondence between the quest for self and the quest for God to substan-
tiate the important and apparently intrinsic connection between
them.

NOTES

[1]An important discussion of this problem and an attractive
solution to it can be found in Giles Gunn, "Threading the Eye of
the Needle: The Place of the Literary Critic in Religious Studies,"
JAAR, 43 (1975), pp. 164-184. He relies heavily on Clifford Geertz
to find something distinctively characteristic about religious

feelings; beliefs, and behaviors--a particular view of reality or
perspective on experience which contains both an ethical and metaphysical component. Gunn finds Geertz's work suggestive because
it manages to link ethos with world view in such a way that one
can see more clearly the connections between religion and literature. "Whatever else one may say about works of imaginative
literature, it is generally agreed at the very least that they represent forms designed to explore, to express, and to criticize
the relationship between what is here [in Geertz] being called
'metaphysics' on the one hand and 'ethics' on the other" (p. 175).

2"Experience of Self and Experience of God," *Theological Investigations XIII* (New York: Seabury Press, 1975), pp. 123-132.

3Dorothy L. Sayers, " . . . And Telling You a Story: A Note
on *The Divine Comedy*," in *Essays Presented to Charles Williams*, ed.
C. S. Lewis (Oxford University Press, 1947), pp. 90-105.

4"The Ethics of Elfland," in *Orthodoxy* (New York: Dodd Mead,
1908), pp. 46-65.

5"On Stories," in *Essays Presented to Charles Williams*, pp.
90-105.

6*The Confessions*, "noverim me ut noverim te."

7James Joyce, *Ulysses* (New York: Vintage Books, 1961 edition),
p. 213.

8See note 2.

9*Paradise*, XXXIII, 100-105, trans. Dorothy L. Sayers and
Barbara Reynolds (Penguin Edition, 1962), p. 346.

10Introduction to *Hell* (Penguin Edition, 1949), p. 49.

11N. Scott Momaday, *The Way to Rainy Mountain* (New York: Ballantine Books, 1969).

12*Purgatory*, XXX, 129-138 (Penguin Edition, 1955), p. 310.

13Ursula LeGuin, *A Wizard of Earthsea* (New York: Bantam Books,
1975; first published 1968).

14*Ibid.*, pp. 180-181.

15Howard E. Smith, "Love Lifted Me" (copyright 1912).

16*The Complete Stories of Flannery O'Connor* (New York: Farrar,
Straus and Giroux, 1971), p. 133.

17Peter Matthiessen, *At Play in the Fields of the Lord* (New
York: Random House, 1965).

18Charles Williams, *Descent into Hell* (Grand Rapids: Eerdmans,
1973).

IGNAZIO SILONE'S POLITICS OF CHARITY

Wayne Lobue

> "We shall not cease from explorations
> And the end of all our exploring will
> be to arrive where we started
> And know the place for the first time."
>
> - T. S. Eliot

The career of Ignazio Silone ended in paradox, almost as it began. In his fictional pieces and autobiographical essays, Silone baffled those who tried to reduce his writing, and thus the meaning of his life, to politics, propaganda, or piety. Not that those characteristics are irrelevant. In fact, it is very much to the point to understand that, as a writer and in his life, Ignazio Silone fully concerned himself with bringing a spiritual vision of reality--what he called religious thinking--to bear on the political dimensions of human life. It is the purpose of this essay to examine Silone as a storyteller who wrote contemporary political parables from an essentially theological perspective.

Silone would not have admitted the theological dimension, even after acknowledging that he considered "the rediscovery of the Christian heritage in the ferment of liberation taking place in contemporary society, our most important spiritual gain."[1] His stories testify to his interest in re-presenting the Christian story in the guise of contemporary struggles for freedom, but to him that was not theology. He associated theology with the narrow interests of the institutional Church that encouraged mere doctrinal abstractions. Christian theology ignored some historic movements, he thought, as well as many current efforts to realize the Kingdom of God and, through such ignorance, became one more ideology preserving an institution at the expense of the people. This judgment is part of his determined opposition to every kind of institutional ideology, not only that of the Church.[2]

Despite his reservations about theology, to deal at all with Silone's writing is to confront the issue of faith at every level, from trust in individuals to belief in God. A man of ultimate faith himself, he struggled past certain orthodox versions of it, first in the form of the institutional Church and then in the form

of the Marxism of his young adulthood. Awakened to social conscience by the ferment of World War I, he shifted his allegiance
from Catholicism to Marxism. He later described this interlude as
his mistaken conviction that Marxism would contribute to a harmonious and just society with greater integrity. During the 1920's
he devoted himself to building a Marxist base in Italy and is commonly recognized as one of the founding fathers of Italian Commu-
nism. After his break with the Party in 1930 and while in Swiss
exile,[3] he continued alone to search for something to believe in
without, what he called, the mindless dedication to some ideological
cause. Despite promises of a better future, both Church and Party
had proven false, representing, in truth, a denial of liberty and
presenting obstacles to the prospect of human community.

What Silone had learned sadly after years devoted to the cause
of justice, he has attempted to explain as the primary motive for
his writing. In 1942 he stated his view that "in ourselves, in
our movements, in our doctrine, side by side with love and respect
for man, resided hate and contempt." Almost bitterly, he noted
"a vocation for tyranny nestled next to the desire for liberty."[4]
There is nothing new in his view of humankind, at the same time
noble and wicked, but the statement marked for him a kind of existential reawakening. As he reflected upon his career and disillusionment, he gradually regained a version of his first faith.
Stripped of its ideology, his term for abstract theological musing,
Silone rediscovered in Christianity's rich and varied heritage the
imagery to express hopefully but realistically the human pursuit
of life here and now. At its center this imagery recalled the
historical Jesus who joined the mystery of God-in-man to suffering
innocence.

A "second naiveté," as it were, brought Silone full circle.
By returning to Christianity, but not the Church, he had come to
see in the old meaning and symbols a much richer and more deeply
instructive answer to the question he had first asked in face of
social and psychological injustice, the question that concluded
his first novel, *Fontamara* (1934), "What must we do?"

The road back to faith in answer to that question was a long
one. It took up most of the rest of his life and would be understood
by a very few, least of all himself, until the publication in
1965 of *The Story of a Humble Christian*.[5] Between *Fontamara* and
Story, his first fiction and his last, Silone probed the nature of
religious faith married to social conscience. His novels and dramas
can be characterized as both a relentless challenge to existing

authority and a slow progress toward the reconstruction of religion with respect to what he saw as the contemporary experience of nihilism. In that sense it may be correct to call Silone a pessimistic optimist. He believed in seeking after a future hope, even as he viewed the contemporary world order in the darkest terms. His pursuit of religious faith enriches as it clarifies the thematic paradox typical of all his fiction, namely, survival and self-sacrifice, life and its tragic betrayal.

The clarification of his thought in this matter moved through stages. In addition to *Fontamara*, the first stage takes in two other early novels, *Bread and Wine* (1937), his masterpiece, and its sequel, *The Seed Beneath the Snow* (1942). These early novels expressed sharply Silone's cultural pessimism. As he explained it, "in the history of human society, we are, alas, still at Good Friday." Nevertheless, he infuses these novels with the prospect of something better. He searches, in fact, for a way to the spiritual center that might humanize life and, in more than mere slogans, free the impulse for a just and equitable society. He acknowledged that his vision is utopian. As a Marxist, Silone had anticipated a material utopia as the inevitable end of history. After his disillusionment with Marxist rigidity, he rediscovered the older Christian notion of the kingdom of God. This image conveyed better his sense that the kingdom must be pursued here and now, while elevating the pursuit to a spiritual quest ever in need of renewal as measured in human time. He shaped his fiction to express that understanding.

Set in southern Italy, these early novels--like all his stories--draw on the rich local legend of the region and reflect the stubborn yet fatalistic independence of its people. His purpose, however, is to state a larger truth about modern life, not to memorialize a people. Through his protagonists, Silone charts the effort in one society to gain some degree of freedom from an oppressive and impersonal system. The quest for freedom usually begins at a point of rebellion, so that the major action in each story centers on the theme of the hunted hero, the rebel and his cause.

This format allows Silone to attach a socio-religious significance to his protagonist's personal crisis. As his anti-heroes challenge the conventional tenets of society, they also inevitably undergo a conversion, "a profound shift of allegiance." In *Fontamara*, a loosely-strung series of anecdotes about the hard life of the *cafoni* (landless peasants), the characterization of the protagonist Berardo is based on a popular legend of a local saint.

Bernardo also serves as the prototype for Silone's later protagonists. After a string of personal tragedies that awaken Berardo
from his apathy, he undergoes a profound change in an encounter
with the "Solitary Stranger" who moves across the countryside urging
the *cafoni* to resistance. In a strange twist, Berardo assumes the
identity of the stranger when he confesses to the other's "crimes."
His subsequent torture and execution in the stranger's place assume
a sacrificial significance and become a sign of hope for the *cafoni*,
who rise in unison when the news of Berardo's execution reaches
them.

What Silone accomplished in this first novel was partial and
incomplete. His description of the effort to arouse the socially
marginal *cafoni* to organize did not characterize sufficiently the
nature of the conversion he wanted to probe. Although sacrificial
heroism continued to dominate his later stories, it was thereafter
merely an indicator of a deeper core of meaning he tried to articulate. Without that deeper meaning giving substance to conversion,
the possibility of a future hope would remain illusory.

In *Bread and Wine* and *The Seed Beneath the Snow*, Silone chron-
icled the saga of Pietro Spina. These novels continued what he
started in *Fontamara*, the representation of how one person's conviction can effect change in society without manipulating people.
Both narratives are appropriately fictional studies into the nature
of conversion. In complementary ways, both also focus on Pietro
Spina, whose personal awakening alters his commitment to changing
social structures. He grows to understand that cosmetic change,
in some new form of ideology, merely sacrifices people once more to
the goal of impersonal power. Spina learns to embody an even more
radical source of change, one that works with and through people.

In working out of this scenario, Silone brings the religious
dimension more fully to the center of his writing and to the heart
of any effective systemic change. *Bread and Wine*, for example, en-
visions the transformation of Christianity to the gospel of liberation for the oppressed and through the oppressed for the oppressors.
The possibility also brings together a disparate complexity of com-
peting images. Its meaning is best expressed thematically as the
emergence of a "new humanity" enunciated through images meant to
fuse the saint with the rebel who "practices politics out of a religious aspiration."[6]

The story describes the flight of Pietro Spina, a political
rebel disguised as a priest. Although Spina is concerned with
political power, he has renounced it in his refusal to collaborate

with a heartless system. He is unprepared, however, to deal with
his isolation or with the unfamiliar role of priest his disguise
forces on him. Yet as he unwillingly fulfills the demands of his
assumed role, Spina reaches a moment of religious insight in which,
still reluctantly, he recognizes God as his true pursuer. The
experience begins vaguely with Spina seriously questioning his
past and extends gradually to the people he serves. Disguised as
a priest, he is touched by the integrity of simple peasants bound
by the thread of region, a common tradition, and their destiny as
pawns of the powerful over long generations. As Spina penetrates
the life of the *cafoni*, he discovers their potential for community
beneath the facade of resignation.

Delineating Spina's struggle for something to believe in--which
was perhaps his own as well--allowed Silone to lay out the conditions for his new humanity. Even when their ties are comically
betrayed, the *cafoni* manage to hang on and occasionally to rise
above the complex strategies of the power brokers and would-be
princes of every variety. He begins to learn from them the hard
lesson that there is something far more salvific than revolutionary
activity. Through their everyday effort to communicate and to provide one another with support in the task of surviving, Spina experiences hope. Yet even in this environment, integrity--with
courage as its boon companion--is an important check against compromising good will to survival for its own sake. As he learns to
be a companion to the *cafoni*, his contribution to their lives together teaches them to be more than passive to the fate that
threatens to engulf them. Against the oppression of anonymous authority, the prospect of self-sacrifice accompanies the effort to
live with courage.[7] In the bond of companionship, self-sacrifice
is not an act of futility or despair but the yeast for the deeper
communion at the very foundation of community.

Bread and Wine is Silone's richest novel, but it is not without flaw. In Pietro Spina, he has created a strong character who
dominates the action, focusses the story, and carries forward the
social and psychological meaning of conversion. As Spina learns
that life is companionship, Silone exposes through him his own
sense of the paradox that exists between the religious and the political. The quality of paradox that juxtaposes personal awakening
to God with an awareness of its social dimension is missing in his
conclusion, however. Spina's flight across the mountains to escape
the authorities is more ambiguous than paradoxical.[8] In the end,
the rebel replaces the priest and Spina seemingly reverts to

fighting a lost cause. The concluding question of *Fontamara* remains unanswered. The necessity of flight overshadows communion
and the rebel once again finds himself alone.

The Seed in the Snow, however, continues Spina's story. In
this sequel, Silone presents a more reflective, less impulsive
Pietro Spina. Still in disguise, he returns to his native village,
where the main portions of the novel involve meditative dialogue
instead of action. One major sequence reunites Spina with the
Donna, his grandmother, with whom he experiences a deep spiritual
rapport despite her otherworldly piety. Later in the novel, a
second important sequence reintroduces the Infante, a deaf-mute
with whom, in *Bread and Wine*, Spina had first experienced the communion of brotherhood. These sequences fittingly parallel the self-
satirizing exchanges within a shallow and corrupt middle class.

The scenes with the Donna and the Infante are important because they join religious faith more intimately to social conscience. Although the faith they exchange is personal, it also
speaks of "the God within" who manifests himself in self-respect
extended to others in equal portion. Spina describes this faith as
"a goodness free of every calculation, an honesty indifferent to
what people will say, and generous acts that are entirely gratu-
itous, not tied to hope of reward or resolution even in the next
world."[9] Later scenes with the Infante draw out some of the implications of this belief applicable to the problem of social sin. In
speaking of this association, Spina describes it as neither traditionally religious nor recognizably political: "A new type of saint
will be born, a new type of martyr, a new type of man. I do not believe there is any other way of saving one's soul today." He goes
on to say that this form of sanctity will not be expressed "in private communion with God, but in an urgent communion with one's fellow man, that it will assuage a little the human sufferings of his
time, not only combatting the miseries of men but sharing in them."[10]

With *The Seed in the Snow*, Silone rounded out his view of conversion and the new humanity. He had begun to recast traditional
Christian ideas in a modern context of moral protest. In more
specific terms, he shed the abstraction of dogma in favor of "gratu-
itous sacrifice" which abandons self-interest to establish "an
opening to the reality of others." Shortly before his death, Spina
challenges the skeptics: "Men of vision won't disappear," he asserts. "When they've died in one place, they'll spring up again
somewhere else."[11]

A long silence followed *The Seed in the Snow*. Silone's next
novel, *A Handful of Blackberries*, did not appear until 1953. This
was followed by *The Secret of Luca* (1958) and *The Fox and the
Camellias* (1961). More than his earlier novels, these are of a
single fabric. No less than before, Silone writes of his new humanity, but his tone is calmer. The clarification of what companionship means predominates, in place of his earlier concern with
the often desperate effort to find companionship. Conversion
deepens to raising consciousness among the already committed. But,
even so, the climate of betrayal and compromise continues, an
abiding counterpoint to Silone's community of faith.[12] For example, the disillusioned party-man Rocco, in *A Handful of Blackberries*, is reminiscent of Spina in his early struggle for faith.
Likewise, in *The Secret of Luca*, the young party organizer must
undergo the gentle persuasion of Luca's secret. Nevertheless, the
intensity of the early quest gives way in these works to a mellower
conviction. Instead of the search for faith, Silone now conveys
evidence of it. With faith comes hope, and these novels are distinctly hopeful, even when Rocco must reassert the sacrificial nature of it. "Love hurts," he tells his doubting companion, "but
life isn't worth living without it. . . . Are you so afraid of
suffering that you think love isn't worth the price?" Similarly,
Luca's secret is about suffering assumed out of love without bit-
terness or the need for vindication.

Each of these novels presents a hopeful view of change from
the bottom up, but one in need of constant reaffirmation. Through
friendship, mutual aid, and the resistance to fate, they expose
and then attack the structures of evil present to the *cafoni*. The
stalwart Gabriele with his symbolic horn in *Blackberries*, for instance, stands prepared to announce any transgression against the
commonweal; and in *The Fox and the Camellias*, Silone's most controlled novel, the rebel-farmer works stubbornly but quietly with
others to uphold their heritage of social companionship. The
rebel speaks more softly now, but he is never in danger of being
lost to the saint.

Prior to completing *The Fox and the Camellias*, Silone returned
to his early fiction in a series of revisions of those first novels.
He later explained his motives:

> I would have liked to spend my life writing and
> rewriting the same story in the hope of understanding
> it, as least, and of making it understood to others.
> In the Middle Ages, there were monks who spent their
> lives painting the Holy Face, always the same face,

> although in reality the faces were never quite
> identical. Now it's clear I'm interested in the
> fate of man, how a certain type of man, a certain
> type of Christian fits into the machinery of the
> world, and I wouldn't know how to write anything
> else.[13]

His revisions, in fact, excised material associated narrowly with
the era prior to World War II. He acted, in part, to save his fiction from the misreading that would place it only against such
threats of the period as Fascism or Stalinism. To the contrary,
Silone has been definite in stating that when he used the term
"totalitarian" he meant it to describe the structures of evil inherent in every ideology. He also did not wish to be understood
in the familiar pattern of exposé some others had adopted.[14] Silone
had rejected the party but not his reasons for going to the party
in the first place.

The revisions, in truth, refocussed what, for him, characterized
the paradox of contemporary life, namely, the struggle between cultural pessimism and alternative versions of society. In retrospect,
these revisions also expressed Silone's desire to trace the organic
progress of his original themes, and, thus, were preparations for
his next work as well, a powerful drama in which his muted rebel
once again raised his voice.

The Story of a Humble Christian highlights the events surrounding the short reign of Celestine V, a fourteenth-century Pope
who abdicated his papacy amid considerable controversy. Celestine
had intrigued Silone for many years. In fact, he admitted that the
drama is the historical version of most of his earlier fiction, but
especially *Bread and Wine*, and its dramatic revision, *And He Hid
Himself* (1946). The story and the long introductory essay that
accompanies it enlighten everything Silone had previously written.

The drama raises yet again the paradox of companionship and
community set against human isolation and sacrifice. Silone believed history had mistreated Celestine by making him a figure of
ridicule and the image of cowardice; in contrast, unofficial legend
supported the virtue of his marginal life. Rejected by history,
Celestine reemerges in Silone's play as a man of the people, out-
standing for the very reasons officialdom rejected him--for his
strict following of Franciscan poverty, his socially marginal life
as a hermit-leader, and, not least, his strongly anticlerical
temperament.

The narrative is straightforward, but with his characteristic
simplicity Silone turns his tale into a parable of universal

significance. Celestine's election to the papacy is a compromise
that follows a deadlocked conclave in which neither of the rival
candidates can muster enough votes to win. Celestine's election
is considered a victory for the people, and he accepts the office
as an opportunity to end the strife within the Church and to open
it to serve all people rather than special interests. After twenty-
seven months, Celestine gives up in frustration. He has discovered
unhappily that institutions refuse to bend to efforts at deepseated
reform, even when they apparently cry out for it. In futility,
Celestine returns to a life of integrity among the people and away
from the centers of power. His successor, the infamous Boniface
VIII, immediately vilifies Celestine and pursues him to his death.

     Despite the theme of isolation and flight, the result is not
defeat or resignation. At the allegorical level, a kind of redemption is achieved that turns Celestine into a figure of hope against
those who disregard the dignity of man. His canonization by popular
acclaim shortly after his death marks his ultimate victory, not a
personal one but, in its preservation of a noble human ideal against
official versions of the truth, a victory for all the people. In
failure, or rather through it, Silone has Celestine represent an
affirmation of life that stretches beyond the boundaries of his
era. The courage of those who fail in pursuit of a utopian faith
in man represents the very possibility of further hope. In Silone's
view, the compassionate Celestine stands as a universal symbol of
love and will seeking meaning.

     The play and the author's commentary leave little doubt as to
Silone's intent. His version of Pope Celestine draws together the
major themes that cut across the entire corpus of his writing.
Like Silone's other protagonists, the free-spirited Celestine disciplines his great energies toward the work of achieving the kingdom
of God. This ideal reflects the great and noble heritage of Christianity awaiting a new cycle of birth in each age. In aid of a
more tangible realization of community, the past could speak of
kindred spirits who have clarified the meaning of human fellowship.
Furthermore, behind all such examples as Celestine, one could ultimately identify the paradoxical Jesus, whose gift of life survived
his apparent defeat.[15]

     For more than forty years, Silone reflected on the fate of man.
Each new work stated and restated what he understood from his reflections. He never deviated from his goal of trying to clarify
the values of the past worthy of those living now. Against the
dehumanization of ideology, he wished to assert what he called "our

paleo-Christian heritage." In other words, against the political
expediencies of our time, Christianity could aid in elevating mankind's communal instincts from the laws of survival "to a permanent
aspiration which thirsts after social justice."[16] In its essence,
Silone believed, Christianity was a type of socialism that aimed
to further humanize life by extending the moral criteria of private
life to every aspect of society.

Put in that way, Silone's fiction, collectively, presents a
redemptive theology of the cross projected toward the establishment
of the kingdom of God. He has commented on the utopian impulse
that gripped Celestine and all his protagonists as somehow deeply
rooted in every person: "In man's consciousness there is an unrest
that no reform and no material well-being can ever subdue. The
history of utopia is the history of an ever disappointed but tena-
cious hope."[17]

Silone left little doubt he understood the kingdom, first of
all, "of this world." Moreover, his is a political kingdom, not
as we usually think of politics, but as a unified social expression
of human solidarity elevated to the level of religion. In short,
he celebrates a politics of charity. For all of the early Marx
in that vision, it is Jesus, not Marx who best exemplifies its inspiration. This politics is what Silone has called "the perennial
hope" and "our common faith in an Age of the Spirit, without church,
without state, without coercion, in an egalitarian society, sober,
humble, benign, based on man's spontaneous charity."[18] The hope for
a politics of charity--however inachievable--persists and is expressed in a variety of historical guises. Its persistence, moreover, keeps the human community from being overwhelmed in ours and
every era by the attraction of selfish interest or the fatalism
of despair.[19]

Against those who would characterize his fiction as mere sentiment, Silone has insisted that what he describes is "an awareness."
It is a "feeling for God" that leads to acts of courage of personal
and social nature--a spirituality that honors God through service
to people. Against the occupational hazard of narcissism and isolation, this "God awareness" pushes outward toward solidarity with
others, independent of any intermediary, that is, institutional ap-
paratus. It occurs first in simple "communion with the other" and
builds by degrees from companionship to community. Silone thought
of solidarity as communion because, in opposition to impersonal
systems, an enduring community develops from "the personal disposi-
tion to be directly sociable, sympathetic and generous, which can

go so far as an awareness that others are really present in us."[20]

The delicacy of the communion Silone speaks of renders its goal of communal solidarity utopian and, in a significant way, aligns this manner of living with the Cross. Challenged by the reality of "the way things are," this utopian notion, at best, struggles to be realized. As Silone's marginal man reaches for something better, he discovers that those who question too far are more likely to be disciplined or cast out by those who have a stake in existing inequities. To successive ages of nihilistic thinking, from the totalitarianism of the 1930's to the narcissism of the present, a politics of charity is--regrettably--utter foolishness. For Silone, this knowledge is itself the final paradox.

NOTES

[1]Ignazio Silone, "The Situation of the Ex," in *Emergency Exit*, ed. Ruth Nanda Anshen (New York: Harper and Row, 1968), p. 105. This book is a representative collection of Silone's essays and short fiction. It covers the period between 1942 and 1964. Ruth Nanda Anshen handled the English version for the World Perspectives series, Volume 39. The titlepiece "Emergency Exit" was added to the English edition.

[2]Although Pope John XXIII's *resorgimento* surprised and pleased him, he never returned to Catholicism. Silone characterized himself as a Christian outside the Church and a socialist outside the party. See *The God that Failed*, ed. Robert Crossman (New York: Bantam, 1965), pp. 101-2.

[3]His account of that break is quite touching and a fine testimony to his sincerity. The best version is his essay in Crossman, *Ibid.*

[4]"The Situation of the Ex," *Emergency Exit*, p. 104.

[5]*The Story of a Humble Christian*, trans. William Weaver (New York: Harper and Row, 1968). Lawrence Cunningham, who has studied Silone's language, has informed me that a more accurate rendering of the title would be *The Story of a Simple Christian*. It was Silone's purpose to hold simplicity in tension against the tendency toward self-interested complexity in contemporary life.

[6]The critic R. W. B. Lewis coined the phrase. See *The Picaresque Saint: Representative Figures in Contemporary Fiction* (Philadelphia: J. B. Lippincott, 1959), p. 157. His essay is an excellent introduction to Silone's early fiction, and I have drawn on his insights throughout this essay.

[7]The culture of anonymity and its problems have been discussed persuasively by Richard Rubenstein, who uses the context of the holocaust. See, for example, *The Cunning of History: Mass Death and the American Future* (New York: Harper and Row, 1975).

[8]In a later revision, a drama entitled *And He Hid Himself* (New York: Harper and Row, 1946), Silone improved on the original ending. Instead of flight, Spina chooses to enlist local people for the purpose of resistance. Among those joining him is the unconventional Giachimo, a wandering monk whose prophetic lamentations had previously punctuated Spina's warnings to the people.

[9]*The Seed in the Snow* (New York: Harper and Row, 1942), p. 185.

[10]*Ibid.*

[11]*Ibid.*, p. 300.

[12]Silone discusses this conflict frequently. See, for example, "Reasons for Living," in *Emergency Exit*, p. 126, and his introduction to *The Story of a Humble Christian*, pp. 28-29.

[13]*The Story of a Humble Christian*, p. 12.

[14]Silone apparently did not see eye to eye with Arthur Koestler and Malraux, as well as others in their circle. Koestler has described Silone as "a kind but very reserved person, wrapped up in himself." Silone later replied that Koestler wanted to make contact on the ground of enthusiasms he (Silone) had never shared very deeply. Silone was never preoccupied with anticommunism. "Our problems," he said, "are post-communism; they are new problems." See Lewis, *The Picaresque Saint*, pp. 160-161.

[15]Silone might have found his views quite consistent with current South American theology. His images of human community parallel closely the "base communities" that have developed there. Many other parallels between Silone and the liberation theologians are evident in Jon Sobrino, *Christology at the Crossroads* (New York: Orbis, 1978), preface, pp. 35-37, 68-74, to cite but a few instances. For his connections with the ideas of European and North American theologians, see Dorothee Soelle, *Political Theology*, trans. John Shelley (Philadelphia: Fortress, 1974) and Gregory Baum, *The Social Imperative: Essays on the Critical Issues that Confront the Christian Churches* (New York: Paulist, 1979).

[16]"Reasons for Living," *Emergency Exit*, p. 126.

[17]"The Situation of the Ex," *Emergency Exit*, p. 108.

[18]*The Story of a Humble Christian*, pp. 25-27.

[19]Silone studied Christian tradition carefully. In his introduction to *The Story of a Humble Christian*, he indicates that he drew considerable inspiration from the heritage that included such models as the first Christian conscientious objectors, the peasant leagues of medieval Europe, and especially the free spirit movement of Benedictines and Spiritual Franciscans as represented by Joachim Fiore. See pp. 21-29.

[20]*Ibid.*, p. 26.

THEOLOGY AND THANATOLOGY:

A CASE HISTORY IN THE RELATIONSHIP

OF RELIGION AND CULTURE

Peter H. Beisheim

We do theology within and upon the human condition. And the
human condition, Peter Berger writes, "fraught as it is with suffering and with the finality of death, demands interpretations that
not only satisfy theoretically but give inner sustenance in meeting
the crisis of suffering and death."[1] Today, however, contemporary
theology is reflecting upon a "taboo" subject in a cultural milieu
which contributes to and affirms societal reactions of denial and
avoidance toward death and the dying process. Death has been
transposed by the separation of the young and the old which has
distorted, if not obstructed completely, the natural human need of
one generation passing on to another its wisdom and insight into
the meaning of history, events, and life.

Death and the process of dying have become *insulated* through
our society's practices of cosmetically hiding the reality, initiating drive-in viewing windows by which death is given a passing
glance, structuring euphemistic language which has finally culmi-
nated in the undertaker becoming the transition-technician, and
separating the dying institutionally which has tended to isolate
individuals from family and children, reduced individuals to the
level of problem--overall, to have dehumanized the individual.
Death has been deprived of a *context* inasmuch as the extended family
has been lost through mobility, and also because of the loss of
ethnic and religious traditions which in the past have traditionally
communicated the knowledge necessary for integrating the "death
experience" into one's life. And, finally, death has been so *tech-
nologized* that now the question is being seriously asked, "Is death
a disease to be overcome or is it essential for personal and societal
growth?"[2]

Reaction to this "pornographic attitude toward death" has given
rise to thanatology which attempts through interdisciplinary dialogue
to study the psychological aspects of dying, reactions to death,
loss and grief and recovery from bereavement, as well as the somatic
process of dying. The Foundation of Thanatology, founded by Dr.
Austin Kutscher of Columbia University in the mid-sixties, posits:

(1) that thanatology recognizes and stresses the importance of the
psychosocial aspects of caring for the terminal patient and his
family; (2) that thanatology is deeply concerned that all aspects
of clinical treatment of the terminal patient be monitored and that
initiation of technology be questioned to avoid dehumanization of
the individual; (3) that thanatology proposes a philosophy of caring
that reinforces alternative ways of supporting the positive qualities in the life of the dying patient; and (4) that thanatology
strives to introduce methods of giving emotional support to the
dying individuals afterwards.[3]

    Paradoxically, this concerted effort during the past fifteen
years has resulted in better human care for the dying patient and
families, but at the same time has become so specialized that death
and the process of dying lose their human dimension.

    Excepting accidental death for the moment, we usually under-
stand the natural event of death to occur at the end of a process
of somatic deterioration. While this factor is integral to understanding death, there is another process which has more significance, that is, "the process of disengagement."[4]

    In this context our life from birth is a steady growth of re-
lationships by which we "identify ourselves." As our world becomes
larger through these relationships, our identity keeps changing,
while our orientation is usually focused on the future in anticipation of accomplishments and realizing our potentialities. Traditionally, societies have marked these significant changes in an individual's identity by rituals in which the changes were experienced
in the context of "dying and rebirth" and this experience was intimately linked to the "cosmic process of dying and rebirth." At some
point in the individual's life, this continual process of expansion
--of widening horizons--ceases, and a process of contraction disengagement begins in which the individual gradually releases a hold
on life and relationships in anticipation of the eventual somatic
disintegration, the ultimate sign of death. The rituals marked
not only a new situation for the individual, but also a new situation
for the community. Thus the process of dying and the event of death
had communal or societal ramifications beyond those of the individual. Contemporary anthropologists have suggested that the "loss of
rituals" in our society has contributed to the societal avoidance of
death and the frightening aloneness for the individual; in short
death has lost its cosmic dimension. In this process of disengagement the individual undergoes a life review that consists of examining one's personal history, accomplishments, failures, and values

which in the face of impending death forces the individual to either
say Yes or No to his personal history. This act of affirmation
or rejection can be viewed (but does not have to be) as a salvific
moment in which one freely chooses in faith to let go of all personal history and relationships and surrender to the incomprehensible God.[5]

While this process of disengagement has lost its traditional
social and ritual dimension it has been observed in the psychosocial dynamics of terminal patients coming to grips with the reality of their impending death. This is provoking the creation of
ecclesial and liturgical expressions which will give support to
the individual and the family undergoing this process. The process
of disengagement has been described by Kubler-Ross as the stages
of dying[6] and by Carl Nighswonger as the dramas of dying.[7] The
sense of process and its theological significance is best grasped
by the familiar schematic presentation of the data:

Stages of Dying	*Dramas of Dying*
1. Denial and Shock ("Not me!")	1. Shock: Denial vs. Panic
2. Anger ("Why me!")	2. Emotion: Catharsis vs. Depression
3. Bargaining ("If I do this, then...")	3. Negotiation: Bargaining vs. Selling Out
4. Depression (life review)	4. Cognition: Realistic Hope vs. Despair
5. Acceptance (live life until...)	5. Commitment: Acceptance vs. Resignation
	6. Completion: Fulfillment vs. Forlorness

There are some additional factors that must be kept in mind when
interpreting this schema: (1) the process is one that is undergone many times during one's lifetime, not just in the context of
impending somatic death; (2) realistic hope is understood in the
context of the significant quality of one's remaining time in contrast to emphasizing cure; and (3) the sixth drama refers to an
overall perspective to the process rather than having a firm basis
in the social and behavioral studies.

The first element of significance for theology concerns the
possible need for *reinterpreting the moment of death*. Instead of
understanding the moment of death as that moment of total somatic
cessation, it is quite possible to understand the moment in the
context of one's consciousness of mortality, the radical confrontation with life in the face of impending death. The moment of death
transcends time, space, and place, so that awareness of death

overwhelms the questions of the length of life-span, the mode of
death, or the setting of death. The moment calls into question
one's past and present in the face of the future. It is my moment,
even though others will also experience their own moments; it is
one which I experience in my aloneness. Even more importantly,
life is confronted possibly for the first time in its ultimacy and
with this the confrontation of my "I" which has been shaped, consciously but more often unconsciously, by the interaction of "life"
and "I." The process of dramas also indicates the active or decisive dimension by which one decides to die. While this can be
seen in agreement with Boros' position on the final option, it does
indicate that the process is one that is undergone innumerable
times, so that the ultimate act by which one decides for eternity,
in an act of unconditional freedom, union, or rejection of God, is
not dealt with in Boros' categories. On the other hand, the mere
process of coping with one's impending death is not guaranteed
completion.[8]

The second element of significance for theology is the support
that thanatological research contributes to the understanding that
in death *one's personal history is consummated*.[9] The intimacy that
this position has with the moment of death becomes quite visible.
For Rahner, life constitutes a personal history which seeks consummation by its own intrinsic nature. The death of an individual is
the event in which the whole of his history as a free being is
brought into immediate confrontation with the mystery of God and
this confrontation is experienced as "blessing or judgment." This
confrontation highlights the accountability and responsibility of
an individual for his participation in the creation of his personal
history, in the creation of the personal history of others and of
the world as either an openness to God in one's neighbor or an ob-
stacle to this realization. It may well be that this factor is
what prompts the anxiety that dying people have for prolonging existence in order to find meaning in their lives.[10] This point is
also highlighted by Erik Erikson in his eighth age of man--ego integrity vs. despair--in which the individual in old age, facing
death, reflects upon his personal history and either says "Yes"
(ego integrity) or "No" (despair).[11] The key element, however, is
that the process moves to completion as one becomes more aware of
having opened up to others through love; through this experience
of love an individual begins to glimpse the power of love in over-
coming the fear of death, the fear of the future, and to glimpse

the power to accept the challenge of life and to experience it more intensely.

The third significant issue addressed in the interaction of theological reflection and thanatological research is *the issue of technologically prolonging life*. Once again, Rahner's concept of life consummation rejects any implications of an indefinite prolongation into an indeterminate future. While life has a beginning, a birth, there is a process of growth towards a completion, a goal--death. In death, the significance of one's life is made conscious to the individual and those intimately linked with the individual. This dimension is achieved through the living of life as contrasted to mere existing which implies the lack of realizing one's potential and lack of openness to the mystery and wonder of reality. Thus it would seem that the moment of full realization of the significance of one's personal history may very well be thwarted by medical technology. Therefore, for Rahner, doctors may struggle to maintain somatic life as long as there is the realistic possibility of realizing for the individual a "truly personal kind of living," that is, on the level of self-awareness, personhood, freedom, responsibility, love and faithfulness." If not, then the moment of somatic termination should be allowed to occur.[12] Within this context of personal history, Rahner sees no difficulty utilizing the definition of brain death (as irreversible coma) in order to decide whether or not medical technology should be utilized in either attempting to resuscitate an individual or terminating treatment.

A fourth issue is related very intimately to the third and that is *the donation of organ tissue* which may be viewed as the final act of love which highlights the consummation of one's personal history. In this act of giving to one's neighbor the possibility of somatic life, one is acknowledging and at the same time making an act of faith in the meaning of life. Thus one gives to another the possibility of fulfilling his personal history and the personal histories of others with whom each person becomes interrelated.

A fifth point of mutual concern which arises from the process of completing one's life in death is the most controversial, that is *the individual choosing to die*. Within the context of the consummation of one's personal history, passive euthanasia, the choice by which somatic death naturally occurs without any human or technical interference, appears to offer no serious problems. The question becomes more controversial when it concerns the right of

another to determine and actively bring about the consummation of
another's personal history. Moreover, this is another situation
which is no longer being encountered in isolated incidents and is
creating the need to redefine the concept of suicide. I am
referring to those individuals who, having completed the process
of letting-go, choose not to continue treatments (e.g., dialysis)
which may serve no other purpose than the prolongation of existence
and in some circumstances seriously affect the quality of life.
Is this man's most decisive act of freedom or man's inability to
assimilate pain and suffering into a theology of life?

   A sixth area of interest between the two disciplines concerns
the meaning and significance of a survivor's "experience of dying"
(falling, near-drowning, car accidents, etc.) These experiences
have been described as a progression of moments. The first moment
is called *resistance* because the individual is searching for ways
to avoid impending death within the limits of the situation. This
struggle to avoid the reality of death ceases when realistically
death dominates totally the consciousness. The second moment is
a *life review*, a panoramic sweep of one's personal history. This
intense re-experiencing of significant personal events (peak experiences?) leads to the last moment of the "dying experience"--
transcendence. The moment of experience has been described in the
following manner: "I felt no conflict or strife; conflict had
been transmuted into love. Elevated and harmonious thoughts dominated and united the individual images and like magnificent music
a divine calm swept through my soul. I became ever more surrounded
by a splendid blue heaven with delicate roseate and violet cloud-
lets. I swept into it painlessly and softly and I saw that now I
was falling freely through the air and that under me a snow field
lay waiting. Objective observations, thoughts and subjective
feelings were simultaneous. Then I heard a dull thud and my fall
was over."[13]

   This phenomenon is not without its questions. What is the relationship of the rational dimension and the irrational in this
experience? Is it merely a sensual experience without cognitive
content? Does this experience of transcendence demand, allow, or
contain, in any manner, a conscious decision of affirmation or rejection to my personal history which has been reviewed?

   Without straining credibility, it may well be possible that
this experience could contribute to the final option theory (dependent upon answers to the above questions). Moreover, this contributes theologically and pastorally to the situation of "death without

dying." Rahner has postulated that the fifth stage of acceptance can be understood as a "situation in which God's merciful providence makes it easy for a man to leave the world, to renounce a sinful attachment to it and to surrender confidently to that incomprehensible mystery which in death man meets more clearly than ever before and which we call God."[14] He further indicates that a sudden and possibly violent death "presumably" does not contain any such phase of acceptance. Does this experience of dying indicate otherwise?

The experience of life review appears to be a very essential element within this context and the context of achieving consummation of one's personal history. Even though this data was experienced in "dramatic circumstances," there does appear, without stretching, a similar process in more "normal circumstances." It is much clearer when seen in schematic fashion:

Experience of Dying	Stages	Dramas
	1. Denial	1. Shock
1. Resistance	2. Anger	2. Emotion
	3. Bargaining	3. Negotiation
2. Life Review	4. Depression	4. Cognition
3. Transcendence	5. Acceptance	5. Commitment

Thus it would appear that, in the process of life review, the events of one's personal history lead either to an affirmation which can be seen as a blessing or rejection which is understood as judgment. The moment of death which makes conscious the process of dying calls into question the meaning of life itself, the significance of birth, personal history, the present, and an openness to the future in a radically new experience of freedom.[15] The experience of freedom which is experienced in anger is prompted by a new-found consciousness of the "more" to life that has been hidden to my "closed" living. The experience of freedom is one in which all previous conceptions and assumptions about God, man, and life are confronted and possibly shattered leaving one with a feeling of aloneness, in which faith is finally understood as an act of risk-taking. The experience of freedom opens up the possibility of truly experiencing the sense of communion with others. My personal history has been intertwined with others, but now I may well experience the others as other because the values, concerns, and priorities that have dominated and governed my decision-making and activity have been "let go."

    A seventh point of mutual interest is the desire to understand
the "why" and "how" of a person's acceptance of death. A colleague
of Kubler-Ross discovered that the individuals who had reached the
stage of acceptance possessed one major common characteristic--a
"holistic view of creation"--supported by two other characteristics:
a standard of ethics which allowed them to put everything into its
proper perspective (and death does that).[16] This holistic view of
creation has been observed in other scientific research. First, in
LSD experiments with terminal patients paralyzed in the stage of
denial, who after having been released from denial in order to
progress through the process of dying, have communicated this "death
of death" as a union of one's personal dying and rebirth with a
"cosmic sense of dying and rebirth." Others have described this
as an experience of mystical union with the Ground of Being, Ultimate Reality, World Soul, God. The researchers themselves have
questioned whether or not this is an insight into reality or a
merciful delusion.[17] Secondly, Maslow's experiments regarding peak
experiences have indicated that a few of the more significant characteristics include: (1) perceiving of the universe as an integrated and unified whole; (2) transcending of the ego, time, and
space; (3) a sensing of one's "real" self or personhood; (4) becoming more of a free agent, more responsible, more creative, more
self-determining; (5) a feeling of being graced; and (6) experiencing "unitive consciousness" in which the sacred is glimpsed in
and through the particular moment.[18]
    It was originally intended that upon discovering what allows
an individual to accept death, these elements would be integrated
into the "environment" (e.g., hospital) in order to guarantee that
all would achieve acceptance and more quickly. Fortunately, this
was not then possible and apparently is not possible. There is a
human, living process that is to be undergone and this should not
be "taken" from me. If this may not be successful then it emphasizes the failure of wrong choices, the de-valuing of life, the
passive attitude to living.
    From a theological perspective can it not be posited that
death is the culmination of my life, not in the sense of looking to
the future, but that, in the face of death, the meaning of all the
decisions of my life leaves me accepting them or despairing of
them, which is the judgment. To live is to lose oneself. The
development of the individual is one from the consciousness of "I"
to personhood, yet for the Christian this development finds its
complete fulfillment in the giving of the "I" for another. Is this

not the search for community today? Meaning in life is realized
in the process of humanization, in the process of "emptying oneself"
in order to be reborn, to be capable of truly living. Thus in
dying my true creative capabilities and powers are realized--I am
what I have become or I am not what I truly could have been.

The growth of thanatology may well signal the continual presence of the overspecialized and fragmented view of life and reality
possessed by technological man. The need for total integration of
life was traditionally the function of religious institutions and
may once again be its role. In this regard, there is the need
for theological contribution, a contribution, however, respectful
of the conclusions being arrived at by the other disciplines. We
can anticipate, I believe, the continual development of a theology
of death.

NOTES

[1] Peter Berger, *A Rumor of Angels* (New York: Doubleday &
Co., 1969), p. 25.

[2] Robert Kastenbaum and Ruth Aisenberg, *The Psychology of Death*
(New York: Springer Publishing Co., 1972), p. 205.

[3] The Foundation of Thanatology, 630 West 168 St., New York,
N.Y. 10032. Newly revised brochure concerning the goals and purposes of the foundation.

[4] Ernest Q. Campbell, "Death as a Social Practice," in *Perspectives on Death*, ed. Liston O. Mills (New York: Abingdon Press,
1969), pp. 209-218.

[5] Karl Rahner, *Christian at the Crossroads* (New York: Seabury
Press, 1975), pp. 84-86.

[6] Elizabeth Kubler-Ross, *On Death and Dying* (New York: Mac-
Millan, 1969).

[7] Carl Nighswonger, "Ministry to the Dying as a Learning Encounter," *Journal of Thanatology*, I (1971), 101-108.

[8] Ladislaus Boros, *The Mystery of Death* (New York: Herder &
Herder, 1965).

[9] Ladislaus Boros, *We Are Future* (New York: Doubleday & Co.,
1973), p. 142.

[10] Karl Rahner, "Theological Considerations Concerning the Moment of Death," *Theological Investigations*, XI (New York: Seabury Press, 1974), pp. 314-315, 318-319.

[11] Erik Erikson, "Eight Ages of Man," *International Journal of
Psychiatry*, 2 (1966), 281-297.

[12]Rahner, *Theological Investigations*, pp. 315, 317.

[13]Russell Noyes, Jr., "The Experience of Dying," *Psychiatry*, 35 (1972), 174-184.

[14]Rahner, *Crossroads*, p. 85.

[15]Jerry Irish, *A Boy Thirteen: Reflections on Death* (Philadelphia: Westminster Press, 1975), pp. 42-55.

[16]Gisbert Greshake, "Towards a Theology of Dying," *Concilium*, 94 (1974), 80-98.

[17]Jerry Avorn, "Beyond Dying," *Harper's* (March, 1973), pp. 56-64.

[18]Abraham Maslow, *Religion, Values and Peak Experiences* (Columbus: Ohio University Press, 1964).

CONTRIBUTORS

PETER H. BEISHEIM is associate professor of religious studies
and Director of the Institute for Justice and Peace at Stonehill
College. He has been involved in thanatological research and
teaching since 1969 and was recently elected chairman of the Old
Colony Hospice in Brockton, MA, which provides multi-dimensional
supportive care to the terminal patient and his family. Professor
Beisheim has contributed essays to the 1971 CTS Annual Publication,
Concilium, and *Death and Ministry: Pastoral Care of the Dying
and the Bereaved* (Seabury, 1975).

MARY COLLINS, O.S.B., is associate professor of religion and
religious education and a member of the liturgical studies faculty
at Catholic University. She is associate editor of *Worship*, an
editorial consultant for the liturgy volumes of *Concilium*, and a
member of the editorial committee of the North American Academy
of Liturgy. Since 1976 she has been president of the Liturgical
Conference. She has contributed to *Worship*, *The Living Light*,
Benedictines, *Proceedings of the Catholic Theological Society of
America*, and several collections.

LAWRENCE S. CUNNINGHAM, professor of religion at Florida State
University, is NEH Visiting Professor of Religious Studies for
1980-81 at the University of Scranton. His most recent book is
The Meaning of Saints (Harper and Row, 1980). In 1981, Holt, Rine-
hart, and Winston will publish volume one of a two volume humanities
textbook, titled *The Humanistic Tradition*, that he has co-authored
with John Reich. The author of over sixty articles, Professor
Cunningham is interested principally in the interplay of religion
and culture. He writes regularly for *Commonweal*, *America*, *Christian
Century*, and *Cross Currents*.

KEITH J. EGAN is associate professor of historical theology
and spirituality at Marquette University and was the vice-president
of CTS from 1978 to 1980. He holds a doctorate from Cambridge
University where he studied under David Knowles. He regularly
teaches undergraduate and graduate courses on mysticism and has
taught Teresa of Avila on the graduate level. He has published
widely in the areas of Christian spirituality, mysticism, and
prayer.

JAMES J. FORSYTH received his Ph.D. in religious studies from
the University of Ottawa, where he has taught since 1969. As an
assistant professor of religious studies, he offers courses in contemporary Christianity and psychology of religion. His primary
area of interest is the dialogue between christian theology and personality theory in general, with particular emphasis on the application of Freudian and Jungian insights to Christian faith experience.
He has published articles on these topics in *Dialog*, *Religion in
Life*, and *Dimension*.

EUGENE M. GEINZER, S.J., whose M.F.A. is in sculpture from
Pratt Institute, is assistant professor of fine arts at Georgetown
University where he teaches sculpture, the graphic processes, and
philosophy of art. Throughout his theological studies, Fr. Geinzer
fixed his attention on ferreting out the equivocal evidence of

213

God's entrance into this world. Most recently he has sculpted a
series of six whimsical rocking chairs that attempt to mimic the
cryptic process by which material forms entice the sentient man
to ask the question: "Can corporeal things be trusted to be the
loadbearers of the spirit?"

MARTIN C. KASTELIC is chairperson of the Department of
Religious Studies at Gilmour Academy, Gates Mills, OH. He received his Ph.D. in religion from Syracuse University in 1979.
Co-chairperson of the Detroit-Cleveland Region of CTS, he will
serve as convener of the religion and culture sections of the annual
meeting of the society from 1981-83. His research in religion and
culture centers on the development of a Christian theology appropriate to a technological worldview.

ROBERT KRESS is associate professor of systematic theology at
Catholic University. With degrees in education, philosophy, and
theology, he has taught at Vincennes University, St. Meinrad College and Seminary, St. Louis University, Notre Dame University, the
University of Evansville, and Indiana University. Fr. Kress is
the author of four books and over ninety articles and reviews in
scholarly and popular journals. His *Whither Womankind: The
Humanity of Women* received the Book of the Year Award of CTS for
1975. He recently completed an introduction to the theology of
Karl Rahner for John Knox Press.

WAYNE LOBUE teaches religious studies at Gilmour Academy and
at Lake Erie College in Cleveland, OH. His doctorate in religion
and culture is from the University of Kansas, through the department of American Studies and the Kansas School of Religion. In
1975 he was awarded an NEH fellowship to study "civil religion"
under Robert Bellah. At Western Washington University, Dr. Lobue
developed and coordinated an undergraduate interdisciplinary program in religious studies. He has published in *Cross Currents* and
serves as one of the coordinators for the Detroit-Cleveland region
of CTS.

MARCHITA B. MAUCK is associate professor of art history at
Louisiana State University. A Ph.D. from Tulane University, she
is a medievalist with particular interest in the relationships
among art, liturgy, and theology. She is presently investigating
the visual evidence for the use of various biblical texts for a
specifically sacramental catechesis. Dr. Mauck, recipient of both
Fulbright and German government grants for international study, is
a member of the Liturgy Commission of the Diocese of Baton Rouge.
She is presently pursuing a second Ph.D. in liturgy at Notre Dame
University.

JOHN R. MAY has a doctorate in theology and literature from
Emory University's Graduate Institute of Liberal Arts. Presently
associate professor of English at Louisiana State University, he
is the author of *Toward a New Earth: Apocalypse in the American
Novel* (1972) and *The Pruning Word: The Parables of Flannery
O'Connor* (1976). He and Ernest Ferlita co-authored *Film Odyssey:
The Art of Film as Search for Meaning* (1976) and *The Parables of
Lina Wertmuller* (1977). An associate editor of *Horizons* from
1975 to 1980, Dr. May is co-editor with Michael Bird of a collection of essays on religion and film, titled *Image and Likeness*, to
be published by the University of Tennessee Press.

GEORGE MUSCHALEK studied philosophy in Pullach and Freiburg, and theology in Enghien, Innsbruck, Freiburg, and Heidelberg, completing his doctorate under Karl Rahner in 1971. He taught at the Universities of Innsbruck and Pullach-Munchen, before being invited to Marquette University, where he was professor of systematic theology from 1973 until 1979. He is presently doing research and writing in Princeton. Dr. Muschalek's work focuses on faith and knowledge as related to existence-bearing decisions. His other areas of special interest include modern and contemporary culture, and the philosophy and theology of man.

RICHARD L. RUBENSTEIN is Distinguished Professor of Religion at Florida State University. He is the author of six books, including *The Cunning of History* (1979), *Power Struggle* (1974), *After Auschwitz* (1966), and *The Religious Imagination* (1968), which won the Portico d'Ottavia Literary Prize for the best book "expressing the Hebraic Spirit" published in Italy between 1975 and 1977. He has lectured at over a hundred universities and theological institutions in the United States, Canada, England, Scotland, Germany, Poland, Korea, Japan, Italy, and Israel; his books and articles have been translated into eight languages. Co-chairman of the Florida State University Institute of the Humanities, Dr. Rubenstein is also currently the director of the university's Center for the Study of Southern Culture and Religion.

MARY JO WEAVER is an assistant professor of religious studies at Indiana University, Bloomington. She received her Ph.D. in theology from the University of Notre Dame in 1973, taught in a seminary for three years, and has been at Indiana University since 1975. She is interested in using literature, especially novels, to understand religious themes and to explore the similarity between the experience of self and the experience of God. She has published a series of articles on pilgrimage, concentrating on Augustine, Dante, Charles Williams, Flannery O'Connor, Thomas Merton, and Dorothy Day.